KNACK
MAKE IT EASY

FABULOUS
DESSERTS

KNACK

FABULOUS DESSERTS

A Step-by-Step Guide to Sweet Treats and Celebration Specialties

Linda Johnson Larsen

Photographs by Viktor Budnik

Guilford, Connecticut
An imprint of Globe Pequot Press

Editorial Director: Cynthia Hughes
Editor: Lara Asher
Project Editor: Tracee Williams
Cover Design: Paul Beatrice, Bret Kerr
Interior Design: Paul Beatrice
Layout: Melissa Evarts
Cover Photos by: Viktor Budnik
Interior Photos by: Viktor Budnik

Library of Congress Cataloging-in-Publication Data

Larsen, Linda Johnson.
   Knack fabulous desserts : a step-by-step guide to sweet treats and celebration specialties / Linda Johnson Larsen ; photographs by Viktor Budnik.
      p. cm.
   Includes index.
   ISBN 978-1-59921-915-8
   1. Desserts. I. Title. II. Title: Fabulous desserts.
   TX773.L3143 2010
   641.8'6—dc22
                                             2010003881

The following manufacturers/names appearing in *Knack Fabulous Desserts* are trademarks:

Bundt®; Callebaut™ Chocolate; Crock-Pot®; Cuisinart®; Famous™ Wafers (Nabisco®); Ghirardelli®; Grand Marnier®; Kahlúa®; Marshmallow Fluff®; Silpat®; Special K®; Sterno®

Printed in China

10 9 8 7 6 5 4 3 2 1

Acknowledgments

Thanks as always to my dear husband, Doug, and my agent, Barb Doyen. And I'd like to thank the wonderful students of the ZED ALC high school in Byron, Minnesota, for liking everything I make.

Photographer Acknowledgments

I would like to say thanks to everyone at KNACK. A real pleasure to be on a team with great people. Thank you to my crew of gifted and talented people—Claire Stancer, a wonderful and talented food stylist—who created beautiful food to shoot. To Celeste for the shopping and keeping us on track—and to Kimmi a great assistant. A special thanks to Jon, Brooke, Bree, and Elliot for letting us shoot in their wonderful kitchens.

CONTENTS

INTRODUCTION

No matter how many diets our nation tries, one thing never changes: We still want rich, delicious, and accessible recipes for dessert. We crave chocolate desserts for Valentine's Day, an elegant cake for birthdays, and an array of perfect cookies for Christmas. A good report card, a telephone call from an old friend, and even the first day of spring all give us reasons to celebrate too, with perfect peanut butter brownies, a cool fruit fool, or some homemade pudding.

Desserts offer the perfect finishing touch to any meal. You can serve desserts for dinner, lunch, and, yes, breakfast! Many people feel a meal isn't complete unless it ends with something sweet. But many people are also intimidated by the thought of baking something from scratch.

Once you understand a bit about the science of baking and have learned some techniques, you will see that baking is not a difficult art. As you gain confidence you can expand your repertoire and create beautiful pies, tarts, cakes, and even candies and ice cream with ease. And you will get so much satisfaction out of the wonderful treats you will be able to offer family and friends. Perhaps the best part is that once you master the basic recipes, variation possibilities are endless!

The most important factor when making desserts is measuring accurately. Baking recipes are not like cooking recipes. When you're cooking soups, creating casseroles, or making salads, you can substitute ingredients or change proportions with very little problem. Baking recipes, however, are precisely calculated formulas that need a certain balance of solids, sugars, fats, liquids, and leavening ingredients. Making a change to this formula increases your chances of failure. It is possible to change recipes slightly but only after you understand how they work.

Most people measure many ingredients incorrectly, with flour measuring the main culprit. Too much flour in a recipe will make that recipe dry and crumbly. Too little flour means the recipe's structure will not hold up, and cakes and bars will collapse or sag in the center.

To measure flour correctly, lightly spoon it into a measuring cup and level off the top with the back of a knife. Never scoop the cup or spoon into the flour or pack the flour down. Brown sugar is measured by packing into a cup or spoon. All other dry ingredients are like flour, spooned into the cup, then leveled off with the back of a knife.

Liquid ingredients are measured with measuring spoons for small amounts, and with glass measuring cups for larger amounts. Always check the measurement by bringing the cup up to eye level. The liquid should be even with the desired line.

Good calibrated measuring cups and spoons are essential to baking success. Dry ingredients should be measured using nested measuring cup and spoons, not coffee cups or the spoons you use to eat. And liquid ingredients need liquid measuring cups, which must be used properly.

Good-quality ingredients are also very important. Fresh eggs, real butter, the best chocolate, fresh nuts, and ripe fruits all contribute their wonderful characteristics to your recipes. Never use unripe or shriveled fruit, low-quality margarine, or cheap chocolate if you want the best result.

So now you know how to measure, and you have good-quality ingredients and measuring equipment. What's next?

More kitchen tools! A high-quality whisk, spoons, a good mixer, a rolling pin, spatulas, and heavy-duty pots, pans, cookie sheets, and knives are all essential to good baking. Parchment paper, heavy-duty foil, a pastry bag, and nonstick baking spray with flour are also important so your creations can be beautifully finished.

Be sure to combine ingredients in the order and manner described in the recipe. When sugar is beaten with butter, small air pockets are formed that create the texture of the dessert. Egg whites, beaten separately and folded into a batter, are necessary for leavening. And cutting butter into a flour mixture creates a flaky piecrust or cookie. Recipes that

call for just combining all ingredients in a bowl do exist, but they are rare.

Finally, you need to learn about doneness tests. An over-baked or underbaked dessert is just not fun to eat. There are several doneness tests, including the fingertip test, toothpick test, observation, and internal temperature. Once you've performed each test, it will become easier, then second nature to tell when your dessert is perfectly done.

It's time to pick out the desserts you want to try. The easiest dessert recipes to start with are trifles and parfaits, where you are just layering ingredients. The next is bar cookies. You mix up a batter or dough and place it in a large pan, then bake until done. These sweets are easier to make than drop cookies because you don't have to individually form each cookie. Now try your hand at fruit desserts like crumbles and

crisps, then cakes and pies. If you've never baked before, be sure to read every recipe carefully and look at the photos of the steps.

One of the best things about baking is that once you understand the basic rules, how to measure, and how to test for doneness, you can vary recipes to create your own masterpieces. You can change the flavor of a dessert from vanilla to chocolate by adding some cocoa powder and melted chocolate. Or you might add a complementary caramel or vanilla frosting to chocolate cookies. Change the shape of a cake by baking a sheet pan recipe in a Bundt pan, or making cupcakes instead.

As long as you continue to follow the basic rules of proportion, measuring, beating, and doneness tests, your desserts will turn out beautifully.

Many recipes are perfect as is; others require some type of finishing touch. There is an entire chapter of frostings toward the end of this book, with flavor variations. When a dessert is frosted, it's important that that frosting complement the texture and flavor of the dish without overpowering it. Most recipes have frosting suggestions in the ingredients list, but you are free to choose your own. When considering pairing frostings and desserts, think about using a really sweet frosting with a tart or bland dessert, and a mild or flavored frosting with very sweet cookies or cakes.

Entertaining with desserts is easy. You can choose one special recipe to end a celebration dinner or offer a couple of complementary desserts for a celebration. Or go all-out and have a dessert party.

You must take the whole meal into consideration when planning which dessert to make. After a very heavy meal of roast beef and potatoes, with vegetables and bread, a lighter recipe such as a sorbet or fruit dessert will be most welcome. But if you're serving something like grilled fish with a fruit salad, go ahead and serve a rich cheesecake or some decadent brownies to end the meal.

A dessert party should have lots of offerings, varied by flavor, texture, appearance, richness, and color. A fruit pie or some tartlets, several kinds of cookies and bars, a special cake or cupcakes, a low-fat option like Floating Island, and some fresh fruit create a satisfying spread that will give everyone choices.

Pair the dessert with the season, too. On a hot day everyone will appreciate a cool frozen or chilled dessert. And when it's cold and blustery outside, a warm and rich dessert will send everyone on his or her way happy and well fed. Use the season's produce in desserts from puddings to crisps, and turn a trip to the farmer's market into the best apple pie.

These are the recipes that everyone wants. They will never go out of style. No matter what occasion you mark, dessert recipes will be made and enjoyed.

Let's start baking these delicious desserts. Fill your cookie jar to delight your children after school. Offer a simple dessert after a weeknight meal, or bring your latest triumph to the school bake sale. Your entertaining will become more effortless as your confidence increases. And you'll become famous for your baking!

SWEET & SALTY
Desserts are flavored with sweet ingredients; salt adds depth

When you think of desserts, you almost always think of something sweet. Chocolate, caramel, vanilla, and fruits are all sweet flavors. Sugar plays an important part in the flavor of desserts, as well as their texture.

But salt is an important flavor, too. Salt is an unusual chemical. It enhances other flavors as well as interacting with your salt taste buds. Salt can make chocolate taste richer, make strawberries seem sweeter, and bring out the flavor of extracts and spices. And the newest trend in desserts is sweet and salty together: Think of a caramel sprinkled with some Fleur de Sel.

Sugar has many functions in dessert recipes. Flavor is the obvious one. Sugar is hygroscopic: that is, it attracts water. This property helps keep desserts moist after they are baked. Sugar crystals help form the structure of cakes and cookies. The sharp crystals cut pockets in fat, which are filled with CO_2

Sugars

- There are many different types of sugars. Granulated sugar is the most commonly used in desserts. It helps create structure.

- Brown sugar is granulated sugar that has some molasses added for richer flavor. It must be measured by packing it into a cup.

- Powdered sugar is finely processed granulated sugar with some cornstarch added. It dissolves quickly for use in frostings and glazes.

- Sanding, or demerara sugar, is used to decorate desserts, especially shortbreads and sugar cookies.

Honey and Syrups

- Honey and other syrups— including corn syrup, maple syrup, and molasses— are used in desserts to create a soft texture and smoothness.

- It's not possible to directly substitute honey for sugar in most recipes because their function is different.

- If honey or other syrups crystallize, just warm them in a saucepan of water over very low heat.

- There are several grades of honey, maple syrup, and molasses, from light to dark. Keep a variety on hand.

from leavening. And sugar helps promote browning of cakes and cookies.

Salt has functions other than flavor as well. It helps strengthen gluten formation in doughs and will make egg whites foam stronger. Measure salt carefully; if you add too much, the recipe will be salty or may not work. Remember that recipes are scientific formulas!

RED ●LIGHT

You can reduce the amount of sugar and salt in a baking recipe, but only up to a point. Since both are important to the baked good's structure, eliminating them completely is impossible. Start by reducing sugar by one-third, up to one-half of the original amount. And reduce salt by one-half. If the dish still tastes good to you, make a note in the recipe of this change and how it worked.

Fruits

- Fresh, frozen, and canned fruits all have their place in dessert recipes.

- The simplest dessert is just some perfectly ripe fruit, drizzled with a simple syrup and topped with mint or other herbs.

- Choose ripe fruits for your dessert recipes, but don't try to use overripe produce in any recipe.

- Prepare fruits as the recipe directs. Many frozen fruits are used frozen; others are thawed. Fruits can be peeled, chopped, or pureed before being adding to a recipe.

Salts

- If you have only used plain table salt in your kitchen, browse through the spice aisle of the supermarket.

- There are many varieties of salt available. Sea salts, or Fleur de Sel, have a more intense flavor than regular iodized salt.

- Because exotic salts have a stronger flavor, you can use less of them.

- Use fine salt in baked goods so it dissolves properly. Special salts can be sprinkled on desserts for a final touch.

TART & SPICY

A contrast of tart or spicy flavors adds interest to desserts

If desserts were just sweet, they wouldn't be very interesting! Even the sweetest recipes, such as chocolate and caramel dishes, have other flavors to balance the overall presentation. We may be born with a sweet tooth, but there is such a thing as a recipe or food that is too sweet.

Some foods are naturally tart. Fruits, especially citrus and stone fruits, have a tart or sour aspect to their flavor along with sweetness. This tart flavor actually enhances the sweetness of the fruit, creating a more enjoyable eating experience.

Lemons, limes, and oranges are commonly used in many dessert recipes. The pulp, juice, and zest of these fruits add tart flavor and floral fragrance to many recipes.

Tart and sour vinegars are used in dessert recipes, both to provide flavor contrast and to help maintain the structure of the recipe. The acid in vinegar helps egg whites stay fluffy longer and turns meringue into Pavlova.

Citrus Fruit

- Always choose citrus fruit based on smooth skin, heaviness for its size, and plumpness.

- Avoid wrinkled or shriveled fruit, which will be dry, and fruit that is light, which also means it won't have much juice.

- Always wash citrus fruits with food-safe soap before zesting and slicing to remove pesticides.

- These fruits can be substituted for one another. The only difference is in amount of juice and zest you'll get from each type.

Tart Fruits

- Tart fruits add nice flavor contrast to many desserts. The tartness level will vary with ripeness and variety.

- More tart apples include Granny Smith, Jonathan, Northern Spy, Pippin, and Winesap.

- Rhubarb is technically a vegetable but is classified as a fruit. It is very tart and has to be cooked with sugar.

- Dried fruits such as currants and raisins have a slightly tart, floral taste and aroma.

And spices are an integral part of baking. Gingerbread cake or cookies must include ginger, cinnamon, nutmeg, and sometimes cardamom. These spices provide a bit of heat on the tongue and create wonderful aromas as the recipes are baked and consumed. Scientists are also discovering that some spices have medicinal qualities.

Vinegars

- There are several types of vinegars that play a part in baking and desserts.
- Plain vinegar is used to sour milk or to help egg whites maintain a firm foam. Apple cider vinegar is milder and slightly sweet.
- Balsamic vinegar comes in several forms. The longer it's aged, the sweeter it gets, and the more expensive it is.
- A simple dessert can consist of a very good balsamic vinegar drizzled over sliced ripe fresh fruits.

Spices

- The best spices are the freshest. Most ground spices have a shelf life of 3 to 6 months.
- Smell the spices before you use them in your recipes. If they don't have a very strong aroma, discard them and buy fresh.
- You can purchase whole spices—cinnamon sticks, gingerroot, and whole nutmeg—and grate them yourself.
- Use a microplane grater or a spice grinder that you reserve solely for this use.

CRUNCHY

Texture is almost as important as flavor in desserts

Always take texture into consideration when considering a dessert or baking recipe. Think about biting into a pecan bar, or an apple crisp with crunchy oatmeal topping. You expect the food to snap between your teeth and create a moderate amount of noise.

Food scientists measure the crunchiness of foods by using displacement curves. All you need to know about this is that a crunchy food will produce a curve with lots of peaks and valleys. The more peaks and valleys, the crunchier the food.

When you eat a dessert, the way your teeth sense texture is called mouth-feel. Crunchy foods should resist the first bite, then shatter with significant noise.

There are several ways to make foods crunchy. Nuts are toasted, cookies baked until they are golden brown, and streusels made with oatmeal and butter. Baking, broiling, grilling, and toasting all produce crunchy products because

Fruit Crisp Topping

- The combination of flour, sugar, and butter creates a crunchy topping on many desserts with or without nuts.

- This mixture usually does not have moisture other than that provided by the butter.

- The dry heat of the oven literally fries the mixture as it bakes, creating the crunchy texture.

- If the proportion of flour and sugar and butter isn't correct in these toppings, it will be tough or gummy instead of crunchy.

Nuts

- Nuts are automatically crunchy. When they are toasted, their crunch factor increases.

- Toasting also brings out the flavor of the nuts. You can toast nuts in the oven, in the microwave, or on the stovetop.

- Different nuts have different levels of crunch. Pecans are less crunchy than almonds, and pine nuts are crunchier than walnuts.

- Think about the amount of crunch you want in your recipe when making desserts with nuts.

these are dry-heat methods. In other words, moisture is removed from the product so it can be crunchy. The opposite of crunchy is soggy.

Unless you're making peanut brittle or toffee, most dessert recipes have other textural characteristics, most notably creamy, chewy, and crisp. Measuring, mixing, and baking techniques are all designed to maximize these textures, so follow them carefully.

• • • • • • • • • • • • RED ● LIGHT • • • • • • • • • • • • •

Crunchy texture results from moisture evaporating from dry ingredients, and the browning of dry ingredients. Make sure that you follow the recipe for a crunchy topping or crust carefully. Storing desserts correctly is also important. If you refrigerate a dessert that isn't meant to be, crunchy toppings and crusts can become soggy as they absorb water. Making good desserts also means knowing how to store them.

Crunchy Cereals

- Crunchy cereals are a good way to add more texture to many desserts.

- You can use cereals in place of nuts or oatmeal in recipes. Substitute them measure-for-measure.

- Always taste cereals before using them in desserts to make sure they have the proper amount of crunch.

- Store cereals tightly covered so they don't absorb moisture from the air. Keep the inner paper packet well sealed.

Streusel

- Streusel is used to top cakes, cupcakes, pies, and tarts. It is also used as a filling for coffee cakes.

- The word *streusel* is a German term that means "sprinkled or scattered." It's made of butter, flour, and sugar and often cinnamon.

- Streusels are baked at relatively high temperatures, so the butter melts quickly and turns the flour and butter into clusters.

- When stored, streusels will become less crunchy after a while.

CREAMY
A creamy and smooth dessert is comforting and satisfying

Of all the dessert textures, creamy is the one that most personifies decadence and indulgence. For example, puddings, fudge, frosting, trifles, and fillings are creamy. Think about spooning a rich rice pudding or chocolate fondue into your mouth. The creamy mouth-feel is described as rich, melting, thick, and smooth. Fat is almost always a prime component in creamy textures, but you can also achieve creaminess with purees and reductions.

Creamy foods also coat the mouth, which allows the taste and aroma of the food to create more impact. A creamy chocolate dessert will taste more intense than one that is crisp or crunchy. No wonder we associate creamy foods with comfort!

To achieve a creamy consistency, lots of stirring or beating is required. A wire whisk is an excellent tool to use when making sauces and puddings, and a stand or hand mixer is

Cooked Pudding

- Cooked pudding is a good example of a creamy dessert. The mixture of fat, sugar, flour, and liquid makes it creamy.

- The fat provides the creamy mouth-feel. And the starch and protein in the flour or cornstarch are suspended in the liquid.

- The combination of these ingredients thickens the mixture and creates a creamy texture.

- Puddings and other creamy mixtures must be stirred constantly over the heat so they thicken evenly.

Frosting

- Uncooked frostings are made from fat, sugar, and liquid. The fat provides the creaminess.

- The sugar and liquid blend and coat the fat particles, creating a suspension.

- It's really difficult to overbeat uncooked frostings.

- The more you beat, the smoother and creamier they will be.

- Always spread creamy frostings on completely cooled desserts, or the frosting will melt. When it subsequently hardens, the consistency will be different.

usually required. Lumps and graininess have no place in a dessert that is supposed to be creamy and smooth.

Melting and cooking ingredients for creamy desserts must be done carefully. Chocolate can seize, or become grainy, when overheated, and cream and other dairy products can curdle.

Desserts can be creamy by themselves, or be combined with crisp, chewy, or crunchy textures. The contrasts among these textures are what make a good dessert.

YELLOW ● LIGHT

Low-fat products can be substituted for full-fat ingredients in desserts, but when you're making a creamy dessert, never use all nonfat substitutions. The texture of the dessert will not be creamy and satisfying. Combine low-fat and nonfat substitutes for best results, or substitute nonfat ingredients for some of the full-fat products.

Fillings

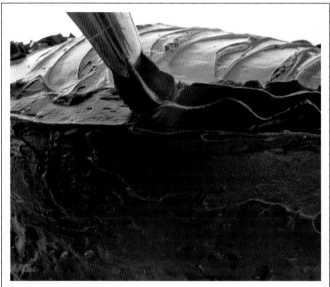

- Fillings are made of whipped cream, a frosting-like mixture of fat, sugar, and liquid, or other ingredients such as cornstarch and eggs.

- Cooked fillings are either cooked on the stovetop or baked in the oven on some type of crust.

- A filling can be made of any mixture that includes fat, sugar, and some type of thickener.

- When baked, creamy fillings will thicken as they cool, so be careful not to overbake them.

Cream

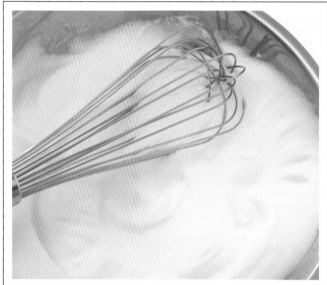

- Only heavy whipping cream will whip to form a foam that is creamy. Make sure you read labels in the supermarket.

- The cream, beaters, and bowls should be very cold for best results.

- Chill all of them in the refrigerator for several hours before beating the cream. The cream can then be folded into other mixtures to increase creaminess.

- You can flavor whipped cream with brandy, powdered sugar and vanilla, caramel, or chocolate.

CRISP

Crisp foods shatter in the mouth, adding another dimension to the recipe

Food scientists differentiate crisp from crunchy in a specific way. Crisp foods break apart in a single stage, but crunchy foods have several stages of disintegration. Acoustic, or sound, research plays a big part in food science. The sounds you hear when you eat a food have an impact on your opinion. Crisp foods should be crisp, soft foods soft.

When you think of a crisp food, the first bite breaks the food apart into smaller, usually flaky pieces. A piecrust is crisp, as is a shortbread cookie, a flaky cereal, or a fresh apple. Crisp food is easy to bite. There is very little resistance to pressure, and the food stays crisp until it is swallowed.

Techniques to making desserts crisp include frying, layering

KNACK FABULOUS DESSERTS

Phyllo

- Phyllo, filo, or fillo, is a paper-thin dough made of flour and water. It's difficult to make at home.

- You can buy phyllo dough in any large supermarket in the frozen pastry aisle. It is thawed overnight in the refrigerator.

- To make phyllo crisp, layer the dough with melted butter and other ingredients such as ground nuts and sugar.

- Baking at a high temperature removes moisture from the dough, and the butter fries the dough, making it crisp.

Meringue Cookies

- Meringues can be soft and tender, chewy and melting, or crisp. The meringue starts out full of moisture.

- Crisp meringues, used as dessert shells or fat-free cookies, are baked at a low temperature until all the moisture is removed.

- This sets the foam into an airy and brittle web that is crisp and tender.

- Follow directions for making meringues carefully and store them tightly covered at room temperature.

fat with flour, baking meringues, and using crisp fruits. There is little moisture in crisp foods, a characteristic they share with crunchy foods.

Crisp foods can become soggy or tough if they absorb moisture, so storage of these foods is critical to maintaining texture. Store in airtight containers. You can bring some crisp foods back to the proper texture by baking them for a short time to drive out the moisture they may have absorbed from the environment.

ZOOM

Crisp is one of the most pleasing textures in food. The texture is apparent in the mouth and in the sounds the food makes. A crisp food has a softer, more muted sound than crunchy foods. Crisp foods are produced with dehydration: removing water from food. Meringues are baked at a low temperature to remove water, while shortbread dough is baked at a higher temperature.

Apples

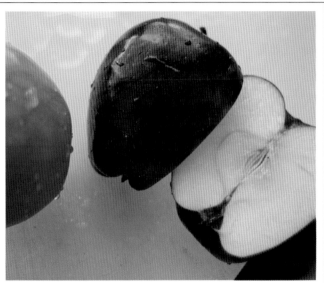

- Really the only crisp fruit that is supposed to be crisp is the apple.

- Crisp as a texture is usually combined with soft fruits for the contrast: Think of toppings for fruit crisps and piecrusts.

- When apples are overripe

or not properly transported from the orchard they can become mealy or mushy.

- Apples lose their crispness and become mealy when their cell structure begins to break down. These apples are older or have been stored at high temperatures.

Shortbread

- Shortbread crispness is produced when flour is layered with fat, either by cutting butter into dry ingredients or by folding dough.

- The dough has to be high in fat or the flour in the gluten will develop, making the shortbread tough.

- Shortbread should be handled gently and baked at a relatively high temperature.

- Always store shortbread in a tightly closed, preferably airtight container at room temperature to preserve texture.

HOT OR COLD
The correct serving temperature is crucial to a dessert's success

The temperature of a dessert in its final form depends on what type of food it is. Fondue is served warm, as are bread puddings and some fruit desserts. Chilled desserts like trifles or chocolate pudding are served at about refrigerator temperature, while ice cream is best served slightly thawed.

Avoid extremes of temperature when serving any food. Food should never be served so hot that it burns the mouth, or so cold that it hurts to eat it.

Desserts meant to be served hot or warm are cooled for a specific amount of time before eating. And you are often advised to let frozen desserts stand at room temperature for a few minutes before serving.

There are good reasons for this: Food tastes best when it is not too cold or too hot. Food that is very cold numbs the taste buds so you don't experience the full range of flavors. And food that is too hot is just unpleasant to eat.

Fondue

- Fondue served as dessert is usually made of chocolate. The mixture is melted over low heat.

- Then the fondue must be kept in a heated container so it remains liquid. You can use a fondue pot that is kept warm with a candle or Sterno.

- Some fondue pots are electric, allowing you to regulate the temperature more closely and prevent burning.

- Crock-Pots, especially the small 1-quart and 2-cup types, are ideal for keeping dessert fondues warm.

Warm Puddings

- Warm desserts are most often served just a few minutes out of the oven or microwave.

- These dishes can be kept warm on serving trays designed to hold heat.

- Or you can serve them warm and they will gradually cool down as they are being eaten.

- The optimal temperature range for these types of desserts is very broad, so you don't have to be overly concerned with timing.

Most dessert recipes are served at room temperature. The only time you really need to consider the temperature of desserts is when you are serving a number of them for a buffet or large party, or when the weather is very cold or hot.

ZOOM

There are special serving items you can purchase to help keep desserts hot or cold. Warming trays are a good choice for buffets or larger parties. A Crock-Pot is a good choice to keep a dessert warm, especially if it has a "keep warm" setting. And you can purchase special trays that can be frozen to keep food cold, or trays with a special thermal oil to keep the dessert at the right temperature.

Chilled Desserts

- Chilled desserts include puddings, trifles, tiramisu, and dishes kept cold for food safety reasons.

- These recipes are fine served straight from the refrigerator, but you may want to let them stand at room temperature for a few minutes.

- If the recipe directs you to store the dessert in the refrigerator, please do so.

- If the recipe has perishable ingredients like sour cream, eggs, or cream cheese, the fridge is the safest place for it.

Ice Cream

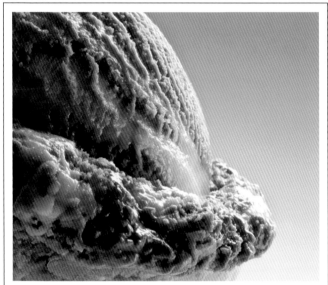

- Ice cream and desserts made from ice cream have to be kept cold. But that doesn't mean they're best eaten at 0°F.

- Any frozen dessert will be more flavorful if you let it stand at room temperature for 10 to 15 minutes.

- This step usually makes the frozen dessert easier to serve too.

- The flavor in frozen desserts is only available as the food melts on your tongue. Ice-cold food doesn't have much flavor.

OVENS

A clean, calibrated oven is essential to recipe perfection

A clean, well-maintained oven is necessary to producing the best dessert recipes. Since recipes are timed, knowing that the oven temperature is accurate means you can relax and trust that you will check the recipe at the right time.

Overbaked and underbaked desserts are a result of ovens that aren't properly calibrated. An oven thermometer is a necessary piece of kitchen equipment. Preheat your oven for 15 minutes, then check the temperature. If it isn't exactly correct, have the oven serviced.

You can calibrate some ovens yourself, usually by changing the tightness of the knob. Check your oven instructions for information. Do not try to service any oven components yourself.

Most dessert recipes and other baked products are baked on the center rack of the oven, right in the middle. Heat can easily circulate around the pan or cookie sheet, for the most

Gas Oven

- Gas ovens heat by igniting a pilot light. The timing for gas ovens is the same as for electric.

- There is one difference: Gas ovens introduce water vapor into the cavity, which can reduce browning.

- Gas stovetops heat mixtures more quickly and are easier to control than electric burners. When you turn them off, they go off.

- Gas ovens may bake less evenly than electric ovens, so you may need to rotate the food during baking.

Electric Oven

- Electric ovens are drier than gas ovens. They bake more evenly, too.

- If you're fitting out a kitchen, you may want to choose electric wall ovens and a gas cooktop.

- Another advantage to electric ovens is that they don't need to be professionally installed, particularly toaster ovens.

- Electric stovetops or cooktops heat up more slowly and cool down slowly, so you need to watch food carefully.

evenly cooked results. Unless a recipe tells you otherwise, bake one cookie sheet or one pan at a time.

If your oven doesn't bake evenly, you can rotate cookie sheets and pans after half the cooking time has elapsed. Rotate the sheets 180 degrees.

The stovetop is another important oven component: No-bake cookies, puddings, and some frostings are cooked over heat.

Microwave Oven

- Microwave ovens range from simple countertop units to over-the-range convection/microwave combos with vent fans.

- The microwave is a wonderful appliance for softening and melting butter, melting chocolate, and softening cream cheese.

- It is possible to bake in the microwave oven, but you do need to take additional steps since the food won't brown there.

- Foods also will not get crisp in a microwave oven unless it's cooked with special equipment.

Convection Oven

- Convection ovens are regular ovens with a fan. The fan moves hot air around the food, cooking it evenly and more quickly,

- Some ovens are microwave/convection combinations. Follow your owner's manual.

- Make sure that you reduce baking time if you use a convection oven. Foods brown better, and you can bake multiple products at once.

- Start by setting the timer to three-quarters of the shortest time, and check the food at that point.

MIXERS & PROCESSORS
Stand and hand mixers make creating perfect desserts easy

You can, of course, mix any recipe by hand. My maternal grandmother made divinity, one of the most difficult candies, by beating the meringue with a wooden spoon. But a hand mixer, stand mixer, blender, and food processor make baking much easier.

There are literally hundreds of types and styles of mixers and processors on the market, at every price point. You can find these appliances at big-box retailers, baking supply stores, grocery stores, and hardware stores.

Buy the best-quality appliances you can afford. The prices of many of these products have declined in recent years; it's possible to buy a good-quality hand mixer for $30 or less.

It's always a good idea to check out reviews and ratings of appliances at online sites like www.ConsumerReports.org and www.Epinions.com. Professional testing is used as the standard at the former site, and regular users rate lots

Stand Mixer

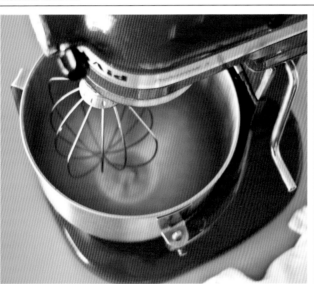

- Stand mixers are made in several incarnations. Lightweight stand mixers are usually available at hardware stores.

- There are also heavy-duty mixers that literally weigh twenty pounds or more for serious bakers.

- These mixers are an investment, so make sure you research before you buy and take care of the appliance.

- Buy more bowls and beaters for your stand mixer so you can bake lots of foods without having to clean first.

Hand Mixer

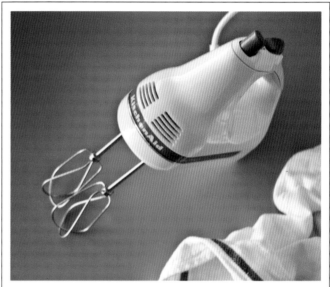

- Handheld mixers are less expensive than stand mixers and are very helpful in the kitchen.

- You can whip egg whites, beat a cake batter, and make creamy frosting with the lightest-duty hand mixer.

- Hand mixers are essential for making Seven Minute Frosting and for smaller kitchen tasks.

- Extra beaters, whisks, and flat beaters for your hand mixer increase its usability and allow you to make multiple dishes without washing beaters.

of products at the latter. These reviews and ratings may be helpful in finding the right small appliance for your kitchen.

Mixers can whip egg whites, make cake batter and cookie dough in seconds, and whip frostings. Stand mixers can do all of those things as well as knead dough.

Blenders can make smoothies, puddings, and light batters; they can also grind and puree foods. Food processors can do all of those things plus puree, slice, and chop food.

Blender

- This ubiquitous wedding gift is a very useful appliance. Most blenders are best at mixing light or delicate mixtures.

- Some new blenders on the market feature wave action.

- These heavy-duty blenders have the ability to blend stiff mixtures and grind and puree almost any food.

- Do your research before purchasing a blender to make sure the product will fit your needs and kitchen tasks.

Food Processor

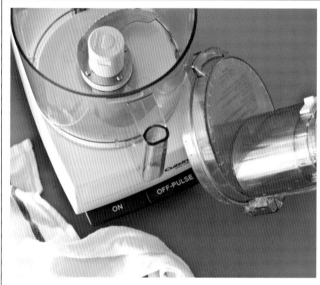

- The food processor is a relatively new addition to consumer kitchens. Until the 1970s the blender reigned supreme.

- Food processors can do everything blenders do and more. Mini food processors are a good addition to any kitchen.

- You can blend, puree, shred, slice, grind, and grate in the food processor.

- Be careful with the blades; they are very sharp. Clean and maintain your processor according to the owner's manual.

UTENSILS

Quality utensils will last a lifetime when properly cared for

Utensils are extensions of your hands, and perform tasks well when properly cared for. Good-quality spoons, whisks, spatulas, knives, and other utensils are essential when cooking and baking.

As with other equipment and appliances, buy the best-quality utensils you can afford. You don't want spoons that bend, whisks that become tangled, spatulas that melt in the heat, or knives that are dull.

Once you find a utensil that you really like, that works well and fits the shape of your hand, buy more than one. Then you can cook and bake your way through several recipes without having to stop and wash your utensils. Since manufacturers are constantly changing their products, buying more than one will also help ensure that you will have your favorite utensils on hand for years.

It's fun to look through hardware or kitchen supply stores

Spoons

- There are various types of spoons for baking. Sturdy stainless-steel spoons with a wide bowl are the most basic.

- Slotted spoons are helpful for lifting marinating fruits out of a liquid or cubed pineapple from a can.

- Wooden spoons are wonderful for stirring stiff batters and working with hot mixtures on the stovetop.

- And teaspoons, coffee spoons, and iced tea spoons can all be used to garnish foods and for serving.

Whisks

- Whisks are essential for beating egg whites and for making smooth sauces and puddings.

- There are several types of whisks: ball whisks, balloon whisks, and combination whisks.

- Balloon whisks are the bulbous type we all know. Ball whisks are made of long strands with tiny balls at the end.

- And combination whisks are balloon whisks with loose balls inside, made to thoroughly mix heavy or thick mixtures.

16

for different types of utensils or something you didn't know about. Or browse online at kitchen sites to get ideas about stocking your kitchen.

There are other utensils too, like nut choppers, swivel-bladed peelers, microplane graters, spice grinders, and specialty tools like cherry pitters, strawberry hullers, apple corers, and honey dippers. Choose the ones you need based on the types of food you handle most often.

YELLOW ● LIGHT

Different kinds of kitchen utensils need different kinds of care. Most knives (except serrated knives) need to be sharpened regularly and become dull when washed in the dishwasher. Wooden spoons should be washed by hand as well, while delicate spatulas can warp in the dishwasher or very hot water. Pay attention to and follow care instructions for any utensil, no matter how small or inexpensive.

Spatulas

- Spatulas are used to move cookies and cakes, to scrape down the sides of a mixing bowl, and to frost cookies and cakes.

- Buy round and square spatulas for moving food, as well as a plastic one for working on nonstick equipment.

- Spatulas for scraping should be sturdy with a well-attached handle and firm bowl.

- And narrow, straight, and offset spatulas smooth frostings while keeping your fingers away from the surface.

Knives

- Knives, when well cared for, can last a lifetime. Choose good-quality knives and take care of them.

- The best knives have a full tang, or length of steel, running right into the wooden or metal handle.

- Sharpen your knives regularly using a knife sharpener, or take them to a metalsmith for upkeep.

- Serrated knives are good for slicing breads and cakes, while paring knives are necessary for peeling and slicing fruit for desserts.

MEASURING TOOLS

You need the proper measuring tools to make flawless desserts

Since baking is an exact science, tools for measuring ingredients are very important. All recipes are fairly tolerant—that is, the measurements can vary slightly, within a few teaspoons, but larger variations will cause the recipe to fail.

You need proper measuring tools to bake desserts correctly. Companies have developed precise measuring cups and spoons that you can be confident work well and will measure accurately.

Dry ingredients should be measured with dry measuring cups. These are usually made of steel or plastic with an attached handle and a straight top. Measuring spoons, which come in sizes ranging from 2 tablespoons down to a pinch, are also used for dry and wet ingredients.

Wet ingredients have special measuring utensils. They are usually made of glass, which allows you to see the level of the liquid inside of the cup. There are new liquid measuring cups

Dry Measuring Cups and Spoons

- Graded measuring cups commonly range from ¼ cup to 1 cup.

- You can find dry measuring sets with amounts ranging from ⅛ cup (2 tablespoons) up to 2 or 4 cups.

- Typical measuring spoons range from ⅛ teaspoon to 1 tablespoon in a set.

- You can find spoons with a larger range, from 2 to 3 tablespoons down to a pinch, which is ¹⁄₃₂ teaspoon.

Liquid Measuring Cups

- These measuring cups are made of plastic or glass. The sizes range from 1 cup to 6 cups, with increments marked on the side.

- When you're measuring sticky liquids like honey or corn syrup, start by spraying the cup with nonstick baking spray and then the

liquid will slide right out.

- Put the cup on the countertop and bend down to read the level. Don't hold it up to your eyes.

- If you have a regular measuring cup, read the amount at eye level.

on the market that have special markings so you can judge the amount by looking straight down into the cup.

And for the most accurate measuring, a scale is best. Many Web sites can tell you the weight of different ingredients by cup or teaspoon. When recipes are evaluated in a test kitchen, the ingredients are weighed for accuracy.

Measuring Equivalents

3 teaspoons = 1 tablespoon = 15 ml

2 tablespoons = $1/8$ cup = 30 ml

4 tablespoons = $1/4$ cup = 50 ml

$5^{1}/_{3}$ tablespoons = $1/3$ cup = 75 ml

8 tablespoons = $1/2$ cup = 125 ml

$10^{2}/_{3}$ tablespoons = $2/3$ cup = 150 ml

12 tablespoons = $3/4$ cup = 175 ml

16 tablespoons = 1 cup = 250 ml

2 cups = 1 pint = 8 fluid ounces

4 cups = 2 pints = 1 quart = 16 fluid ounces

Scale

- A food scale should have a removable bowl that you can spoon the ingredients into and that is easily washed.

- The best scales can be zeroed out. That means the scale automatically subtracts the weight of the measuring bowl for an accurate weight.

- Look for a scale that is digital and weighs in ounces, pounds, and grams.

- Many recipes from Europe and other countries use measurements by weight. With a scale you can make these recipes easily.

PANS & SHEETS

Heavy-duty, high-quality pans and baking sheets are a kitchen necessity

Cake pans, saucepans, tart pans, and cookie sheets are all important in dessert recipes. As with other utensils and equipment, buy the best you can afford. Cheap pans (not inexpensive pans, but cheaply made) can warp in the oven's heat, which will deform the food and ruin your dessert. It's also important to have a good variety of this equipment so you can make different desserts.

Cookie sheets can be found in any grocery or hardware store. But if you venture into a baking supply store, you'll find a lot more choice. These sheets can be found made with aluminum and stainless steel; some come with nonstick coatings, and some are double-layer insulated sheets.

Cookie Sheets

- Insulated cookie sheets first appeared in the 1980s. These utensils are made of two sheets fastened together, with an air space in between.

- The sheets are excellent for baking cookies, especially at high temperatures.

- The cookie bottoms will not overbrown by the time the tops are baked.

- For uninsulated sheets, look for heavy-duty aluminum so they don't warp in the heat. The sheets should have very low or no sides.

Two-Part Pans

- Tart pans with removable bottoms and tube pans are unique utensils.

- You must handle them carefully and lift them only from the sides when filled with batter or they can fall apart.

- These pans make it easy to serve tarts and large cakes. Remove the side from the tart pan and serve from the base.

- Run a knife around the tube pan and push the cake up, then remove the base.

Tart pans and tube pans have removable bottoms for ease in serving. These pans have to be handled carefully, but create excellent products.

Cakes can be made in round layer pans, in sheet pans, Bundt pans, cupcake tins, and other molds. And pie pans are available in everything from nonstick aluminum to heavy-duty ceramic.

Take care of your pans. Grease them when directed, and clean them as soon as they have cooled down. Dry them well, store in a dry place, and they will last a lifetime.

··········· RED ● LIGHT ···············

Nonstick pans are convenient, especially when you're working with sticky recipes like upside-down cakes and caramel. But there are some health warnings with these pans. Never put them over heat without oil or food. The Teflon coating can emit harmful gases when overheated. Never use these pans at temperatures higher than 500°F. They reach these temperatures faster than you think, after about 5 minutes on high heat.

Cake Pans

- Standard cake pans come in 8- and 9-inch sizes, both round and square, as well as 13x9 inch.

- Specialty pans for making wedding cakes are available, from 4 inches in diameter up to those larger than 13 inches.

- Other specialty pans include hexagonal, Bundt, and heart-shaped pans. Some pans have a design to shape the cake.

- Browse through baking supply stores and Internet sites like www.CooksDream .com to find more cake pan shapes and sizes.

Jelly Roll Pan

- A jelly roll pan is usually 15x10 inches, although there are half sheet pans that are 12x18.

- These pans have very low sides; they're used for making thin cakes to roll up with a filling. You can also use them to bake cookies.

- Since the pans have such short sides, it's very important that you purchase heavy-duty models that will keep their shape in the oven.

- Good-quality cake pans can be very expensive, costing more than $40 each, but they are worth it.

SERVING FUN

Serve your delicious desserts using beautiful and interesting stands and plates

Now that you have all of the serious equipment and tools for baking, it's time for some fun! There are so many wonderful serving pieces to display your delicious dessert recipes.

Look for these objects everywhere: at garage sales, antiques stores, novelty shops, home stores, department stores, and baking supply stores.

In fact, when you find something you love that can be used to serve a dessert, think about starting a collection. Many collections have been built around Candlewick plates, themed cookie jars, Fire-King serving ware, or Lusterware plates.

There is one thing to watch out for, however: lead content. Many older dishes and serving plates were decorated with

Cake Stands

- Cake stands with a high, domed, securely fitting lid are great for presenting and storing your cakes.

- They don't have to be expensive; a good glass stand with a domed lid can cost around $20.

- Use your cake stand for displaying desserts other than cakes too, especially on a buffet table. Changing heights of serving pieces adds interest.

- Some cake stands can be inverted on their base to make an elegant trifle or tiramisu server.

Pretty Plates

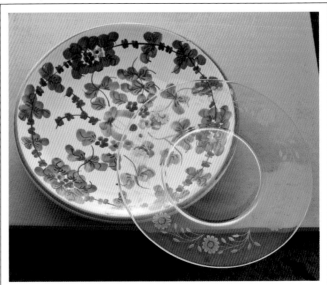

- A mismatched collection of large and small plates can be a wonderful way to display desserts.

- Follow cleaning directions carefully and make sure items are dishwasher-safe before you clean them.

- Collect serving plates in different colors or complementary periods. If you think it looks pretty, it will.

- Don't be afraid to mix different genres and styles of serving plates and utensils. You're creating your own unique style.

lead paint in the twentieth century. You can buy a lead testing kit to make sure your serving dishes are safe. Or, if you line the plates with napkins or doilies, or serve only cupcakes in paper liners, you can use these dishes.

Care for these dishes, especially older dishes, gently. Think twice about putting them in the dishwasher, and store them with felt squares or napkins between them so they don't scratch.

Have fun mixing and matching fun serving pieces. Use them to develop or accent your own style.

Cookie Jars

- There is an entire community dedicated to collecting cookie jars. Some are quite valuable.

- There are cookie jars that commemorate historic events, that were given as promotions, and that are just plain whimsical.

- Famous cookie jar collections include McCoy, Disney, Christopher Radko, Lenox, and Metlox.

- The cookie jar is not in actuality a very good place to store cookies. Place the cookies in a plastic bag inside the jar.

Special Servers

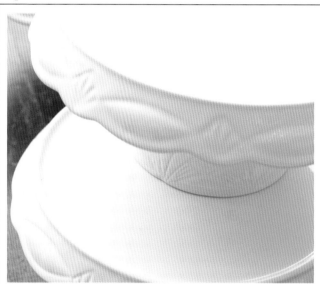

- Browse through any kitchen supply or fine dining catalog and you'll see lots of special serving equipment.

- Serving sets usually offer a large plate or bowl paired with matching smaller plates or bowls, and spoons, servers, or knives.

- Some pieces are made of china, others ceramic, and still others sterling silver.

- Think about the types of desserts you serve most often and then about creating a collection of special serving pieces.

BAKING BASICS
Learn the basics of baking techniques

Before you can bake you need to understand what some of the terms mean. Baking is like any other science. Before you can understand it, you need to learn the language.

Begin by reading the recipe straight through. Make sure you have all the ingredients, the utensils, tools, and appliances on hand. The recipe begins with the ingredient list, arranged in the order used.

Make sure that you measure all of the ingredients correctly,

not only spooning flour and other dry ingredients into the cups and leveling them off, but using the proper tools as well.

Most baking recipes require that you add ingredients in certain steps and at certain stages. Don't think you can just throw everything in a bowl and mix it. Most products need to have their structure created in a certain way.

Usually, fat and sugar are combined to begin the recipe.

Cream Butter and Sugar

- *Creaming* butter and sugar together is a term that means beating the ingredients in the same bowl.

- Use a sturdy spoon or a hand or stand mixer for this step. You're creating small holes in the fat, which will become the "crumb" of the product.

- These little holes, cut into the fat with the sharp edges of the sugar crystals, will fill with CO_2 in the oven.

- When the ingredients are properly combined, the mixture will look lighter in color and fluffy.

Sift Flour

- To sift flour, spoon it into a sieve or a mechanical sifter. Then sift it onto a piece of waxed paper or a bowl.

- When a recipe calls for sifted flour, sift the flour first, then measure it for best results.

- Sometimes you'll need to sift the flour after it has been measured, together with other ingredients.

- This blends the ingredients and aerates the flour. Do not skip this step if the recipe calls for it.

Then eggs and flavorings are added, and finally flour and liquid ingredients are added, sometimes in a particular way. The last step in putting together a baked product is often folding in beaten egg whites.

All of these steps are critical to the recipe's success. There are some recipes where all of the ingredients are combined. Even then, measuring and baking or cooking instructions must be carefully followed.

Add Dry and Wet Ingredients

- Adding the dry and wet, or liquid, ingredients to the egg-and-sugar mixture helps build the product's structure.

- The protein and starch from the flour and liquids form a web around the holes in the fat.

- Add these ingredients alternately. That means you add a quarter of the flour mixture and beat until it's combined.

- Then add a third of the liquid ingredients and beat the mixture until combined. Begin and end with the dry ingredients.

Fold Egg Whites

- Let egg whites stand at room temperature for 30 minutes, then add cream of tartar or lemon juice.

- Start beating; when foamy, start adding the sugar. Add the sugar gradually, beating constantly.

- Soft egg white peaks will droop when the beater is lifted. Stiff peaks will not droop.

- First stir a dollop of whites into the batter to lighten it, then fold in the rest, using an over-and-under motion.

TECHNIQUES

MEASURING
Measuring correctly is key to baking success

When a baking recipe fails, the most common cause is improper measuring. If there isn't enough flour, the recipe's structure will be weak and the dessert will collapse or fall. Too much flour means a tough or dry cake or cookie.

Too much liquid and a cake will never set; too little and it will be dry. Too much sugar and the recipe will be too sweet and may overbrown. Too little sugar and the recipe will be tough and won't brown enough, or the structure will collapse.

Correct measuring is a skill that comes with practice. Before long you won't even need to think about it. Practice with a scale until you're very accurate.

Different ingredients have to be measured different ways, but it's not that difficult. To measure dry ingredients, spoon them into calibrated measuring cups then level off the top. Liquid ingredients are measured using glass or plastic cups with graduated measurements on the side. Use the proper

Spoon Flour into Cup

Level Off the Top

- There's no need to sift flour before measuring as a matter of course, unless the recipe calls for it.

- Stir first, if that step is necessary. Then spoon the flour into the measuring cup. Keep adding flour until it heaps up over the top of the cup.

- Don't tap the cup on the counter or press down on the flour with the spoon.

- Measure whole wheat flours, granulated sugar, powdered sugar, and corn-starch this way too.

- Once the flour or other ingredient is in the cup, you need to level off the top for accurate measurement.

- Hold a cup containing flour over the canister or bag so you don't make a mess.

- Sweep the back of a knife over the excess flour on the top of the cup. Now you're ready to use the flour in your recipe.

- Use measuring spoons just like measuring cups: Add the ingredient and level off the top even with the spoon.

KNACK FABULOUS DESSERTS

equipment and you will have success.

Buy multiples of all your measuring cups to make baking easier and more fun. Then just drop them into the sink or the dishwasher as you work.

Enjoy the results of your new measuring skills.

More Measuring Tips

- Brown sugar is measured in a special way because it is relatively high in moisture.

- Pack the sugar into the cup or spoon firmly, and level off the top. The sugar should hold its shape when unmolded.

- Shortening or other solid ingredients are also measured by packing into the measuring cup or spoon, then leveling off the top.

- Buy lots of measuring spoons so that, as you use them, you can just drop them in a sink of soapy water and keep working.

Measuring Liquid Ingredients

- You can use dry measuring cups to measure liquid ingredients, but you'll get better results using a standardized liquid measuring cup.

- Pour the liquid into the cup and place it on a solid surface.

- Bend down so your eyes are even with the measurement level you're trying to achieve. Don't hold the cup up to your eyes.

- The liquid should be just at the mark on the cup, whether it's ¼ cup, 1 cup, or 2 cups.

TECHNIQUES

MIXING
Mixing, stirring, folding, and creaming: What's the difference?

There are many terms that describe how ingredients are combined in dessert recipes. And they all have distinct, specific definitions that are basically about adding air to batters and doughs. Learning how to perform these functions isn't difficult, but it does take some practice.

Ingredients are combined with different amounts of energy. Adding energy to the food changes its characteristics. *Mixing* and *stirring* basically mean the same thing. These generic terms just mean you are manipulating the food with a spoon or mixer.

Beating and *whipping* are higher-energy actions, usually performed with a whisk, or a hand or stand mixer. These are used when air must be added to the batter, as when whipping egg whites or beating heavy cream.

Creaming means combining fats with sugar. This action is performed with a spoon or mixer and helps add air to the fat

Stirring

- Stirring is a gentle method of mixing, usually done with a wooden or metal spoon.

- Move the spoon around the ingredients in the bowl, stopping several times to scrape down the sides of the bowl.

- Keep going until the mixture becomes smooth, or as long as the recipe directs. Don't use much force, and be consistent in the mixing speed.

- You can stir with a hand mixer set to the lowest possible speed.

Beating

- Beating involves more effort, more speed, and more energy. To beat, stir vigorously and quickly.

- You are adding air into the ingredients, so tilt the bowl a little bit as you beat.

- The protein and starch in flour, cornstarch, and eggs will begin to form a web that will trap the air being beaten into the batter.

- Beating is most efficiently done with an eggbeater or a hand or stand mixer. Scrape down the sides of the bowl frequently.

to create the recipe's structure.

And *folding* is the gentlest of all the mixing actions. Fold in egg whites or whipped cream by cutting a spoon or spatula down through the center of the ingredients, scraping along the bottom, and turning the food over until the mixtures are combined.

Once you understand these differences, making and baking desserts will become very easy.

ZOOM

Cut in is a very specific baking term that applies to only one action: adding fat to flour to make a piecrust. A pastry blender, a utensil made of a handle with attached parallel blades, is used to cut the fat into tiny pieces. You can use two knives to work the ingredients together. Cutting in creates layers of fat and flour in the finished product, which become flaky layers when baked.

Folding

- Folding is a very gentle action, usually used to combine a delicate mixture into a sturdier one, such as egg whites into a batter.

- Begin by stirring a dollop of the lighter mixture into the heavier mixture to lighten it.

- Add the rest of the lighter mixture. Cut through the center of the mixture in the bowl down to the bottom.

- Then scrape the bottom of the bowl, turning the two mixtures together. Turn the bowl slightly and repeat.

Whisking

- Whisking is accomplished with a wire or plastic whisk. This tool is designed to make smooth sauces.

- When you're adding a liquid to a roux (a cooked fat-and-flour mixture), you need a whisk to beat out any lumps.

- Hold the whisk by the handle and move it quickly through the ingredients, being careful to reach into edges and corners.

- You can use a whisk to beat egg whites into a meringue. This takes work, but can be quite satisfying.

TECHNIQUES

DONENESS TESTS

When a recipe is done, there are clues to watch for

Beautifully browned cakes, tender, delicate cookies, and crisp and flaky piecrusts all have one thing in common: They have been baked to the perfect doneness point.

Doneness tests are important because underdone cakes can fall, while overdone cakes are dry and tough. Underdone cookies will fall apart, while cookies baked too long can burn or become dry.

Once you learn how to perform doneness tests, your confidence in baking will increase. After all your hard work making the recipe, the final step of baking or cooking it must be carefully monitored.

Use the baking and cooking times given in recipes as general guidelines. Start checking the food about 5 minutes before the earliest time. If the recipe isn't done, continue checking at 4- to 5-minute intervals until it is finished. Make sure to write down the final baking or cooking time on the

Toothpick Test

- Insert a clean toothpick into the cake or torte, at the center or near the center of the food.

- Pull it out. If the toothpick is dry and clean, the recipe is done. If moist or wet crumbs stick to the toothpick, keep baking.

- You can also use a skewer, and stainless-steel reusable cake testers are available at kitchen supply stores.

- Don't reuse the toothpick; Use a clean one each time you perform the test.

Finger Touch

- Lightly touch your finger to the top of a cake or cookie. When it is done, the cake will spring back with no indentation.

- Don't press down too hard on the cake or the test will not be accurate.

- If you do press down too hard, and the cake is not done, return it to the oven immediately.

- The part where you pressed your finger might not expand in the oven, even when the cake is properly baked. Just fill with frosting.

recipe so that you can be more accurate next time.

Basic doneness tests include the toothpick tests, a finger touch, internal temperature, and observation. Some recipes call for more than one doneness test to make absolutely sure the recipe is baked or cooked correctly. This helps ensure the accuracy of the recipe.

A well-calibrated oven is essential to recipe timing and recipe doneness, as is an accurate oven thermometer.

•••••••••••••••• RED ● LIGHT ••••••••••••••••

If you do remove a food from the oven, the microwave, or the stovetop before it is done, it can't always be returned to the heat to finish cooking. Cakes may start to fall quickly if they are underbaked, and the leavening will not work if the cake is rebaked. Cookies can sometimes be returned to the oven, however, and puddings and custards cooked on the stovetop can be recooked.

Internal Temperature

- Any recipe that contains raw eggs should be cooked to an internal temperature of at least 160°F for food safety reasons.

- Custards, puddings, and cheesecakes should reach this temperature too.

- Cakes are finished when their internal temperature reaches 200°F.

- All foods will continue cooking slightly after they are removed from the oven. This is known as residual cooking. It stops after a few minutes out of the oven.

Observation

- The doneness test for brownies, especially those that are fudgy or include additional ingredients like chocolate chips, is to observe a shiny, dry crust.

- Cakes are done when they are evenly golden brown and the sides pull away from the pan.

- Cookies are done when they are light golden brown. The centers of the cookies should still be moist.

- Cheesecakes will look set, with golden edges. The centers will jiggle slightly when the cake is moved.

TECHNIQUES

FINISHING TOUCHES

Frosting, glazes, and other garnishes finish your desserts beautifully

Now that your desserts are perfectly made and baked, it's time to add the finishing touches. Glazes, frostings, decorations, and garnishes are all fairly easy and add so much to the appearance of your desserts.

A finishing touch is a wonderful way to add another dimension to your dessert. If you're serving a creamy dessert, garnish with something crisp or crunchy. A cold dessert is enhanced with a warm sauce, and a crunchy dessert is even better with

a soft or creamy garnish. Or use a tart garnish, like lemon zest, on a very sweet dessert.

A finishing touch can be as simple as a sprig of fresh mint, or as complicated as homemade ice cream and chocolate sauce.

In the 1980s plate painting became a popular way to serve a dessert beautifully. Fruit sauces, jam, and ice cream toppings can be used to draw a design on a plate that showcases a

Frost Two-Layer Cake

- To frost a two-layer cake, place the first layer upside down on a serving plate that has been lined with waxed paper on the edges.

- Frost the top of that layer with about a cup of frosting. Place the second layer on top, right-side up.

- Frost the top of the cake, pushing the frosting over onto the sides, then frost the cake sides. An offset spatula works well for this task.

- Now carefully pull the waxed paper strips out from under the cake for a clean serving plate.

Piped-Frosting Decorations

- Frosting can be used in simple ways to decorate a cake. A pastry bag with attached tip can be used to pipe a border, swags, rosettes, or simple flowers.

- An easy way to garnish a chocolate dessert is to pipe whipped cream stars in an even and dense layer on the top.

- Directions that come with your pastry bag can give you lots of ideas and quick tips for decorations.

- And you can find premade frosting roses and flowers at kitchen supply stores.

32

torte, pie, or cake. Use a small squeeze bottle to draw a pattern on the plate, or make a spiral. Stars and hearts are also easy designs to create.

Citrus peel and zest, chocolate-dipped fruits, strawberry fans, and plain or sugared fruits and flowers are more excellent garnish ideas to perfectly finish your gorgeous desserts.

Garnishes and Sauces

- Toasted coconut and chopped nuts are an excellent garnish for desserts.

- To toast coconut or nuts, spread them on a baking sheet. Toss with spices like cinnamon or nutmeg.

- Bake at 350°F for 10 to 14 minutes for coconut, or at 400°F for 8 to 10 minutes for nuts. Toast nuts whole or chopped; let whole nuts cool before chopping.

- Edible flowers include pansies, violets, nasturtiums, roses, and orange blossoms. Be sure they are safe for food use.

Sprinkle a Garnish

- Sprinkle powdered sugar on a cake or pie for a garnish. You can place a doily or stencil atop the dessert first for an even more elegant finish.

- Or add chopped or shaved chocolate. Use a swivel-bladed vegetable peeler to create chocolate shards.

- Dust the plate with cocoa powder or powdered sugar before you add the dessert to create another garnish.

- And crumbled cookies or a light sprinkling of coarse sea salt can be the perfect finish for a pudding or custard.

TECHNIQUES

CHILLING & FREEZING
Chilling and freezing food has special rules to follow for best results

Whether you are freezing or chilling a dessert meant to be served frozen or cold, or are preserving your efforts in the kitchen, there are some rules to follow.

Most dessert recipes are allowed to cool at room temperature. Exceptions to that rule include cooked puddings and custards, ice cream, and other frozen desserts.

To cool baked goods, follow the recipe directions. Some foods are cooled in or on their baking pans, while others need to be removed from the pan or they will continue to cook. Make sure that the cooling food is not placed in a draft, which can adversely affect delicate cakes and cookies.

When you're chilling cold and frozen desserts, cooling the food quickly is key to the best results. Transfer the food from a pan used to heat it to another to cool it. Or spread the food out in a single layer to place in the refrigerator or freezer.

Storing frozen food properly is also key. The freezer is a very

Cooling Food

- Cool food on a wire rack. This utensil allows air to circulate around the food so it cools evenly and doesn't become soggy.

- When hot foods are placed on a cool surface, condensation can occur at that border.

- This condensation can ruin baked goods with a wet layer at the bottom, which can make them fall apart or ruin their texture.

- Cool foods according to the recipe instructions, then cover or wrap them to store.

How to Freeze

- Foods should be frozen as quickly as possible after preparation. Be sure that your freezer is set at 0°F or below.

- Freeze individual foods in a single layer until hard, then wrap well, using freezer bags, containers, wrap, and freezer tape.

- Frozen desserts should be placed in the coldest spot in the freezer. Check your freezer manual for this information.

- Follow the recipe directions to see whether the food should be frozen covered or uncovered.

dry place. Any food that is not properly covered and sealed can develop dried spots, commonly known as freezer burn.

Finally, thawing and serving frozen food takes special knowledge. Follow directions and your cold desserts will have great texture.

Serving Frozen Food

- Very cold temperatures dull the flavors of food. It's harder for your tongue to taste food that is frigid.

- Most frozen foods should stand for a few minutes at room temperature before serving.

- This standing time thaws the food very slightly, which also makes it easier to cut or scoop and serve.

- The recipe should tell you whether the food should be thawed before serving or served frozen.

Storing Frozen Food

- Have a thermometer in the freezer to make sure it is set at the correct temperature.

- A full freezer is most efficient, but be sure to leave some space around the food so the cold air can circulate.

- You can store the food for up to 3 or 4 months. Make sure you write the preparation date directly on the package.

- To keep track of what's in your freezer, keep a small notebook nearby. Update it every time you take something out or put it in.

TECHNIQUES

CHOCOLATE CAKE

The best chocolate cake is creamy and light with an intense flavor

Chocolate cake is a classic recipe everyone should know how to make. The best cake is creamy, with an intense chocolate flavor and an even, delicate crumb.

Cocoa powder comes in two forms: Dutch processed and regular. Dutch-processed cocoa powder is treated with an alkaline compound to reduce its acidity. It won't react with baking soda, like regular cocoa powder will. This type of cocoa powder has a lighter flavor. Read labels and use regular cocoa powder in this simple recipe.

Make sure that the chocolate chips are finely ground. The tiny particles melt in the cake as it bakes, adding a creamy texture. Frost this cake with any frosting: vanilla for contrast, or chocolate for a rich chocolate sensation. *Yield: 1 two-layer 9-inch cake or 1 13x9-inch cake*

KNACK FABULOUS DESSERTS

Ingredients

2 cups sifted flour

2/3 cup cocoa powder

1 teaspoon baking powder

1/2 teaspoon baking soda

1/2 teaspoon salt

1/2 cup butter, softened

1 cup granulated sugar

1 cup packed brown sugar

3 eggs, separated

2 teaspoons vanilla extract

1/2 cup milk

1 cup water

1 cup semisweet chocolate chips, finely ground

Easy Buttercream Frosting (see page 212) or Silky Chocolate Frosting (see page 213)

Chocolate Cake

- Preheat oven to 350°F. Spray two 9-inch-round pans with nonstick baking spray.

- Sift flour, cocoa, baking powder, soda, and salt. In bowl, beat butter with granulated sugar until fluffy.

- Add brown sugar, egg yolks, and vanilla; beat. Alternately add flour mixture with milk and water.

- Add unbeaten egg whites; beat 2 minutes; fold in ground chocolate. Pour into prepared pans. Bake 20 to 25 minutes, until done; remove to racks; cool. Fill and frost.

White Cake: Make cake as directed, except omit cocoa powder. Increase flour to 2⅓ cups sifted. Use 4 egg whites in place of separated eggs; add at end of mixing, as directed. Omit semisweet chocolate chips. Grind ½ cup white chocolate chips and fold them in as directed. Bake cake as directed, cool completely, and then frost as desired.

Yellow Cake: Make cake as directed, except omit cocoa powder. Increase flour to 2½ cups sifted. Omit semisweet chocolate chips. Add another teaspoon of vanilla extract, or scrape seeds from a vanilla bean and add those with liquid. Bake cake as directed: 20 to 30 minutes for 9-inch pans, 35 to 45 minutes for 13x9 pan. Cool cake completely, and then frost as desired.

Beat Butter with Sugar

- When butter is beaten with sugar in a method called creaming, the sugar creates tiny holes in the fat.

- These holes help form the structure of the cake, and create the crumb in the baked product.

- This step is very important in creating a fine, even crumb, or texture, in the finished cake, so don't skimp on this process.

- Ground chocolate, as a finely divided solid, makes the finished cake creamy and smooth.

Test Cakes for Doneness

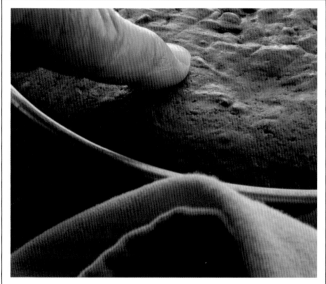

- A toothpick inserted in the center of the cake will come out mostly clean, with a few crumbs clinging.

- The cake will also spring back when lightly touched in the center, and the edges will start to pull away from the pan.

- Let 9-inch cakes cool in the pan 5 minutes, then gently shake the pans to loosen. Turn out onto wire racks and cool completely.

- Bake a 13x9-inch cake for 35 to 45 minutes; cool in the pan.

CAKES

MARBLE CUPCAKES

Vanilla and chocolate batter swirl together in these pretty cupcakes

Everyone loves cupcakes; they are fun to make and eat. For a nice presentation, place a lot of cupcakes on a tiered cake stand. This can even substitute for a fancy layered cake at a birthday or wedding celebration.

When you make cupcakes, be sure that each little tin is filled with an equal amount of batter so they bake evenly in the same time frame. Use a measuring cup to scoop the batter from the bowl into the tins.

Have fun with your cupcakes. Decorate each one with a different color of frosting, or use sprinkles or sugar flowers to add a personal touch. For a child's birthday party, a cupcake-decorating bar is a wonderful activity. *Yield: 24 cupcakes*

Ingredients

$^3/_4$ cup butter, softened

$1^1/_2$ cups granulated sugar

$^1/_2$ cup packed brown sugar

4 eggs

$2^3/_4$ cups flour

$2^1/_2$ teaspoons baking powder

1 teaspoon baking soda

$^1/_2$ teaspoon salt

2 teaspoons vanilla

$^1/_2$ cup milk

$^1/_2$ cup buttermilk

$1^1/_2$ (1-ounce) squares unsweetened chocolate, melted

Silky Chocolate Frosting (see page 213)

Marble Cupcakes

- Preheat oven to 350°F. Spray 24 muffin tins with nonstick baking spray.

- In bowl, beat butter with sugars. Add eggs, beat.

- Mix flour with baking powder, soda, and salt. Combine vanilla, milk, and buttermilk; add alternately with flour mixture to batter.

- Remove a third of batter to another bowl; blend in melted chocolate. Spoon plain and chocolate batters into prepared tins, filling three-quarters full; swirl once with knife. Bake 13 to 19 minutes, until done. Cool on racks.

Marble Frosting: Frost cupcakes with marble frosting. Make one batch Easy Buttercream Frosting; divide in half. Add 1½ squares unsweetened chocolate, melted, to half and beat until combined. Spoon both frostings into piping bag; pipe onto cupcakes, turning bag slightly as you pipe to create a braided effect.

Do not use self-rising flour unless a recipe calls for it specifically. This type of flour, which is actually a mixture of flour, baking powder, and salt, is used primarily in the South. The proportions are generally 1 teaspoon baking powder and ½ teaspoon salt per cup of flour. This is usually too much salt for most baking recipes. If you use this flour when the recipe doesn't call for it, the recipe will probably fail.

Beat in Flour and Milk

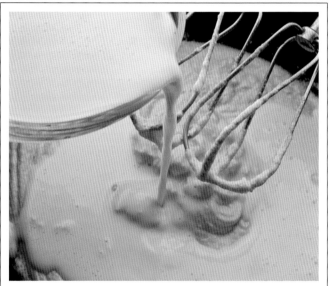

Marble Batter with Knife

- Adding liquid and dry ingredients alternately to a cake batter helps build the structure.

- To accomplish this task properly, the dry ingredients and then the liquid must be fully incorporated into the butter-sugar-egg mixture before you add the other ingredient.

- An electric mixer is the best appliance for this job, but you can mix the batter by hand with a wooden spoon.

- Beat the batter firmly, about 10 to 20 strokes after each addition, until it is smooth and creamy.

- The two batters should be spooned carefully and evenly into the cupcake tins. Don't under- or overfill.

- Then gently run the tip of a knife through the batter in a simple pattern to marble the two mixtures together.

- Don't overdo this, or the batters will combine too much and you'll lose the color and flavor contrast.

- These pretty cupcakes can be served plain, frosted with your favorite icing, or dusted with powdered sugar.

CAKES

RED VELVET CAKE

This classic southern cake is actually flavored with cocoa powder

Anyone who has eaten food at a southern celebration has had a Red Velvet Cake. The cake is actually red in color, with a texture that can be described as creamy and, well, velvety.

The red color comes from two sources: red food coloring and the interaction of acidic cocoa powder with alkaline baking soda. Traditionally, the cake has a very mild chocolate flavor.

The classic recipe is finished with Old-Fashioned Frosting, which gets its creamy texture from a cooked paste. This may sound odd, but the frosting is as velvety as the cake! You can use Easy Buttercream or Cream Cheese Frosting if you'd like.

Enjoy this cake with a tall glass of milk, on the porch under a ceiling fan, with friends. *Yield: 1 two-layer 9-inch cake*

Ingredients

2 teaspoons cocoa powder, for pans

2 cups cake flour

1/2 cup all-purpose flour

1/4 cup cocoa powder

1/2 teaspoon salt

1/2 cup unsalted butter, softened

1/4 cup vegetable oil

1 cup granulated sugar

3/4 cup packed brown sugar

2 eggs

1 tablespoon red food coloring

2 teaspoons vanilla

1 cup buttermilk

1 1/2 teaspoons baking soda

1 tablespoon vinegar

Old-Fashioned Frosting (see page 208)

Red Velvet Cake

- Grease two 9-inch-round cake pans with unsalted butter; dust with 1 teaspoon cocoa powder. Preheat oven to 350°F.

- Sift together flours, cocoa, and salt. In bowl, beat butter with oil and sugars.

- Add eggs, one at a time, then food coloring and vanilla. Add flour mixture alternately with buttermilk.

- Mix baking soda and vinegar in small bowl; stir into batter. Pour into pans. Bake 26 to 32 minutes, until done. Fill and frost with Old-Fashioned Frosting.

- **Red Velvet Cupcakes:** Make recipe as directed, except line 24 muffin tins with paper cupcake liners. Fill tins two-thirds full with batter. Bake at 350°F for 19 to 23 minutes, until a toothpick inserted in center comes out clean. Immediately remove from muffin tins; cool on wire rack. Frost cupcakes using Cream Cheese or Old-Fashioned Frosting (see pages 204 and 208.).

GREEN ● LIGHT

Cakes need to cool in the pan for a few minutes before removing in order to make sure that the structure is set. If the cake is left in the pan too long, it may stick. Let the cake stand, in its pan, on a wire rack 5 to 10 minutes. Then gently shake the pan to loosen the cake and remove it. Cool it completely on a wire rack.

Add Flour and Buttermilk

Pour Batter and Bake

- Because this batter should be acidic, so the baking soda will work well, use regular and not Dutch-processed cocoa powder.

- This reaction between the acidic vinegar, buttermilk, cocoa powder, and the alkaline baking soda accentuates the reddish brown color of the cake.

- Add the dry ingredients and buttermilk alternately to the butter mixture.

- Add one-quarter of the dry ingredients, then one-third of the buttermilk; repeat until all of the ingredients are incorporated.

- When making a layer cake, having an equal amount of batter in each pan is important to the finished product. You can weigh the pans as you pour the batter for the most precise results. Place the pans on a scale and zero it. Then add batter. Or you can use a measuring cup to divide it.

- This cake, although moist and tender, is quite sturdy. Use the toothpick test for testing doneness, cool completely, then frost.

- For a beautiful presentation, coat sides of cake with coconut and sprinkle with crushed nuts.

CAKES

41

CHIFFON CAKE
This light and fluffy cake is easy to make

Cakes that are truly a new creation are rare. Chiffon cakes are a combination of sponge cakes and shortening cakes. The texture is very delicate. Be careful when you fold the egg whites into the batter, spoon the batter carefully into the pan, and be sure to invert the cake when it comes out of the oven.

Chiffon cakes are typically served unfrosted, but you can frost them or drizzle with a glaze. For another option, cut off the top 1 inch of the cake and set aside. Gently scoop out the center of the cake, creating a tunnel. Fill with sweetened whipped cream or berries, then replace the top. *Yield: 1 tube cake*

KNACK FABULOUS DESSERTS

Ingredients

1 cup all purpose flour

$^3/_4$ cup cake flour

2$^1/_2$ teaspoons baking powder

$^1/_4$ teaspoon salt

6 eggs, separated

$^1/_4$ cup granulated sugar

$^1/_2$ cup packed brown sugar

$^1/_2$ cup vegetable oil

$^3/_4$ cup water

2 teaspoons vanilla

$^1/_2$ teaspoon cream of tartar

$^1/_2$ cup granulated sugar

Chiffon Cake

- Preheat oven to 325°F. Sift flours, baking powder, and salt into large bowl.

- In medium bowl, beat egg yolks 5 minutes. Beat in ¼ cup granulated sugar, ½ cup brown sugar, oil, water, and vanilla.

- Beat into flour mixture with wire whisk. Beat egg whites with cream of tartar until foamy.

- Add ½ cup granulated sugar gradually, beating until stiff. Fold into batter; pour into 10-inch tube pan. Bake 55 to 65 minutes, until set. Invert; cool.

A man named Harry Baker developed the chiffon cake in 1927. The food giant General Mills bought the secret recipe from him in the 1940s and made it public. The cake is made with vegetable oil instead of butter, making it lighter in texture and flavor. The eggs are separated and the whites beaten until fluffy, which makes the cake airy and light.

• • • • RECIPE VARIATION • • • •

Spice Chiffon Cake: Make as directed, but omit brown sugar. Increase granulated sugar beaten with egg yolks to ¾ cup. Sift 1 teaspoon cinnamon, ¼ teaspoon nutmeg, and ⅛ teaspoon cardamom with flour mixture. Make cake. Mix 1 cup powdered sugar, 2 tablespoons maple syrup, ½ teaspoon cinnamon, and 2 tablespoons melted butter; drizzle over cake.

Add Liquid to Dry Ingredients

Invert Cake

CAKES

- It's important that the liquid ingredients are added to the dry ingredients all at once.

- Beat the mixture just until the batter is smooth and all of the ingredients are incorporated. Overbeating will develop the gluten and result in a tough cake.

- When folding egg whites into cake batter, first stir a spoonful of the whites into the batter to lighten it.

- Then add the remaining egg whites and fold, using an over-and-under motion, to incorporate the batter.

- Cakes are inverted when the structure is so delicate it can collapse as it cools.

- Keep the cake in the pan; invert over a funnel or pop bottle. Inverting the cake helps stretch the protein and starch in the structure, so as it cools it will set.

- The cake pans are never greased so the cake stays in the pan.

- When cooled, use a sharp knife and carefully loosen the cake from the pan, then ease it out. Cut around the center hole and bottom of the cake and remove the pan.

CARROT CAKE

Carrot cake is rich and velvety, with a wonderful texture and flavor

Carrot cake is a classic recipe that is hearty and moist, perfect for a celebration dinner or a snack.

The trick to making the best carrot cake is to grate the carrots finely. Pre-shredded carrots have no place in this cake; they are too tough and won't dissolve into the batter. Baby carrots are an excellent choice because they are sweeter and more tender than regular carrots.

You can bake this batter as a sheet cake or a layer cake. The classic Cream Cheese Frosting stands up to this cake's assertive flavors and perfectly complements the delicious flavor and texture.

Serve this cake with a tall glass of cold milk after a dinner of roast chicken and scalloped potatoes. *Yield: 1 9-inch layer cake*

Ingredients

- 1 (16-ounce) bag baby carrots
- 4 eggs
- ³/₄ cup vegetable oil
- ¹/₃ cup butter, softened
- ¹/₄ cup carrot baby food
- 1 cup packed brown sugar
- 1 cup granulated sugar
- 1 tablespoon vanilla
- 1 (8-ounce) can crushed pineapple, well drained
- 2 cups flour
- 1¹/₂ teaspoons baking powder
- 1 teaspoon baking soda
- 1 teaspoon cinnamon
- ¹/₄ teaspoon salt
- ¹/₂ teaspoon nutmeg
- 1 cup chopped pecans
- Cream Cheese Frosting (see page 204) or Broiled Frosting (see page 210)

Carrot Cake

- Preheat oven to 350°F. Coat 2 9-inch pans with nonstick baking spray.

- Grate baby carrots in food processor until very fine; set aside. In large bowl, beat eggs, oil, butter, baby food, and sugars until blended.

- Add vanilla and pineapple.

- Stir in flour, baking powder, soda, cinnamon, salt, and nutmeg. Stir in carrots and pecans.

- Spread into pan. Bake 28 to 33 minutes, until done. For 13x9-inch pan, bake 40 to 50 minutes. Cool, then frost with Cream Cheese Frosting.

Carrot Cupcakes: Make recipe as directed, except spray 24 regular muffin tins with nonstick baking spray. Spoon batter into tins. Bake at 350°F for 18 to 23 minutes, until tops spring back when lightly touched with finger. Cool in pans 5 minutes; remove from pans and cool on wire rack. Frost with Cream Cheese Frosting; sprinkle with toasted coconut.

Zucchini Cake: Make recipe as directed, except substitute 2 cups grated zucchini for baby carrots. Reduce eggs to 3; add ⅓ cup flour. Omit nutmeg, and add 1 cup chopped walnuts in place of pecans. Bake cake as directed until it springs back when touched. Cool completely and top with Cream Cheese Frosting.

Prepare Carrots

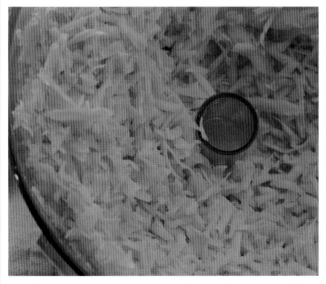

- Baby carrots are more tender than regular carrots. They are actually large carrots trimmed down to a small size.

- But the carrot variety is different from regular carrots; it is sweeter, with less of the bitter middle part.

- Process the carrots until they are finely chopped; do not process until they are mushy or too soft.

- You can also grate the carrots manually on the large holes of a box grater. This takes more time; be careful for your fingers.

Prepare Batter

- For the batter to be properly blended, the butter must be quite soft.

- Let it stand at room temperature for at least 1 hour before combining with the oil, eggs, sugars, and baby food.

- This moist cake is best tested for doneness by observing a deep golden brown crust. The cake will start to pull away from the sides of the pan.

- Store the cake in the refrigerator because of the Cream Cheese Frosting; let it stand 15 minutes before serving.

CAKES

45

LEMON BUTTER CAKE

This dessert combines sponge cake, crunchy toffee, and velvety frosting

If you want a special cake for a celebration, this is it! The light and tender sponge cake is complemented with a fluffy lemon frosting and crunchy butter toffee.

Lemon zest is used in cake batters because it contains lots of essential oils. This adds concentrated flavor to the cake without the bitter flavor juice can sometimes impart.

You can frost this cake using Easy Buttercream Frosting (see page 212); just add a teaspoon of lemon zest to the frosting and use lemon juice instead of milk or cream.

This cake is also excellent as a base for English trifle or tiramisu. Serve it at the end of a special dinner with some flavored coffee and tea in bone china cups. *Yield: Serves 12*

Ingredients

- 1 cup butter, softened
- 1 teaspoon lemon extract
- 1¼ cups sugar
- 2 tablespoons lemon juice
- 1 teaspoon grated lemon zest
- 6 eggs
- 2¼ cups cake flour
- 1½ teaspoons baking powder
- ½ teaspoon baking soda
- ½ teaspoon salt
- Lemon Seven Minute Frosting (see page 215)
- 1 cup finely crushed butter toffee

Lemon Butter Cake

- Beat butter with extract and sugar. Beat in lemon juice, zest, and then eggs.

- Sift cake flour, baking powder, soda, and salt; fold into butter mixture. Spoon into 10-inch angel food pan. Bake at 325°F 50 to 60 minutes.

- Let cool 10 minutes. Remove sides of pan; cool completely. Make Seven Minute Frosting with Lemon.

- Remove cake from pan; cut into three equal layers. Spread bottom with one-third frosting; sprinkle with one-third toffee; repeat.

Easier Lemon Butter Cake: Make cake as directed; bake and cool. Remove cake from pan; do not cut into layers. Frost outside of cake and inside center hole with Lemon Seven Minute Frosting. Press butter toffee into top and sides of cake. You can bake in 12-cup Bundt pan instead of tube pan if desired.

Filled Lemon Butter Cake: Bake and cool cake as directed. Remove cake from pan; do not cut into layers. Remove top 1 inch of cake and set aside. Cut ring into cake, leaving 1-inch sides and bottom; reserve cake for another use. Fold together 1½ cups Lemon Seven Minute Frosting and butter toffee; fill ring. Replace top of cake; frost top and sides with remaining frosting.

Beat in Eggs

Pour Batter into Pan

- For best results, have the eggs at room temperature before beating them into the butter-and-sugar mixture.

- You can let the eggs stand at room temperature for 1 hour, or place them in a bowl of lukewarm water for 20 minutes.

- Break the eggs, one at a time, into a shallow saucer and add to the batter so you can make sure every egg is perfect.

- If some eggshell gets into the egg, use another piece of eggshell to remove it.

- The angel food pan, also known as a tube pan, is round and tall, with a cone extending up the center.

- This cone helps hot air circulate around the center of the cake so it bakes evenly.

- Spread the batter evenly into the pan. Wipe off any spills or drips, which can burn and affect the cake's flavor.

- Be careful when you pick up the pan to put it in the oven. Never pick up a tube pan by the center tunnel or the pan will fall apart.

CAKES

CHOCOLATE CHIP COOKIES

The best chocolate chip cookies are chewy and crisp, with a rich caramel flavor

Everyone loves chocolate chip cookies. But not everyone has had the best chocolate chip cookies! This recipe makes a tender cookie full of rich flavor.

Ground white chocolate chips, in food science language, are called finely divided solids. This type of ingredient adds creamy texture and lots of flavor to cookie doughs and cake batter. Make sure the chocolate is very finely ground.

You can use chocolate chips or chocolate chunks in this recipe, and vary the combination of semisweet, dark chocolate, and milk chocolate to create your own signature cookie. Nuts like pecans or walnuts can also be added. Serve with lots of cold milk! *Yield: 48 cookies*

Ingredients

- 1 cup butter, divided
- 1 cup packed brown sugar
- 2/3 cup granulated sugar
- 2 eggs
- 1 egg yolk
- 1/2 cup white chocolate chips, finely ground
- 2 teaspoons vanilla
- 2 1/2 cups flour
- 1 teaspoon baking soda
- 1/4 teaspoon salt
- 2 cups semisweet chocolate chips
- 1 cup milk chocolate chips

Chocolate Chip Cookies

- Melt half of butter in small saucepan; cook over low heat 6 to 9 minutes, until brown. Transfer to bowl; chill 30 minutes.

- Add remaining butter and sugars and beat until fluffy. Beat in eggs and egg yolk.

- Stir in ground chips and vanilla, then stir in flour, baking soda, and salt. Stir in chips.

- Cover; chill 4 hours. Drop by tablespoons onto greased cookie sheet. Bake at 325°F 10 to 13 minutes, until set; cool on wire racks.

Chocolate Chip Sandwich Cookies: Make cookies as directed; cool completely. Then make sandwiches of the cookies using any filling, including Easy Butter-cream Frosting, Creamy Chocolate Frosting, or Seven Minute Frosting. Store at room temperature. Or you can make ice cream sandwiches, using ⅓ cup of any flavor ice cream between two cookies; freeze until solid.

Ruth Wakefield, a dietitian who owned the Toll House Inn in Massachusetts, invented chocolate chip cookies. She thought that the chopped chocolate added to cookie dough would melt to create chocolate cookies. Instead, the chocolate stayed in discrete pieces, and a brand-new cookie was born.

Browning Butter

- Browned butter has a much more complex flavor than plain butter. It develops a rich nutty and caramel taste.

- It's important to chill the browned butter before you mix it with the other ingredients.

- You can make the browned butter a day or two ahead of time; just store it in the refrigerator. Let it soften before using it in the cookies.

- Beat the butter and sugars together well before adding the egg and egg yolk for the best texture.

Form and Bake Cookies

- The cookies will be more tender and will not over-bake when the dough is chilled.

- This step is important: It helps the gluten in the flour relax. The cookies will be tender and chewy, with crisp edges.

- Watch the cookies carefully in the oven. They should be just done when you remove them—barely set in the middle.

- Let the cookies stand on the baking sheets for 2 minutes, then remove with a spatula to a wire rack to cool completely.

COOKIES

SHORTBREAD COOKIES

Shortbread should be crisp but melt-in-your-mouth tender

Shortbread is named because the dough used to make it is "short," or high in fat and sugar and relatively low in flour. It is crumbly and delicate and very tender.

There are several ways to form shortbread cookies. You can roll them out and cut with a cookie cutter, or roll the dough into a square and cut into rectangles, or roll the dough into balls and flatten with a fork or the bottom of a glass.

The coconut oil is solid at room temperature. It will add a crisp texture to the cookies, and it doesn't taste like coconut. You can use all butter if you'd like.

Shortbread cookies are different from sugar cookies in that they are thicker and more tender. *Yield: 36 cookies*

KNACK FABULOUS DESSERTS

Ingredients

- ³/₄ cup butter
- ¹/₄ cup coconut oil
- ¹/₃ cup granulated sugar
- ¹/₄ cup powdered sugar
- 2 teaspoons vanilla
- 1 ³/₄ cups all-purpose flour
- ¹/₄ cup cornstarch
- Pinch salt

Shortbread Cookies

- In food processor, combine butter with coconut oil; process until well blended. Place in large bowl.

- Add sugars to butter mixture and beat until smooth. Add vanilla, flour, cornstarch, and salt; mix until dough forms. Chill dough 1 hour.

- Preheat oven to 350°F. Roll dough onto lightly floured surface until ½ inch thick. Cut with cookie cutters or cut into 2-inch squares.

- Bake 9 to 11 minutes, until golden brown. Cool 5 minutes and remove from pan; cool on rack.

Chocolate Shortbread Cookies: Make recipe as directed, except add 1 square unsweetened chocolate and ⅓ cup semisweet chocolate chips, melted together and cooled, to butter-and-sugar mixture. Increase flour to 2 cups minus 2 tablespoons. Chill dough at least 8 hours, and watch carefully when cookies are in oven so they don't burn.

Chocolate-Dipped Shortbread: Make cookie dough as directed; cut into 3x1-inch rectangles. Prick dough with fork and bake as directed. Cool cookies completely on wire rack. Melt 1 cup semisweet chocolate chips and ½ cup milk chocolate chips. Dip half of each cookie into melted chocolate; place on waxed paper and let stand until set.

Process Fats

- Coconut oil may be solid at room temperature, but it's also much harder than butter.

- The two fats have to be processed together to make the coconut oil manageable. Don't chill this mixture after the two fats are blended.

- The sugar cuts small holes in the fat, making the cookies crisp and tender.

- When you add the flour, stir just until the dry ingredients are incorporated so the gluten doesn't develop.

Cut Out Dough and Bake

- Try to cut out as many cookies as possible from the first roll. When you reroll the scraps, gluten forms and the cookies will be tougher.

- It's easiest to just cut the dough into squares or rectangles. Use a wavy-edged pastry cutter for a pretty look or use a shaped cookie cutter, like a star.

- You can also just press the dough into a rectangle on the cookie sheet.

- Score the dough into squares, rectangles, or triangles and bake, then break apart when cool.

COOKIES

FROSTED GINGER COOKIES
Three kinds of ginger give these soft cookies a burst of flavor

Children's stories are written about these excellent old-fashioned cookies. They're the perfect cookie to eat with a glass of milk for an after-school treat.

There are two types of ginger cookies: soft and crisp. The crisp cookies are also called gingersnaps. The soft, or cake-like, kind are usually topped with a simple white frosting or glaze.

A jar is not the best place to store these cookies. Instead layer them, with a sheet of waxed paper between the layers, in an airtight box. To keep the cookies soft, you can add an apple slice to the box. This will add moisture to the cookies over a few days. *Yield: 36 cookies*

Frosted Ginger Cookies

Ingredients

³/₄ cup butter, softened

¹/₂ cup granulated sugar

1 cup packed brown sugar

¹/₄ cup light molasses

1 egg

1 teaspoon vanilla

2¹/₄ cups flour

1 teaspoon baking soda

¹/₄ teaspoon baking powder

¹/₈ teaspoon salt

1 teaspoon cinnamon

2 teaspoons ground ginger

2 tablespoons minced candied ginger

2 teaspoons minced fresh gingerroot

Easy Buttercream Frosting (see page 212) or Old-Fashioned Frosting (see page 208)

- Preheat oven to 350°F. Line cookie sheets with parchment paper.

- In large bowl, beat butter with both sugars until fluffy. Beat in molasses, then add egg and vanilla.

- Sift together flour, soda, baking powder, salt, cinnamon, and ground ginger; add to batter and mix.

- Stir in candied ginger and gingerroot. Shape into 1-inch balls and place on cookie sheets. Bake 9 to 12 minutes, until light golden. Cool completely on wire racks, then frost.

KNACK FABULOUS DESSERTS

Add Molasses to Batter

Form and Bake Cookies

- There are several different types of molasses on the market. They range from mild to very strong.

- For these cookies, use fancy or unsulfured molasses unless you really like a molasses flavor. Blackstrap molasses is very strong and dark.

- For an even milder cookie, you could use honey in place of the molasses.

- Stir in the flour mixture until combined, but do not beat, so the cookies stay tender. You can chill this dough up to 24 hours before baking.

- It's important that the cookie dough be formed into a very round shape so the inside stays moist while the outside is slightly crisp.

- For a nice finish on the cookies if you aren't going to frost them, roll in granulated sugar just before baking.

- Don't overbake the cookies or they will be dry. Remove from the oven when slightly underbaked in the center.

- Make sure that the cookies are completely cooled before you frost them.

COOKIES

OATMEAL COOKIES

Chewy oatmeal cookies are crisp on the edges, but honey keeps them soft

Oatmeal cookies are best when they are slightly chewy and slightly crisp. A combination of butter and vegetable oil, along with honey and brown and granulated sugars, helps achieve this texture contrast.

These cookies take their wonderful taste from cinnamon, nutmeg, and more vanilla than usual. For even more flavor,

toast the pecans before you chop them.

These cookies can stick like the dickens, so it's best to bake them on Silpat-lined cookie sheets. These silicone sheets help prevent overbaking, and the cookies will release perfectly. These cookies freeze well; let them defrost at room temperature *Yield: 36 cookies*

Ingredients

- ²/₃ cup butter, softened
- ¹/₃ cup vegetable oil
- ¹/₂ teaspoon salt
- 1¹/₂ teaspoons cinnamon
- ¹/₄ teaspoon nutmeg
- 2 teaspoons vanilla
- 3 tablespoons honey
- 1 cup packed brown sugar
- 1 cup granulated sugar
- 2 eggs
- 2 cups flour
- 1¹/₂ teaspoons baking soda
- 3 cups rolled oats
- 1 cup chopped pecans

Oatmeal Cookies

- In large bowl, combine butter, oil, salt, cinnamon, nutmeg, vanilla, honey, brown sugar, and granulated sugar; beat well.

- Add eggs, one at a time, beating well after each addition. Stir in flour and baking soda.

- Add oats and pecans. Cover and chill 3 hours; preheat oven to 350°F.

- Drop dough by teaspoons onto Silpat-lined cookie sheets. Bake 10 to 13 minutes, until light golden brown. Remove from sheets after 3 minutes; cool on wire racks.

Oatmeal Bar Cookies: Make recipe as directed, except grease 13x9-inch pan with shortening and dust with flour. Press dough into prepared pan. Bake at 350°F 23 to 28 minutes, until bars are set. Cool completely. Melt 2 cups semisweet chocolate chips with ½ cup peanut butter and pour over bars; spread to cover. Let cool, then cut into bars.

Oatmeal Raisin Cookies: Make recipe as directed, except instead of pecans stir in 1 cup dark or golden raisins, or 1 cup chocolate-covered raisins. Shape and bake cookies as directed. You could also stir in 1 to 2 cups of semisweet or milk chocolate chips in place of the raisins. Or use dried sweetened cranberries or cherries in place of the raisins. Or a mixture of any of the above!

Stir Oats into Dough

Bake Cookies

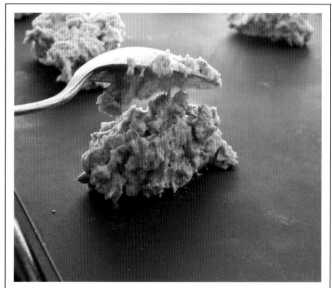

- The character of these cookies will change depending on the type of oats you use.

- Quick-cooking oats make a softer cookie with a more even texture. Rolled oats will create a firmer cookie with a chewier texture.

- Do not use instant or steel-cut oats in an oatmeal cookie recipe because the texture will be wrong.

- Toast pecans by baking at 350°F 8 to 14 minutes, until fragrant. Cool before chopping or mincing.

- Don't overbake these cookies or they will lose their chewy texture.

- Bake just until the edges are golden brown; the center will look slightly underbaked. Let cool on the sheet 3 minutes, then cool on wire rack.

- Store the baked cookies in an airtight container at room temperature.

- If you want to store them in a cookie jar, line it with a plastic food storage bag and seal shut at the top.

COOKIES

NANAIMO COOKIES

These rich little cookies have the same flavors as the famous bar

Nanaimo cookies were created in Canada, named after the city in British Columbia. The recipe is usually made as a no-bake bar cookie, with a layer of sweetened crumbs topped with custard, then frosted with melted chocolate chips.

This version transforms the bar cookie into delicate individual cookies. They look wonderful on a tray with other cookies, or served all by themselves on a pretty platter.

No-bake cookies are nice for hot summer days when you don't want to turn on the oven. Of course you do still have to heat up the base mixture on the stovetop.

Serve these cookies with some hot tea flavored with lemon, on your prettiest china. *Yield: 36 cookies*

Ingredients

¹/₂ cup butter, divided

¹/₄ cup packed brown sugar

¹/₂ cup semisweet chocolate chips

1 egg, beaten

2 tablespoons flour

1 teaspoon vanilla

Pinch salt

1¹/₂ cups finely crushed graham cracker crumbs

¹/₂ cup chopped pecans

1 (3-ounce) package cream cheese, softened

¹/₄ cup caramel topping

2 cups powdered sugar

1¹/₂ cups semisweet chocolate chips

2 tablespoons heavy cream

Nanaimo Cookies

- In medium saucepan, combine ¼ cup butter with brown sugar, ½ cup chocolate chips, egg, flour, and vanilla; bring to boil, stirring constantly.

- Cook 4 to 5 minutes, stirring constantly, until thick. Remove from heat and add salt, crumbs, and pecans.

- Drop by teaspoons onto waxed paper; let stand until set. Make indentation in each cookie.

- Beat ¼ cup butter with cream cheese, caramel topping, and powdered sugar. Frost cookies. Melt 1½ cups chocolate chips with heavy cream; drizzle on top.

Nanaimo Bar Cookies: Make recipe as directed, except press graham cracker crumb mixture into greased 9x9-inch pan. Spread cream cheese mixture over all and top with melted chocolate mixture. Cover and chill 2 to 3 hours before serving. Cut into small squares. Recipe can also be doubled and placed in 13x9-inch pan.

Legend has it that a Nanaimo housewife created these cookies for a recipe contest four decades ago. Whether or not this is true, these bars are inextricably linked with Canada in general and the city of Nanaimo in particular. The original recipe used custard powder mixed with cream and butter. Variations include sweetened cream cheese or vanilla pudding,

Cook Mixture

Cookie Frosting

- It's important to whisk the butter-and-sugar mixture constantly when it's cooking so the egg doesn't curdle.

- This step helps bind the fat in the butter so it stays incorporated in the custard. Otherwise the bottom layer can become greasy.

- Make sure that the graham crackers are finely crushed. They give the cookie structure.

- If there are large pieces of graham crackers in the base, it will not hold its shape and the cookies won't hold together.

- The cookies should be thickly frosted. Make an indentation with your thumb in the top of each cookie.

- This will hold the right amount of filling, and will be a nice contrast with the chocolate glaze.

- For a light chocolate frosting, use chocolate or fudge ice cream topping in place of the caramel topping.

- You can use dark or milk chocolate chips for the glaze. Let the cookies stand until the glaze is firm.

COOKIES

SUGAR COOKIES

Classic sugar cookies are crisp and tender; frost them if you like

These are the cookies everyone wants for the holidays. For Valentine's Day, make heart-shaped cookies and frost with peppermint glaze. For Christmas, there's nothing better than a big batch of sugar cookies cut into star, Christmas tree, and Santa shapes, decorated with sprinkles and edible glitter.

Sugar cookie dough is a great make-ahead recipe. It freezes and thaws very well, so you can make a double or triple batch and freeze it. Let it thaw in the fridge, then have a cookie-making party. The baked cookies freeze beautifully too, but freeze them unfrosted for best results. Pack the cookies into boxes, separating layers with waxed paper.

Have fun making, frosting, and decorating these delicious cookies for holiday parties and entertaining. *Yield: 48 cookies*

Ingredients

- 1 cup butter, softened
- 1 cup granulated sugar
- 1/2 cup powdered sugar
- 2 teaspoons vanilla
- 1 egg
- 2 1/2 cups flour
- 2 tablespoons cornstarch
- 1/2 teaspoon baking powder
- 1/2 teaspoon baking soda
- 1/2 teaspoon salt
- 2 tablespoons orange juice
- 2 tablespoons milk

Sugar Cookies

- In bowl, beat butter with sugars and vanilla until light and fluffy. Add egg and beat well.

- Sift flour with cornstarch, baking powder, soda, and salt. Add to butter mixture alternately with orange juice and milk.

- Cover dough well and chill 8 to 24 hours. Then preheat oven to 350°F.

- Dust surface with half flour and half powdered sugar; roll out dough 1/8 inch thick. Cut with cookie cutters. Bake 8 to 10 minutes, until light golden; cool on rack.

Cookie Glaze: In medium bowl, combine 2 cups powdered sugar with 2 tablespoons light corn syrup, 1 tablespoon milk, 1 tablespoon water, and ½ teaspoon vanilla—clear vanilla if possible. Spread over cookies; let dry. You can pipe this mixture around the edges of the cookies, then fill in for a perfect edge. This glaze can be colored using a paste of liquid food coloring.

• • • • • YELLOW ● LIGHT • • • • •

Try to cut out as many cookies from the first rolled-out batch as possible. At specialty baking stores, you can find rollers made up of intertwined cookie cutters that cut whole batches with no wasted dough. At the very least, place the cookie cutters as close to each other as possible so you don't have many scraps to reroll.

Add Flour to Dough

- With this ratio of flour to fat, it's very important to work the dough as little as possible.

- Do not knead this dough or work it too much with your hands.

- The powdered sugar will help make the cookies more tender, since it contains cornstarch to prevent clumping.

- Chilling the dough is a very important step. It will help the gluten relax so the dough is easy to roll out.

Cut Out Cookies

- Sprinkle the board with powdered sugar instead of flour. This adds a touch of sweetness and helps the cookies brown.

- Divide the dough in half; keep one half in the refrigerator so it doesn't soften too much.

- Dip the cookie cutter in powdered sugar occasionally as you work so it doesn't stick to the dough.

- Bake the cookies just until light brown around the edges. Don't overbake or they will become too hard.

COOKIES

CLASSIC BROWNIES

These brownies start with sugar syrup so they are creamy and rich

Everyone loves brownies. They are creamy and rich and full of chocolate. They can be made with nuts, or chocolate chips, frosted or plain.

There are two basic kinds of brownies: cake-like and fudgy. To make cake-like brownies, which are less dense and usually thicker, just add an extra egg, and bake the brownies for a few more minutes. Fudgy brownies are best a bit underbaked.

This recipe uses melted chocolate and cocoa powder to add a wonderful depth of flavor. The cocoa powder, in addition to pumping up the chocolate content, also helps give the brownies a wonderful velvety texture.

Bake a selection of different brownies and offer them as a dessert buffet for any festive gathering. *Yield: 36 brownies*

Ingredients

1 cup granulated sugar

1 cup packed brown sugar

1 cup butter

1/3 cup water

4 (1-ounce) squares unsweetened chocolate

1/4 cup cocoa powder

4 eggs

2 teaspoons vanilla

1 1/2 cups all purpose flour

1/4 teaspoon baking powder

1/4 teaspoon baking soda

1/4 teaspoon salt

Classic Brownies

- Preheat oven to 350°F. Coat 13x9-inch pan with non-stick baking spray.

- In large saucepan, combine sugars, butter, and water; bring to boil, stirring occasionally. Remove from heat and add chocolate and cocoa; stir until melted.

- Add eggs, one at a time, beating well. Stir in vanilla, then add flour, baking powder, soda, and salt.

- Turn into prepared pan. Bake 25 to 35 minutes, until set. Cool completely; frost if desired.

• • • • RECIPE VARIATIONS • • • •

Easy Brownie Frosting: Combine ½ cup sugar, ½ cup packed brown sugar, ⅓ cup butter, and ⅓ cup light cream in medium saucepan. Bring to boil over medium heat. Remove from heat and immediately stir in 1 cup semi-sweet chocolate chips; stir until melted. Add 1 teaspoon vanilla, stir well, and pour over warm brownies. Let stand until set.

Marshmallow Fudge Brownies: Make recipe as directed, except stir in 1 cup milk chocolate chips and 1 cup semisweet chocolate chips with flour mixture. Bake brownies as directed. When brownies are done, sprinkle with 2 cups miniature marshmallows and return to oven. Bake 2 minutes longer, until marshmallows puff. Pour Easy Brownie Frosting over brownies immediately.

Boil Sugar Mixture

- One of the big problems with brownies is that they can be sugary.

- The amount of sugar is necessary to offset the bitter flavor from the chocolate and to create the brownie structure.

- Boiling the sugar in a syrup of water and butter is an excellent way to make sure that the brownies are smooth.

- Don't skip this step, and make sure that the mixture comes to a complete boil, or the brownies will be grainy.

Add Flour and Bake

- Flour, salt, baking powder, and baking soda all make important contributions to the best brownies.

- Flour provides structure and makes the brownies chewy. Leavening, just a little bit, also provides texture.

- And all sweet baked goods need a bit of salt to bring out the flavor.

- Don't overbake the brownies. A toothpick inserted near the center should come out with a few wet crumbs attached.

61

PEANUT BUTTER BROWNIES

Creamy brownies are flavored with peanut butter and topped with a rich frosting

Peanut butter adds wonderful flavor and richness to chocolate brownies. This versatile ingredient adds more fat to the recipe, which makes the brownies creamier, and the peanut flavor adds richness.

This brownie recipe is so good because the sugar is combined with water and butter and boiled to form a syrup before the remaining ingredients are added. With the sugar thoroughly dissolved, the brownies will be creamy.

You can top the basic brownie with anything: marshmallow crème and melted chocolate, fudge frosting, or white chocolate frosting. Or you can just eat them plain, dusted with a bit of powdered sugar. *Yield: 36 brownies*

Ingredients

- 1¼ cups sugar
- ⅓ cup water
- ⅔ cup butter
- 1 (1-ounce) square unsweetened chocolate, chopped
- ¼ cup cocoa powder
- 1 cup semisweet chocolate chips
- ½ cup peanut butter
- 4 eggs
- 1½ cups flour
- ¼ teaspoon salt
- ½ teaspoon baking soda
- 2 teaspoons vanilla
- 2 cups semisweet chocolate chips
- ½ cup peanut butter

Peanut Butter Brownies

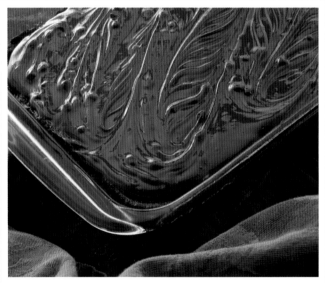

- Preheat oven to 350°F. Grease 13x9-inch pan. In saucepan, combine sugar, water, and butter. Bring to boil over high heat.

- Remove from heat; stir in unsweetened chocolate, cocoa, and 1 cup chips. Beat in ½ cup peanut butter, then eggs.

- Add flour, salt, baking soda, and vanilla; beat well. Pour into pan. Bake 25 to 35 minutes or until just set.

- In heavy saucepan, combine 2 cups chocolate chips and ½ cup peanut butter. Melt until mixture is smooth and glossy. Pour over brownies; cool.

• • • • RECIPE VARIATIONS • • • •

Peanut Butter Layered Brownies: Make recipe as directed, except don't frost brownies. Beat ¾ cup peanut butter, 2 cups powdered sugar, and 2 tablespoons softened butter together. Spread over cooled brownies. Sprinkle with 1½ cups chopped salted peanuts. Then make glaze and pour over peanut butter layer; let stand until set.

Just Peanut Butter Brownies: Make recipe as directed, except omit chocolate, cocoa powder, and 1 cup semisweet chocolate chips. Increase peanut butter to ¾ cup and add 1 cup peanut butter chips. Bake brownies as directed. Let cool, then make Easy Buttercream Frosting, but add ½ cup peanut butter to frosting. Frost brownies and cut into squares.

Boil Sugar Mixture

- Stir the sugar mixture frequently while it's cooking on the heat.

- As soon as the mixture comes to a boil, remove it from the heat so the sugar proportion doesn't concentrate.

- Too much sugar, either in measuring or from evaporation, will make the brownies crusty and hard.

- The peanut butter helps cool the mixture down a bit so the eggs don't cook when beaten into the warm mixture.

Pour Glaze over Brownies

- It's important to make the glaze when the brownies come out of the oven to cool.

- Hot glaze poured on top of warm brownies helps them meld together, and it keeps the brownies moist.

- The peanut butter softens the semisweet chocolate and makes it taste slightly sweeter.

- The peanut butter also keeps the glaze soft so it's easier to cut the brownies and the mouth-feel is very smooth.

WHITE CHOCOLATE BLONDIES

Browned butter, ground white chocolate, and brown sugar add flavor to these delicious bars

These delicious brownies do not contain any dark chocolate or cocoa powder, so they are called blondies. They make a wonderful addition to a cookie tray for a party or during the holidays.

White chocolate has a very low melting point. This means that it will soften in your mouth and, unfortunately, that it will seize easily when exposed to too much heat. So you have to watch white chocolate carefully.

Browned butter adds a caramel flavor to these brownies, and brown sugar adds a nice depth of flavor. For a contrast, try drizzling them with melted dark chocolate, or a combination of dark and white chocolate. *Yield: 36 bar cookies*

Ingredients

³/₄ cup butter

1 (12-ounce) package white chocolate chips, ground, divided

¹/₂ cup packed brown sugar

¹/₄ cup granulated sugar

4 eggs

2 teaspoons vanilla

¹/₂ teaspoon salt

2¹/₂ cups flour

1 teaspoon baking powder

White Chocolate Blondies

- Preheat oven to 325°F. Coat 13x9-inch pan with non-stick baking spray; set aside.

- In saucepan, melt butter over low heat. Cook, stirring frequently, until butter browns lightly, about 8 to 12 minutes. Pour into bowl.

- Stir in half of ground chocolate until smooth, then add sugars. Beat in eggs, one at a time. Add vanilla.

- Add salt, flour, and baking powder; fold in rest of chocolate. Pour into pan. Bake 30 to 40 minutes, until set. Cool completely.

• • • • RECIPE VARIATION • • • •

Black and White Brownies: Make recipe as directed, except stir 1½ cups dark chocolate chips (darker than semisweet chocolate chips) into batter just before baking. Bake brownies as directed; cool. Melt 1 cup semisweet chocolate chips with 3 tablespoons heavy cream until smooth; pour over brownies and let cool.

ZOOM

White chocolate is very different from dark or regular chocolate. It does not contain any cocoa liquor, which means it cannot officially be called chocolate. Chocolate liquor is made when cacao beans are processed. White chocolate is made from cocoa butter, sugar, milk, and vanilla.

Brown Butter

- When butter browns, the proteins and sugars in the milk solids break down and recombine to form other compounds.

- These compounds give the browned butter a rich taste and deep caramel color.

- It will take about 8 to 12 minutes for butter to turn brown. Watch it carefully and don't let it burn.

- If the butter does burn, you must throw it out and start over, or it will ruin the flavor of the blondies.

Add Ground Chocolate and Bake

- To grind the chocolate chips, place them in a food processor or blender.

- Pulse, checking the consistency frequently, until the chocolate is ground into very small pieces.

- Do not process until the mixture starts melting or turns into a paste; that will change the texture of the finished product.

- Bake these brownies just until set; be careful not to overbake or the chocolate will get too hard. Cool on a wire rack, then cut into bars.

NO-BAKE CRISP CEREAL BARS
A rich, crisp date filling tops a graham cracker crust in these lovely bars

No-bake bars are a great choice for warm summer days. They're also a wonderful way to introduce kids to baking.

Follow directions carefully so the bars turn out well. The graham crackers in the crust and the nuts must be an even consistency and finely crushed and chopped. They will absorb some of the butter and create the structure of the base.

The date mixture is creamy, chewy, and crunchy. The dates will literally melt into the butter-and-sugar mixture as they cook. Be sure to stir the filling constantly as it cooks.

And the frosting adds a sweet and elegant finish to the bar cookies. Drizzle in an even pattern so the filling shows through. *Yield: 36 bar cookies*

Ingredients

2 cups finely crushed graham cracker crumbs

$^1/_2$ cup finely chopped walnuts

$^2/_3$ cup butter, melted

$^3/_4$ cup butter

$^1/_2$ cup granulated sugar

1 cup packed brown sugar

$1^1/_2$ cups chopped dates

1 egg, beaten

$1^1/_2$ teaspoons vanilla

1 teaspoon grated orange zest

$3^1/_2$ cups crisp rice flake cereal, such as Special K

$1^1/_2$ cups powdered sugar

2 tablespoons butter, melted

2 tablespoons orange juice

No-Bake Crisp Cereal Bars

- In bowl, mix crumbs, walnuts, and ⅔ cup melted butter; press into 13x9-inch pan.

- In saucepan, mix ¾ cup butter, sugars, dates, and egg.

- Cook over medium heat, stirring frequently, until dates melt and mixture thickens, about 9 to 10 minutes.

- Remove from heat; add vanilla, zest, and cereal. Spread over crust. Cool completely. Mix powdered sugar, melted butter, and orange juice; drizzle over bars. Chill in refrigerator until set.

• • • • RECIPE VARIATIONS • • • •

No-Bake Cereal Cookies: Make recipe as directed, except omit graham crackers, walnuts, and ⅔ cup butter. Make filling as directed, except add 1 cup chopped walnuts to mixture along with crisp rice flake cereal. Let cool 15 minutes, then drop onto waxed paper to form cookies. Cool completely; drizzle with frosting as directed.

No-Bake Chocolate Bar Cookies: Make crust as directed. For filling, combine 1 (14-ounce) can sweetened condensed milk with 1 cup finely chopped dates. Cook over low heat until dates melt. Stir in 2 cups semisweet chocolate chips and remove from heat. Stir until mixture is smooth. Add 2 cups crisp rice flake cereal. Pour over crust and sprinkle with 1 cup chopped walnuts. Chill.

Cook Date Mixture

- Chop the dates fairly fine so they melt into the filling. Dates are sweet, but with a floral undertone.

- The best dates to choose for this recipe are Medjools—the smoothest kind, with the richest flavor.

- Make sure that you use rice flake cereal, not puffed rice or crisp rice cereal.

- Any cereal other than flaked rice cereal will absorb liquid from the bars and become soggy. The cereal must remain crisp to give the bars character.

Drizzle Icing over Bars

- Don't make the icing until the bars are completely cool. If the filling is hot, the icing will melt into it.

- You can flavor the icing with other citrus fruits as well. Think about using blood orange juice or lemon juice.

- Use a whisk to blend the icing mixture. Stir until the icing is completely smooth.

- You can put the icing in a small plastic bag; cut a small bit off the corner to use as a piping bag.

KEY LIME BARS
Key limes, those tiny yellow orbs, add wonderful flavor to these easy bars

Key limes are very different from regular limes. Found only in tropical climates, particularly the Florida Keys, these little citrus fruits are very tiny and yellow, not green.

Since the limes are only about 1 or 2 inches in diameter, it takes a lot of them to make ¾ cup of juice. Each fruit creates less than a tablespoon, so you'll need at least 13 key limes.

Some baking supply stores do carry bottled key lime juice. If you use this, use ½ cup of key lime juice and add ¼ cup of fresh regular lime juice.

These bar cookies should be stored in the refrigerator for best results. Let them stand at room temperature 20 minutes before serving. *Yield: 36 bar cookies*

KNACK FABULOUS DESSERTS

Ingredients

2 cups flour

¹/₃ cup packed brown sugar

¹/₄ cup powdered sugar

³/₄ cup butter, softened

¹/₂ cup finely chopped macadamia nuts

5 eggs

1¹/₂ cups granulated sugar

¹/₃ cup flour

¹/₈ teaspoon salt

¹/₂ teaspoon baking powder

2 teaspoons lime zest

³/₄ cup key lime juice

Key Lime Bars

- Preheat oven to 325°F. In bowl, mix 2 cups flour, brown and powdered sugars, and butter until dough forms. Stir in nuts.

- Press in greased 13x9-inch pan. Bake 14 minutes; remove from oven and set aside.

- In bowl, beat eggs with granulated sugar until fluffy, 5 to 6 minutes. Sift in ¹/₃ cup flour, salt, and baking powder, then add zest and juice.

- Pour over crust. Bake 27 to 35 minutes, until just set. Cool completely; sprinkle with powdered sugar.

• • • • RECIPE VARIATIONS • • • •

Frosted Key Lime Bars: Make bars as directed. Bake and cool completely. In small bowl, combine 2 cups powdered sugar, 2 tablespoons melted butter, ½ teaspoon grated lime zest, and 3 tablespoons lime juice. Mix until smooth with wire whisk, then pour over bars. Spread gently to cover. Let stand until set, then cut into bars.

Coconut Lemon Bars: Make recipe as directed, except substitute ¾ cup freshly squeezed lemon juice for lime juice, and 2 teaspoons lemon zest for lime zest. Substitute ½ cup coconut for macadamia nuts in crust, and add 1 cup flaked coconut to filling mixture along with zest and juice. Bake as directed, then cool, sprinkle with powdered sugar, and cut into bars.

Baked Crust

- Because the filling is so liquid, the crust must be completely baked in the first step.

- If it isn't, the filling will soak into the crust in the oven, and the bars will not have distinct layers.

- Bake the crust until it is light golden brown. Do not bake until golden brown or it will overbake when the filling is added.

- You can bake the crust ahead of time and add the filling up to 6 hours later.

Beat Eggs with Sugar

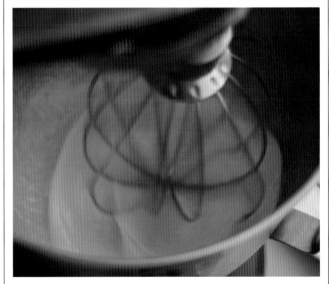

- It's important that the egg and sugar mixture be very well beaten.

- This will ensure that the sugar dissolves in the filling and will be creamy. The air beaten into the eggs also helps make the silky texture.

- Do not do this ahead of time, or the eggs will break down and the filling will be runny.

- Bake the bars until the filling is set. It will be light golden brown in a lacy pattern on the top of the filling.

ALMOND FINGERS

This crunchy bar cookie has a rich almond filling

Fingers are bar cookies that have been cut into a rectangular shape. This is an easy way to make a big batch of elegant cookies in a hurry.

Of course, you can cut the bars into any shape you'd like: squares, triangles, or even circles (and you get to eat the scraps!). But the rectangular shape is pleasing to look at on a cookie tray, and nice to eat.

Almond filling is a mixture of ground almonds, sugar, and eggs. You can make your own filling, or buy it in the baking aisle of the supermarket. It gives a rich almond taste and smooth texture to these bar cookies.

Serve these cookies with some hot tea flavored with nutmeg. *Yield: 27 bar cookies*

Ingredients

1 1/2 cups flour

1/2 cup packed brown sugar

1/3 cup ground almonds

1/2 teaspoon cinnamon

1/2 teaspoon baking powder

1/8 teaspoon salt

1/2 cup butter

1 egg yolk

1/2 teaspoon almond extract

1/2 cup almond filling (not paste)

1 cup sliced almonds

Almond Fingers

- Preheat oven to 350°F. In large bowl, mix flour, brown sugar, almonds, cinnamon, baking powder, and salt.

- Cut in butter until particles are fine. Add egg yolk and almond extract; mix until crumbs are moist.

- Pat two-thirds of crumbs firmly into 9-inch-square pan. Gently spread evenly with the almond filling.

- Sprinkle with remaining crumbs and sliced almonds. Bake 24 to 29 minutes, until bars are golden. Cool and cut into 3x1-inch pieces.

• • • • RECIPE VARIATIONS • • • •

Pecan Fingers: Make recipe as directed, except omit almond filling. For filling, grind 1 cup chopped pecans in food processor with 2 tablespoons butter and ⅓ cup packed brown sugar. Add 1 egg and process until smooth. Spread over bottom crust, then add ½ cup chopped pecans to remaining crumb mixture and sprinkle over filling. Bake as directed.

Homemade Almond Filling: In food processor, combine ¼ cup almond paste with 2 tablespoons butter, 1 egg, and 2 tablespoons packed brown sugar. Process until smooth. You can also grind ½ cup slivered almonds until finely chopped. Add 2 tablespoons granulated sugar, 1 tablespoon butter, and 1 egg; grind until smooth. Use immediately or freeze up to 3 months.

Cut Butter into Flour

- To cut butter into the flour mixture, first make sure it is cold. Warm butter will not form the even particles needed to make a crisp crust.

- Then cut the butter into ½-inch pieces and scatter over the flour mixture. Toss gently with your fingertips.

- Use a pastry blender and work the butter into the flour until particles are even and fine.

- Or you can use two knives. Cut across the mixture in different directions until the mixture is even.

Spread Filling on Dough

- Almond filling is literally pie filling in a can. This is very different from almond paste, which is much more concentrated.

- So read labels and be sure that you are using almond filling in this recipe. If you can't find almond filling, make Homemade Almond Filling (see variation).

- To spread the filling, spoon it onto the crust in small dollops and, using an offset spatula, spread gently.

- When the bars are done, the crumbs and almonds on top will be golden brown. Cool completely.

NEW YORK CHEESECAKE

This is the richest, creamiest cheesecake in the world

When you ask a group of people what the most decadent dessert is, cheesecake will probably be at or near the top of the list. And for good reason!

The perfect cheesecake is very smooth and creamy, with a rich mouth-feel and well-blended flavors. It is made from cream cheese, sweetened with sugar, and flavored with everything from vanilla to chocolate to liqueurs.

Most cheesecakes have a crust made from sweetened graham cracker crumbs. This one, also known as New York–style cheesecake, has a cookie crust. The crust provides a wonderful contrast to the silky-smooth filling.

Top your cheesecake with fresh fruit or chocolate sauce, or serve it plain, garnished with an edible flower. *Yield: Serves 12*

Ingredients

1 cup flour

1/2 cup butter, softened

1/4 cup packed brown sugar

1 egg yolk

5 (8-ounce) packages cream cheese, softened

1/4 cup butter, softened

1 1/2 cups granulated sugar

3 tablespoons flour

4 eggs

2 egg yolks

1 tablespoon vanilla

1/3 cup heavy cream

1/2 cup sour cream

New York Cheesecake

- Preheat oven to 350°F. Mix 1 cup flour, 1/2 cup butter, brown sugar, and 1 egg yolk.

- Press half of dough on bottom of 10-inch springform pan. Bake 9 minutes; cool. Press dough on sides. Increase oven to 450°F.

- Beat cream cheese with 1/4 cup butter. Add sugar and flour; beat. Add eggs and 2 yolks; beat. Stir in vanilla, cream, and sour cream.

- Pour into pan. Bake 15 minutes; reduce heat to 300°F. Bake 40 to 50 minutes.

Miniature Cheesecakes: Make recipe as directed, except cut filling in half and omit cookie crust. Combine 1 cup graham cracker crumbs and 3 tablespoons melted butter in bowl; divide among 15 greased muffin tins; press down. Divide filling over crusts. Bake at 325°F 22 to 28 minutes, until filling is set. Cool completely in muffin tins. Top with cherry pie filling.

Graham Cracker Crust: Combine 2 cups finely crushed graham crackers crumbs, ½ cup finely chopped walnuts, and ⅓ cup melted butter. Press into bottom and up sides of 10-inch springform pan. Do not bake. Fill with cream cheese filling and bake as directed. You can also use chocolate cookie crumbs or chocolate chip cookie crumbs.

Bottom Crust Baked, Sides Are Not

- The bottom of the cheesecake is baked so the filling doesn't melt into the crust.

- Make sure the bottom crust and the pan are completely cool before you press dough onto the pan sides.

- It's important to not overbeat the cheesecake

mixture. You don't want to incorporate much air, or the cheesecake will rise too much.

- Then it will fall as it cools, creating cracks. If this does happen, just top the cheesecake with sweetened sour cream.

Bake and Cool Cheesecake

- Rap the pan on the counter to remove air bubbles before you bake the cheesecake.

- Make sure your oven temperature is accurate. Preheat the oven for at least 15 minutes.

- When the cheesecake is golden brown and 2 inches of the center still jiggles, remove it from the oven. Cover with a towel and cool 15 minutes.

- Run a knife around the edge of the cheesecake; cool 2 hours. Wrap in foil and refrigerate 6 hours.

RICOTTA CHEESECAKE

Ricotta makes a lighter cheesecake with a velvety texture

Cheesecakes can be made of any soft white cheese: cream cheese, cottage cheese, Neufchâtel, mascarpone, and ricotta. A cheesecake made from the last two ingredients has a lighter texture and more subtle taste.

Ricotta is actually a cheese by-product. The name literally means "recooked." The whey that is left over when cheese is made is cooked with more milk to create ricotta. The cheese is grainier than cream cheese, with a lighter taste.

Mascarpone cheese is a double- or triple-cream cheese made from cow's milk. It is fresh, not ripened. The cheese is very rich and smooth, with a deep milk flavor.

Serve this cheesecake with a sweet red dessert wine at the end of an Italian meal. *Yield: Serves 8–10*

Ingredients

2 cups amaretti cookie crumbs

1/2 cup butter, melted

3 cups whole-milk ricotta cheese

1 cup mascarpone cheese

1/2 cup granulated sugar

1/2 cup packed brown sugar

2 tablespoons cornstarch

4 eggs

2 teaspoons vanilla

1/8 teaspoon salt

1/4 cup amaretto liqueur

Ricotta Cheesecake

- In bowl, mix cookie crumbs and butter. Press into bottom and sides of foil-lined 9-inch springform pan.

- Place ricotta in double layer of cheesecloth, set in colander, weigh down with can, and refrigerate 1 hour.

- Preheat oven to 325°F. Beat ricotta, mascarpone, and sugars until smooth. Beat in cornstarch, eggs, vanilla, salt, and amaretto.

- Pour into crust. Bake in water bath 70 to 80 minutes, until just firm. Cool on wire rack, then chill in refrigerator 4 to 6 hours.

•••• RECIPE VARIATION ••••

Mascarpone Cheesecake: Make recipe as directed, except substitute an 8-ounce package softened cream cheese for ricotta cheese, and increase mascarpone cheese to 3 cups. Omit brown sugar and amaretto; increase granulated sugar to ¾ cup and reduce eggs to 3. Bake in water bath 45 to 55 minutes, until set. Cool at room temperature 1 hour, then chill.

ZOOM

Amaretti Cookies: Amaretti cookies are crisp little Italian cookies made from almonds, sugar, and egg whites. They crumble easily and have a wonderful nutty taste. You can find them packaged in bags in the international foods aisle of the supermarket or online through specialty food shops. Make sure you choose the crisp, not chewy variety of the cookies for this recipe.

Drain Ricotta

- Because ricotta cheese has such a high moisture content, it must be drained before being used in cheesecake and many other baking recipes.

- Discard the whey that drains from the ricotta, or save it to use in soups or as the liquid when making fresh bread.

- Let the ricotta and mascarpone stand at room temperature for 30 minutes before beating together.

- Add the eggs, one at a time, beating just until combined. You can omit the amaretto if desired.

Add Filling to Crust

- Because this cheesecake bakes in a water bath, it's important to wrap it in foil.

- This prevents the water from seeping into the cheesecake as it bakes, which would ruin it.

- The foil also helps shield the cheesecake from the heat of the oven so the edges don't overbake before the center is done.

- The cheesecake will firm up as it cools. You can top it with sliced sweetened strawberries or peaches just before serving.

DOUBLE CHOCOLATE CHEESECAKE

This chocolate cheesecake is sublime and rich

Chocolate cheesecake takes a good thing and makes it even better! It's important to use the best-quality chocolate you can find in this recipe since the flavor is crucial to its success.

Three different kinds of chocolate are used in this rich and elegant cheesecake. They all improve the recipe in different ways. Unsweetened chocolate intensifies the flavor, while semisweet chocolate adds richness. And cocoa powder makes the filling silky and velvety smooth.

When you're combining melted chocolate and dairy products, it's important that the two mixtures be close in temperature so they blend completely.

Garnish this cheesecake with fresh strawberries or orange sections and serve after a special dinner. *Yield: Serves 8–10*

Ingredients

- 21 chocolate sandwich cookies, crushed
- 1/3 cup butter, melted
- 7 (1-ounce) squares semisweet chocolate
- 1 (1-ounce) square unsweetened chocolate
- 1/2 cup heavy cream
- 3 tablespoons cocoa powder
- 2 teaspoons espresso powder
- 4 (8-ounce) packages cream cheese, softened
- 1 cup granulated sugar
- 1/3 cup packed brown sugar
- 4 eggs
- 2 egg yolks
- 1/2 cup sour cream
- 1/4 teaspoon salt
- 2 teaspoons vanilla
- 1/4 cup heavy cream
- 1 cup semisweet chocolate chips

Double Chocolate Cheesecake

- Mix crumbs and butter; press on bottom and sides of 10-inch springform pan. Preheat oven to 325°F.

- In saucepan, combine chocolates and cream; melt, stirring, until smooth. Beat in cocoa and espresso.

- In large bowl, beat cream cheese with sugars until smooth. Add eggs and egg yolks; beat until smooth.

- Stir sour cream, salt, and vanilla into chocolate mixture; beat into cream cheese mixture. Pour into crust. Bake 70 to 80 minutes. Melt 1/4 cup cream with chips; top cheesecake.

•••• RECIPE VARIATION ••••

No-Bake Chocolate Cheesecake: Make recipe as directed, except cut filling ingredients in half. Omit brown sugar, eggs, and sour cream. Beat cream cheese with sugars, salt, and vanilla. Add melted chocolate mixture to cream cheese mixture. Increase cream to 1 cup; beat with 2 tablespoons powdered sugar and fold into cream cheese mixture. Pour into crust. Chill.

YELLOW ● LIGHT

Chocolate Bloom: Chocolate has to be handled carefully and kept within certain temperature parameters after it is made. If your chocolate develops a white or grayish covering or streaks, this is bloom. The most common cause of bloom is storage at high temperatures. The bloom doesn't affect the quality of the chocolate, however; you can still use it in recipes.

Melt Chocolate

- To make the chocolate melt more evenly and quickly, chop it into smaller pieces.

- Use a large knife and cut into the chocolate on a cutting board. The chocolate will splinter and break apart.

- Watch the chocolate carefully when it is melting and stir frequently to make sure it doesn't burn.

- The cream will help protect the chocolate from the heat as it melts and makes the cheesecake super-smooth.

Beat Chocolate into Cream Cheese

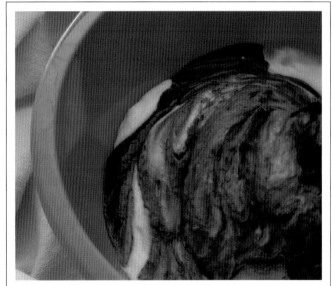

- Add the chocolate mixture slowly to the cream cheese mixture while beating constantly.

- You don't want any lumps of cream cheese or chocolate to appear in the finished cheesecake.

- If you are using a stand or hand mixer, scrape the bottom and sides of the bowl to be sure everything is incorporated.

- When the cheesecake comes out of the oven, immediately run a knife between the crust and pan sides so the top doesn't crack.

GOLDEN PRALINE CHEESECAKE

Sweet potatoes make the filling rich, and a praline topping adds more flavor

Cheesecakes don't have to be made of just cheese, sugar, and eggs. Other ingredients, from vegetables to chocolate to fruits, add interest and flavor to a basic cheesecake recipe.

This cheesecake is perfect for the holidays, especially as the end to a Thanksgiving dinner. Sweet potatoes make the cheesecake dense and add a slightly floral note to the rich filling. And the praline topping is a wonderful texture and flavor contrast.

Make sure that you use sweet potatoes, not yams, in this recipe. Sweet potatoes have bright orange flesh and are sweet, while yams are lighter in color and neutral in flavor. *Yield: Serves 10–12*

Ingredients

2 medium sweet potatoes

1 1/2 cups gingersnap cookie crumbs

1/2 cup finely chopped pecans

1/2 cup butter, melted

1 cup mascarpone cheese

3 (8-ounce) packages cream cheese, softened

1 cup packed brown sugar

1/2 cup granulated sugar

4 eggs

1 egg yolk

1 teaspoon cinnamon

1/4 teaspoon cardamom

1/2 cup heavy cream

1/4 teaspoon salt

2 teaspoons vanilla

1/2 cup packed brown sugar

1/4 cup butter

2 tablespoons heavy cream

1 cup whole pecans

Golden Praline Cheesecake

- Bake sweet potatoes at 350°F 60 to 70 minutes. Cool, peel, and cube.

- Mix crumbs, ground pecans, and melted butter; press into 9-inch spring-form pan.

- In food processor, combine potatoes and mascarpone; blend. Add cream cheese, 1 cup brown sugar, sugar, eggs, egg yolk, spices, cream, salt, and vanilla; blend. Pour into crust.

- Bake 55 to 65 minutes. Mix 1/2 cup brown sugar, 1/4 cup butter, and cream in sauce-pan. Simmer 3 minutes; pour on top. Add pecans.

• • • • RECIPE VARIATIONS • • • •

Pumpkin Cheesecake: Make recipe as directed, except substitute 1 (15-ounce) can solid-pack pumpkin (not pumpkin pie filling) for sweet potatoes. You can use mixer instead of food processor: Beat mascarpone with cream cheese and sugars, then add pumpkin. Add eggs, yolks, and remaining ingredients, pour into piecrust, and bake and top as directed.

Mini Praline Cheesecakes: Make recipe as directed, except use 18 regular-size muffin tins. Divide gingersnap crumb mixture among tins. Make filling as directed, and divide among muffin tins. Bake 20 to 25 minutes, until filling is just set. Make praline topping and spoon over cheesecakes; top each with a pecan half and cool.

Puree Sweet Potatoes

- It's important that the sweet potatoes be completely smooth with no chunks or lumps.

- If you don't have a food processor, mash the sweet potatoes well, then mash in the mascarpone cheese.

- Beat the cream cheese with sugars, then gradually beat in the sweet potato mixture and continue with the recipe.

- Don't beat the mixture too much or you'll add air to the cheesecake; it will rise, then fall and crack.

Pour Topping on Cheesecake

- Start preparing the praline topping when the cheesecake comes out of the oven.

- The mixture must simmer until it blends. This will dissolve the sugar and make the topping into a smooth glossy coating.

- Toast the pecans before you put them on the cheesecake. Bake at 350°F 7 to 9 minutes, until fragrant.

- You can also toast the pecans in some butter on the stove; sprinkle lightly with salt for a sweet and salty flavor.

CHEESECAKE

RASPBERRY CHEESECAKE BARS

Cheesecake in bar cookie form is easy to make and serve

Cheesecake doesn't have to be made in a springform or pie pan. These bars are a more informal way of serving cheesecake. They are also lighter, because the filling is only about an inch thick—not 2 or 3 inches, as in most cheesecakes.

These bars are easier to make than regular cheesecakes, so they're a good choice for beginning cooks. Doneness tests are easier, and there's no fooling around with water baths or covering pans with foil.

You can make these bars plain if you'd like. Just omit the preserves and frozen fruit. Add ¼ cup sour cream to the filling in place of the fruit.

These bar cookies are wonderful on a cookie tray, or served after an Italian meal. *Yield: 36 bar cookies*

Raspberry Cheesecake Bars

Ingredients

1 ²/₃ cups crushed vanilla wafer crumbs

¹/₂ cup finely chopped pecans

¹/₂ cup butter, melted

4 (8-ounce) packages cream cheese, softened

¹/₂ cup packed brown sugar

¹/₂ cup granulated sugar

2 tablespoons flour

¹/₄ cup heavy cream

¹/₃ cup sour cream

1 tablespoon vanilla

3 eggs

1 cup seedless raspberry preserves

1 cup frozen raspberries, thawed

- Preheat oven to 350°F. Combine crumbs, pecans, and butter in bowl; press into 13x9-inch pan. Bake 8 minutes. Cool.

- In large bowl, beat cream cheese, sugars, and flour until smooth. Add cream, sour cream, and vanilla.

- Beat in eggs, mixing until blended. Spread preserves over crust. Pour two-thirds cream cheese mixture over crust. Beat frozen raspberries into remaining mixture.

- Drop raspberry mixture over cream cheese; marble with knife. Bake 35 to 45 minutes, until set. Chill.

• • • • RECIPE VARIATION • • • •

Strawberry Cheesecake Bars: Make recipe as directed, except use 1 cup strawberry preserves in place of raspberry preserves. Instead of frozen raspberries, use 1 cup frozen strawberries, thawed and drained. Omit brown sugar; add ½ cup granulated sugar. Bake bars as directed. Store, covered, in refrigerator. Garnish with fresh strawberries when serving.

• • • • GREEN ● LIGHT • • • •

Frozen Fruit: Frozen fruit is a great ingredient to use in baking. The fruit is very good quality; in fact, since it's processed right in the fields, it is fresher than fresh fruit. The freezing process breaks down the fruit somewhat, making it ideal for pureeing and using in recipes or as a sauce. You can thaw the fruit on the counter, in the refrigerator overnight, or in the microwave. Or just simmer it on the stovetop until thickened.

Spread Preserves over Crust

Marble Plain and Raspberry Mixtures

- To spread preserves over crust, drop by small spoonfuls evenly over the cooled crust mixture.

- Using the back of a spoon or an offset spatula, gently spread the preserves, being careful not to lift the utensil from the preserves.

- If some of the crust does come up or you disturb it as you're spreading, just press back into place.

- Don't spread preserves over the crust until just before you add the filling so the crust stays crisp.

- Marbling means to partially combine two mixtures, leaving each discrete, to create a look like real marble.

- The two mixtures have to be about the same consistency to successfully marble.

- Use the tip of a knife and gently draw the tip through the cheesecake mixtures. Do not overmix.

- Bake the bars until the cheesecake mixture is set. Do not bake until browned, or the bars will be overbaked and the cheese may curdle.

81

WHITE CHOCOLATE CHEESECAKE

A no-bake cheesecake is perfect for a quick dessert

White chocolate is the perfect ingredient to use in a no-bake cheesecake. When melted, white chocolate becomes silky and velvety, taking the place of eggs in the cheesecake batter.

The white chocolate is melted with heavy cream to form a ganache. This mixture, which is also used to make truffles, is chilled in the refrigerator until firm, then beaten to make a fluffy base for the cheesecake.

You can make this no-bake cheesecake with any type of chip. Milk chocolate chips, semisweet chocolate, even peanut butter chips will make an intriguing cheesecake.

Top this cheesecake with fresh fruit, or with a simple sauce made by pureeing frozen thawed raspberries. *Yield: Serves 8*

Ingredients

1 1/2 cups chocolate cookie crumbs

1/3 cup butter, melted

1 (11-ounce) package white chocolate chips

1 1/2 cups heavy cream

3 (8-ounce) packages cream cheese, softened

1/3 cup sugar

1/4 cup powdered sugar

2 teaspoons vanilla

1/8 teaspoon salt

2 cups sliced strawberries

White Chocolate Cheesecake

- Combine cookie crumbs with melted butter; press into bottom and up sides of 9-inch springform pan.

- In heavy saucepan, combine chips with heavy cream; cook over low heat, stirring frequently, until melted. Chill 4 hours in refrigerator.

- In bowl, beat cream cheese with both kinds of sugar, vanilla, and salt. Beat heavy cream mixture until fluffy; fold into cream cheese mixture.

- Spoon into prepared crust and smooth top. Chill 4 to 6 hours until firm. Top with strawberries before serving.

White Chocolate Cheesecake Truffles: Melt together white chocolate chips with heavy cream; chill until firm. Beat 1 (8-ounce) package cream cheese with 2 teaspoons vanilla and 1 cup powdered sugar. Beat white chocolate mixture until fluffy; beat into cream cheese mixture. Chill until firm, then roll into balls. Coat in melted semisweet chocolate; store in refrigerator.

Strawberry Sauce: Wash and slice 1 pint fresh strawberries; remove stems. Place in saucepan with ¼ cup granulated sugar and 2 tablespoons honey. Mash some strawberries. Cook over low heat, stirring frequently, until mixture thickens. Remove from heat and stir in 1 teaspoon vanilla. Store in refrigerator. Can be made with fresh raspberries or blueberries; use same proportions.

CHEESECAKE

Make Crust

- To crush cookies, place them in a heavy-duty plastic bag and seal, leaving a small area open.

- Crush with a rolling pin or meat mallet, pounding the cookies gently until even.

- You can also place the cookies in a food processor. Process by pulsing until the mixture is even. Don't overprocess to mush.

- You can make several of these crusts at a time; cover and freeze up to 3 months. To thaw, let stand at room temperature.

Beat White Chocolate Mixture

- Stir the melting white chocolate mixture frequently, paying special attention to the bottom of the pan.

- White chocolate can burn easily, so keep an eye on it. If it burns, you must throw it out and start over.

- The mixture will whip to a fluffy and light consistency after it has chilled. This gives texture to the cheesecake.

- Make sure that the cream cheese is well softened so it's about the same consistency as the white chocolate mixture.

83

CLASSIC APPLE PIE

A flaky crust and tender apples in a spicy filling make the classic pie

We've all heard the saying *As American as apple pie*. Yet apple pie wasn't invented in America! One of the earliest recipes came from one of the cooks of King Richard II. The first American cookbook, *American Cookery*, written in 1796, had two recipes for apple pie.

But America has embraced this pie as a symbol of good taste and plain living. In its most basic form, the pie is made of sweetened apples and a piecrust. The apples release their juices as they cook, creating the perfect sauce and complement to the tender apples and crisp and flaky crust.

A few simple additions make this pie perfect: cinnamon, lemon juice, and apple cider. *Yield: Serves 8*

Ingredients

Classic Piecrust (see variation)

$1/2$ cup frosted flake cereal, crushed

5 Granny Smith apples, peeled and cored

2 McIntosh apples, peeled and cored

2 tablespoons lemon juice

$1/2$ cup granulated sugar

2 teaspoons cinnamon

$1/2$ cup packed brown sugar

$1/3$ cup butter, melted

2 tablespoons flour

1 tablespoon cornstarch

$1/4$ teaspoon cardamom

$1/2$ teaspoon nutmeg

$1/4$ teaspoon salt

$1/3$ cup apple cider

Classic Apple Pie

- Prepare piecrust. Line 9-inch pan with one crust; sprinkle with cereal. Preheat oven to 350°F.

- Thinly slice apples into large bowl. Sprinkle with lemon juice as you work. Add granulated sugar and cinnamon; toss and set aside.

- In small saucepan, combine brown sugar, butter, flour, cornstarch, cardamom, nutmeg, and salt; mix well. Add cider; simmer 5 minutes.

- Place apples in crust and top with butter sauce. Add top crust; flute edges; cut three slits. Bake 60 to 70 minutes, until brown.

Classic Piecrust: In bowl, combine 2½ cups flour, ½ teaspoon salt, and 1 teaspoon sugar. Cut in ½ cup butter and ½ cup solid shortening until fine particles form. Mix 2 tablespoons milk and 3 tablespoons cold water in small bowl; sprinkle over flour mixture, tossing until particles clump. Gather into a ball; cover and refrigerate 2 hours. Divide in half and roll out into two 12-inch rounds.

Sour Cream Apple Pie: Make recipe as directed, except omit frosted flakes and butter sauce. Chop half of apples. Combine apples with lemon juice, granulated sugar, cinnamon, and nutmeg. Stir in 1 cup sour cream, 1 teaspoon vanilla, and 1 beaten egg; pour into crust. Top with second crust. Seal edges, flute, and cut vent holes. Bake as directed.

Prepare Piecrust

Pour Sauce over Apples

- There are a few rules to making the best piecrust. One is, keep all the ingredients cold.

- The fat must not soften or melt in the flour mixture or the crust will be mealy instead of flaky.

- It may help to chill the flour mixture before you add the butter and shortening. And always chill the dough before rolling it out.

- Don't pull or stretch the dough when placing it in the pie plate or it will shrink when baked.

- As the apples sit in the sugar-and-lemon-juice mixture, they will start to release some juice. Add that to the pie, too.

- The butter sauce adds rich flavor and some creaminess to the pie filling.

- As soon as the butter sauce goes over the apples, top with the top crust.

- Fold the two crusts together at the edges, then pinch so they stand up. Flute by pressing your fingers on either sides of the crust edges.

PUMPKIN PIE

Pumpkin pie is an easy and classic dessert

Thanksgiving wouldn't be the same without pumpkin pie. It's been the traditional holiday dessert since the first American settlers served Thanksgiving dinner.

That dessert, however, wasn't like the pie as we know it. It was most probably a sweetened pumpkin filling baked right in the pumpkin shell. The first true pumpkin pie probably came from France.

You can make pumpkin pie from a fresh pumpkin or from canned pumpkin. Be sure to use solid-pack pumpkin, which is made from real pumpkins cooked to a puree. Pumpkin pie filling has sweeteners and other ingredients added and won't work in this recipe.

Serve this pie with some whipped cream sweetened with brown sugar, and toasted pecans. *Yield: Serves 8*

Ingredients

1 Classic Piecrust (see page 85)

1 (15-ounce) can solid-pack pumpkin

2 tablespoons butter

1 cup packed brown sugar

3 tablespoons granulated sugar

2 tablespoons flour

$1/2$ teaspoon salt

1 teaspoon pumpkin pie spice

1 teaspoon cinnamon

2 eggs

1 cup heavy cream

Pumpkin Pie

- Place crust in 9-inch pie pan; flute edges and set aside. Preheat oven to 375°F.

- In large bowl, combine pumpkin with butter, brown sugar, and granulated sugar; mix well.

- Beat in flour, salt, pumpkin pie spice, and cinnamon. Then add eggs and cream; beat until smooth.

- Pour into piecrust. Bake 50 to 60 minutes, until pie is set and crust is golden brown. Cool; refrigerate overnight. Slice to serve the next day.

Fresh Pumpkin Pie: Make recipe as directed, except substitute 1 2-pound sugar pumpkin and 2 tablespoons butter for canned pumpkin. Cut pumpkin in half, brush with butter, bake 90 minutes at 375°F. Cool, scoop out flesh and seeds, and puree. Use 2 tablespoons honey in place of granulated sugar. Add ½ teaspoon ground nutmeg. Bake as directed in recipe.

Pecan Streusel Topping: Make pie as directed, except top with this mixture: In medium bowl, combine ⅓ cup packed brown sugar, 3 tablespoons flour, 1 teaspoon cinnamon. Cut in 3 tablespoons butter until crumbly. Stir in 1 cup chopped pecans. Bake 15 minutes, then sprinkle topping over pie. Continue baking until done.

Mix Pumpkin with Butter and Sugar

Pour Filling into Crust

- The solid-pack pumpkin is rather stiff and should be beaten before the butter and sugar are added.

- Work the mixture together well so there are no lumps or pieces of pumpkin unincorporated into the filling.

- Don't overbeat the mixture; you don't want too much air in this pie.

- If the pie rises too much in the oven, it will fall and crack when cooled. If this happens, just top it with whipped cream.

- Pour the filling evenly into the crust and smooth it out with the back of a spoon.

- At this point you can top the filling with a streusel or sweetened nut mixture.

- Bake the pie until the crust is deep golden brown. You may need to cover the crust edges with foil to prevent overbrowning.

- The pie will have better flavor and will cut better if it is made the day before and refrigerated overnight.

PIES & TARTS

LEMON MERINGUE TARTLETS
Tartlets are fun to serve at a dessert buffet

Tartlets are simply small pies. They can be made in mini muffin tins, about 1½ inches wide, or in 4-inch tart pans. These little pies are fun to make and serve. Children especially love them.

You can transform any pie recipe into a tartlet recipe. A basic 9-inch pie recipe will make six to eight 4-inch tartlets or about 24 mini tartlets. Adjust the baking time accordingly.

This smooth, cooked lemon filling is a classic, rich with egg yolks and butter. You can make the filling alone and serve it as lemon curd, for that is what it is.

This recipe can be used to make Lime Meringue Tartlets or Orange Meringue Tartlets; just substitute lime juice and zest, or orange juice and zest, for the lemon ingredients. *Yield: Serves 6*

Lemon Meringue Tartlets

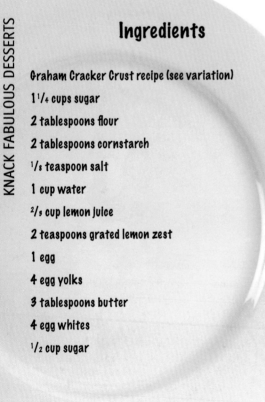

KNACK FABULOUS DESSERTS

Ingredients

Graham Cracker Crust recipe (see variation)

1¼ cups sugar

2 tablespoons flour

2 tablespoons cornstarch

⅛ teaspoon salt

1 cup water

⅔ cup lemon juice

2 teaspoons grated lemon zest

1 egg

4 egg yolks

3 tablespoons butter

4 egg whites

½ cup sugar

- Prepare crust.

- In saucepan, combine 1¼ cups sugar, flour, cornstarch, and salt. Add water, lemon juice, and zest; mix.

- Cook over medium-low heat, stirring constantly, until mixture boils. Beat ½ cup hot mixture into whole egg and yolks; return to pan. Simmer 3 minutes, then stir in butter until melted.

- Pour into tartlet shells; cool 1 hour. Beat egg whites with ½ cup sugar until stiff; top tartlets. Bake at 400°F 6 to 8 minutes; cool.

Graham Cracker Crust: Place 1 paper package graham crackers in zip-lock bag. Seal bag and crush crackers. Pour into bowl. Add ½ cup finely chopped walnuts and 1 tablespoon packed brown sugar; mix. Add 6 tablespoons melted butter and mix well. Press into bottom and up sides of six 4-inch tartlet pans. Bake at 375°F 5 to 6 minutes, until set; cool completely.

Lemon Meringue Pie: Make recipe as directed, except press crust mixture into bottom and up sides of 9-inch pie pan. Bake 7 to 9 minutes; cool completely. Make filling and meringue. Pour filling into cooled crust and let cool, then top with meringue, making sure meringue is sealed to edges of crust. Bake pie 9 to 13 minutes, until meringue is lightly browned. Chill; store in refrigerator.

Cook Filling

- The dry ingredients are combined before the liquid ingredients are added so the filling is well blended.

- Use a wire whisk to stir the filling as it cooks. This will remove any lumps and make the smoothest filling.

- Some of the hot mixture is beaten into the eggs before they are cooked; this is called tempering.

- The mixture must simmer for a few minutes so the egg yolks are cooked. This creates a stable filling.

Seal Meringue

- Beat the meringue until you can no longer feel the grains of sugar when you rub a bit of meringue between your fingers.

- The meringue must be beaten until stiff peaks form: The meringue will stand up without drooping when the beaters are lifted.

- It's important that the meringue be sealed to the edges of the piecrust.

- The proteins in the egg whites will start to shrink in the oven's heat. If the meringue isn't touching the crust, it will shrink.

LAYERED BLUEBERRY PIE

A press-in-the-pan crust, cream cheese, and blueberries make a fabulous pie

Pies don't have to be made with just one layer. A combination of custard or cheesecake with a cooked or plain fruit filling makes a delicious pie that combines two desserts in one.

This recipe can be made with other fruits as well. Raspberries and strawberries are perfect substitutions. Be sure that the fruits are ripe, not soggy or wrinkled. Pick them over carefully and wash them before using.

Sweetened condensed milk takes the place of sugar in the creamy filling. Do not use evaporated milk in its place or the filling will not set up properly. Read labels carefully!

Serve this fresh-tasting pie after a dinner of roast chicken and scalloped potatoes. *Yield: Serves 8*

Ingredients

Cookie Crust (see variation)

3 cups blueberries

1/2 cup packed brown sugar

3 tablespoons cornstarch

2 tablespoons lemon juice

1/3 cup water

1/2 teaspoon cinnamon

1 tablespoon butter

1 (8-ounce) package cream cheese, softened

1 (3-ounce) package cream cheese, softened

1 (14-ounce) can sweetened condensed milk

1/3 cup lemon juice

2 teaspoons vanilla

1/2 cup heavy whipping cream

2 tablespoons powdered sugar

Layered Blueberry Pie

- Bake crust; cool completely. In saucepan, combine blueberries, brown sugar, cornstarch, lemon juice, water, and cinnamon.

- Bring to simmer; cook, stirring frequently, until mixture thickens and liquid becomes clear. Stir in butter and cool completely.

- In medium bowl, beat cream cheese until fluffy. Add condensed milk gradually. Add lemon juice and vanilla.

- Beat cream with powdered sugar; fold into cream cheese mixture. Place in crust. Top with blueberry mixture; chill 4 to 6 hours.

ZOOM

There are several thickeners to use when making a fruit filling for a pie or cake. Cornstarch is a good choice, since it turns clear when cooked and doesn't change the flavor of the fruit. Flour can also be used; sift it first so the filling stays smooth. Both of these thickeners need to be cooked. Tapioca is another option.

PIES & TARTS

Cook Blueberry Mixture

- You can substitute frozen blueberries for fresh in this recipe; don't thaw them before cooking with the sugar mixture.

- The blueberries will start to pop after a few minutes. This helps thicken the filling and releases blueberry flavor throughout.

- The lemon juice accents the blueberries' tartness and gives the filling a bright flavor.

- You can make this mixture ahead of time; store it in the refrigerator up to 24 hours ahead.

Assemble Pie

- The cream cheese mixture is basically a no-cook cheesecake. You can use it by itself in tart shells or a larger pie.

- The lemon juice will react with the proteins in the sweetened condensed milk and cream cheese to thicken the mixture.

- Make sure that the blueberry mixture is completely cooled before adding it to the pie.

- A hot blueberry mixture will melt the cream cheese, and the pie will not have distinct layers.

COCONUT PUDDING PIE
This no-bake pie is creamy, smooth, and full of flavor

Pudding pies are made from a crisp crust and creamy filling. The pies are usually not baked in the oven; rather, the pudding or filling is cooked on the stovetop.

A crumb crust is a good vehicle for this type of filling because it's sturdier than regular piecrusts.

You can make these pies using a packet of instant pudding with some other ingredients folded in, but it's so much better when the pudding filling is made from scratch. And it's not difficult.

Again, you're learning another skill. The pudding can be served on its own as, well, pudding. Change the flavors however you'd like by adding chocolate, fruits, extracts, caramel, or other ingredients. *Yield: Serves 8*

Ingredients

Vanilla Crumb Crust (see variation)

1 2/3 cups coconut milk

1/3 cup heavy cream

1 cup light cream

2 eggs

1 egg yolk

3/4 cup sugar

1/3 cup cornstarch

2 tablespoons flour

1/4 teaspoon salt

2 teaspoons vanilla

1 1/3 cups flaked coconut

1 cup shredded coconut, toasted

1 cup heavy cream

1/4 cup powdered sugar

Coconut Pudding Pie

- Make crust as directed; cool completely and set aside. In large saucepan, combine coconut milk, 1/3 cup heavy cream, and light cream.

- Beat in eggs, egg yolk, sugar, cornstarch, flour, and salt. Cook over medium heat, stirring constantly, until mixture comes to boil and thickens.

- Stir in vanilla and flaked coconut; pour into piecrust.

- Chill 4 hours. Top with toasted shredded coconut. Beat 1 cup heavy cream with 1/4 cup powdered sugar until stiff; serve with pie.

• • • • RECIPE VARIATIONS • • • •

Vanilla Crumb Crust: Crush 28 vanilla wafers until fine crumbs form. Place in bowl with ¼ cup ground almonds. Melt ⅓ cup butter; add ½ teaspoon vanilla. Drizzle over crumbs, stirring to coat. Press into bottom and up sides of 9-inch pan. Bake at 350°F 8 to 10 minutes, until set; cool completely.

Chocolate Cream Pie: Make recipe as directed, except make crust with chocolate sandwich cookies. For pudding, omit coconut milk; use 1½ cups light cream and 1½ cups heavy cream. Add ⅓ cup cocoa powder along with sugar. After pudding thickens, remove from heat and stir in 1 cup semisweet chocolate chips. Omit coconut. Chill pie and top with whipped cream.

Beat Pudding Mixture

- The combination of egg yolks, cornstarch, and flour will thicken the cream to the correct consistency.

- Cornstarch or flour alone doesn't do the job as well. The flour adds more protein, while the cornstarch adds starch.

- Beat the mixture well when adding the eggs and dry ingredients to the cream mixture.

- Don't combine the ingredients ahead of time without cooking it or it may not thicken properly.

Cook Pudding Mixture

- A wire whisk is the best tool to use when cooking any pudding or custard mixture on the stovetop.

- Use medium heat and watch the mixture carefully. If you don't stir constantly, it could burn or get lumpy.

- The mixture is done when it thickens and coats a spoon evenly and thickly.

- For a fluffier pie, chill the pudding mixture until it is cold, then fold in the sweetened whipped cream instead of using it to top the pie.

PIES & TARTS

PECAN PIE

Pecan pie should be rich, nutty, and sweet with a smooth texture

Nut pies are another type of traditional American pie. Most pecan pies have a few nuts suspended in a sweetened clear custard. The best pecan pie has more nuts with less custard to hold it together.

Traditional pecan pie uses corn syrup to make the filling smooth and creamy. You can substitute honey or maple syrup for the corn syrup for a more authentic, nutty taste.

This recipe reduces the corn syrup amount usually used in pecan pies to give the filling more substance. The tiny bit of apple cider vinegar helps cut the sweetness of the filling and makes it more tender.

Serve on special china plates with a selection of teas. *Yield: Serves 8*

Ingredients

1 Classic Piecrust (see page 85)

$^1/_3$ cup finely chopped pecans

3 eggs

$^3/_4$ cup packed brown sugar

$^1/_4$ cup granulated sugar

Pinch salt

$^1/_4$ cup melted butter

$^1/_3$ cup dark corn syrup

$^1/_2$ teaspoon apple cider vinegar

2 teaspoons vanilla

$1^1/_2$ cups coarsely chopped pecans

1 cup whole pecans

Pecan Pie

- Prepare crust but do not bake. Press $^1/_3$ cup finely chopped pecans into bottom; set aside. Preheat oven to 350°F.

- In large bowl, beat eggs until light and fluffy; add brown sugar, granulated sugar, and salt.

- Stir in butter, corn syrup, vinegar, vanilla, and chopped pecans. Pour into piecrust.

- Place whole pecans on top in decorative pattern. Bake 55 to 65 minutes, until knife inserted in pie comes out clean. Cool.

Brown Sugar Pecan Pie: Make recipe as directed, except increase brown sugar to 1 cup, increase melted butter to ½ cup, omit dark corn syrup and add 2 tablespoons milk and 2 tablespoons flour to filling. Reduce chopped pecans in filling to 1 cup. Bake at 375°F for 15 minutes, then reduce temperature to 350°F. Bake 35 to 45 minutes longer until pie is set.

Chocolate Walnut Pie: Make recipe as directed, except substitute chopped walnuts for the ⅓ cup pecans pressed into piecrust and the 1½ cups chopped pecans used in filling. Omit whole pecans. Melt 1 cup semisweet chocolate chips and add to filling along with corn syrup. Bake pie as directed. Melt ½ cup milk chocolate chips with 2 teaspoons oil; drizzle over cooled pie.

Toast Nuts

- This pie is easy to make because all you have to do is stir the filling ingredients together.

- For more flavor, you can toast the chopped pecans before adding to the filling.

- Toast them at 350°F for 4 to 6 minutes, watching carefully, until the nuts are fragrant.

- Chop them before you toast them, or toast whole nuts and cool completely before chopping, or they will become mushy.

Doneness Tests

- There are several doneness tests for pecan pie. One is to insert a knife near the center of the pie.

- If it comes out clean with no soft custard sticking to it, the pie is done.

- The pie will also jiggle just a bit when moved. This slight jiggling is what you want; the filling will set up as the pie cools.

- You can also test the doneness by observation. The crust will be very browned and the pecans on top will be toasted.

PEACH COBBLER

Fresh peaches bake with a crunchy and velvety cake topping

Cobblers are classic old-fashioned desserts. They were originally invented by settlers and farmers as a way to use fruits and turn them into a hearty and filling dish. They were often served at breakfast for a hearty start to a long day in the fields.

Other names for this classic American dish include *buckle*, *slump*, *grunt*, and *pandowdy*. These regional names all mean the same thing: a fruit filling cooked with a pastry topping.

A cobbler is a deep-dish pie that can have a cake topping or tops a cake mixture with a fruit filling. Juicy fruits like peaches, pears, and berries provide a sauce to accompany the cake.

Serve this recipe with vanilla ice cream or sweetened whipped cream. *Yield: Serves 6–8*

Ingredients

5 large peaches, peeled

1 tablespoon lemon juice

1 teaspoon lemon zest

$^1/_2$ cup packed brown sugar

$^1/_4$ cup granulated sugar

1 teaspoon cinnamon

$^1/_2$ cup butter, melted

$1^1/_2$ cups flour

$^1/_2$ cup granulated sugar

$^3/_4$ cup packed brown sugar

$1^1/_2$ teaspoons baking powder

$^1/_2$ teaspoon baking soda

$^1/_4$ teaspoon salt

$^1/_3$ cup peach nectar

$^1/_2$ cup light cream

2 eggs

1 teaspoon vanilla

Peach Cobbler

- Preheat oven to 375°F. Slice peaches ½ inch thick into large bowl; sprinkle with lemon juice and zest. Combine ½ cup brown sugar, ¼ cup granulated sugar, and 1 teaspoon cinnamon; sprinkle over fruit.

- Melt butter in 13x9-inch pan in oven for 5 minutes; remove. In bowl, combine flour, ½ cup sugar, ¾ cup brown sugar, baking powder, soda, and salt.

- In bowl, beat nectar, cream, eggs, and vanilla; add to flour mixture. Pour batter over butter in pan; spoon peaches over. Bake 45 to 55 minutes, until golden.

96

To peel peaches, the easiest way is to blanch them. Bring a large pot of water to a boil, then add the peaches, two or three at a time. After 40 seconds, remove the peaches and place in an ice-water bath; let sit 15 seconds. The peel will then slip right off the peach. Cut in half, remove the pit, and use as directed.

RECIPE VARIATION

Cranberry Pear Cobbler: Make recipe as directed, except substitute 6 Bosc or Anjou pears, peeled and sliced, for peaches. Toss with lemon juice as you work. Combine pears with ½ cup dried sweetened cranberries and ½ cup chopped fresh or frozen cranberries. Substitute pear nectar for peach nectar in cake topping. Assemble dessert and bake as directed.

Peel Peaches

Assemble Dessert

- Blanching is the easiest way to remove the peel from peaches. It also helps slow down the enzymatic browning process.

- Look for freestone peaches; the pit is easy to remove. Cling peaches are called that because the flesh clings to the pit.

- You can peel the peaches with a swivel-bladed peeler or a sharp paring knife.

- The knife must be sharp or you'll bruise the fruit as you work. Work slowly and don't remove much of the flesh.

- You can substitute frozen, thawed peach slices for the fresh in this recipe.

- The butter in the pan helps prevent the cake from sticking and helps the cake start browning quickly.

- The hot butter and the hot pan also ensure that the cake will have a slightly crisp bottom crust.

- The peaches are baked on top of the cake in this recipe. You can turn the recipe upside down: Add the peaches first, then pour the batter over.

COBBLERS & CRISPS

MIXED FRUIT COBBLER
Sweet fruits are topped with tender biscuits

This type of cobbler consists of fruits mixed with sugar and cornstarch, topped with tender drop biscuits made with cinnamon and sour cream.

This old-fashioned dessert is homey and comforting, perfect for a cold winter night. Because it has so much fruit, it's also relatively good for you. This recipe has lots of vitamins A and C and is low in fat.

You can use any combination of fruits you'd like in this easy recipe. Make sure that they are ripe and juicy, and use at least one fruit that is slightly tart.

Serve this dessert warm from the oven, topped with vanilla ice cream or Hard Sauce (see page 183). It's a good ending to a dinner of roast chicken and scalloped potatoes. *Yield: Serves 8*

Ingredients

2 peaches, peeled and pitted

3 pears, peeled and cored

2 tablespoons lemon juice

2 cups pitted bing cherries

2 teaspoons grated lemon zest

1/3 cup sugar

2 tablespoons cornstarch

1 1/4 cups flour

1/3 cup packed brown sugar

1 teaspoon cinnamon

1 teaspoon baking powder

1/2 teaspoon baking soda

1/4 teaspoon salt

1/3 cup butter, cut into pieces

3/4 cup sour cream

1 teaspoon vanilla

2 tablespoons demerara sugar

Mixed Fruit Cobbler

- Preheat oven to 400°F. Grease 2-quart baking dish with unsalted butter.

- In dish, toss peaches and pears with lemon juice. Add cherries; sprinkle with zest, sugar, and cornstarch; toss. Bake 12 minutes.

- In medium bowl, combine flour, brown sugar, cinnamon, baking powder, soda, and salt; cut in butter. Add sour cream and vanilla and mix just until blended.

- Remove fruit from oven; drop topping over. Sprinkle with demerara sugar. Bake 25 to 35 minutes longer.

Cobbler with Rolled Biscuits: Make recipe as directed, except when making biscuits, increase flour to 1¾ cups. Place dough on lightly floured surface and sprinkle with flour. Roll or pat out to ½-inch thickness. Cut into 2- or 3-inch rounds with cookie cutter. Brush biscuits with melted butter and sprinkle with demerara sugar. Place on hot fruit and bake as directed until done.

Peach Cobbler: Make recipe as directed, except omit pears and bing cherries. Increase peaches to 6 or 7 large fruits. Peel peaches and remove pits; slice into ½-inch slices. Toss with lemon juice, lemon zest, ½ cup sugar, and cornstarch; place in pan. Bake 10 minutes, then top with biscuits and continue baking 25 to 30 minutes longer, until peaches are bubbling and biscuits are golden.

Fruit in Baking Pan

Drop Biscuits onto Fruit

- Lemon juice will help to stop the enzymatic browning in the peaches and pears.

- This browning occurs when air is exposed to enzymes within the fruit's cells. The brown color is a result of this process.

- Lemon juice slows down the enzyme's reaction. It won't completely stop the browning, but it does reduce it.

- Toss the fruit in the pan gently so it doesn't bruise but mixes together thoroughly.

- You can combine the dry ingredients for the biscuits before you prepare the fruit.

- But don't add the sour cream and vanilla to the biscuits until the fruit is in the oven.

- Using a large spoon, drop about 2 tablespoons of dough for each biscuit onto the bubbling fruit.

- Leave a bit of space between the biscuits because they will rise as they bake. Bake until the biscuits are golden brown.

COBBLERS & CRISPS

CRANBERRY APPLE BETTY

Finely cubed cinnamon bread makes the crunchy topping on this simple dessert

A betty is a simple fruit dessert that is topped with a sweetened and buttered bread mixture. The dessert is sometimes made with applesauce instead of the whole fruit, and sometimes with bread crumbs instead of cubed bread. The choice is yours!

This is an economical dessert, designed to use up stale bread. You can use any type of bread for the topping, but cinnamon swirl or raisin bread makes the dessert a bit more special.

Use tart apples for baking in this easy recipe. They should be crisp with a firm texture to stand up to the relatively long baking time. *Yield: Serves 6–8*

Ingredients

4 Granny Smith apples, peeled and chopped

²/₃ cup sweetened dried cranberries

2 tablespoons orange juice

¹/₂ cup granulated sugar

¹/₈ teaspoon salt

4 slices cinnamon swirl bread

¹/₄ cup packed brown sugar

1 teaspoon cinnamon

¹/₃ cup butter, melted

2 tablespoons apple cider

¹/₂ cup finely chopped walnuts

Cranberry Apple Betty

- Preheat oven to 375°F. Combine apples and cranberries in 2-quart baking dish. Toss with orange juice, granulated sugar, and salt.

- Cut bread into ¼-inch cubes; place in medium bowl. In separate bowl, mix brown sugar, cinnamon, butter, and cider.

- Drizzle butter mixture over bread cubes, tossing to coat. Add nuts and spread apple mixture.

- Bake 40 to 50 minutes, until apples are tender and bubbling and topping is crisp. Serve warm with ice cream.

Applesauce Brown Betty: Combine 2 cups chunky applesauce with 1 peeled and grated Granny Smith apple, 1 tablespoon lemon juice, and 2 tablespoons packed brown sugar in place of apples and cranberries. Bake bread slices in a 300°F oven for 15 to 20 minute until dried; crumble, then drizzle with butter-and-cider mixture. Assemble dessert and bake.

ZOOM

The best apples for baking are those with a strong sweet-tart taste and a firm texture that doesn't become soft or mushy in the heat. These varieties include Granny Smith, Cortland, Empire, Golden Delicious (*not* Red Delicious), Jonathan, Jonagold, and Winesap. Choose smooth and firm apples that are heavy for their size, with no bruises or soft spots.

Mix Fruits

- The orange juice provides the same function as lemon juice: preventing enzymatic browning.

- You can thinly slice the apples instead of chopping them, but do remove the peel.

- The apples will become quite soft during the long baking time, but the peel won't soften enough.

- You can substitute dried cherries, golden raisins, or dried currants for the dried cranberries if you'd like.

Assemble Dessert

- The cinnamon swirl bread should be a good-quality bread, firm and not too soft.

- You can make bread crumbs from the bread instead of cutting it into cubes. Tear the bread into small pieces.

- Any other type of bread can be used, including firm white bread or whole wheat bread.

- Bake the dish until the fruit mixture is bubbling and the apples are soft. The bread topping should be crunchy and golden brown.

BUTTERSCOTCH APPLE CRISP

Tender apples nestle under a sweet crisp topping

A crisp is a combination of baked fruits and streusel topping. The streusel is usually made from flour, oatmeal, and butter, sweetened with brown sugar. Granola can also be used as a shortcut.

Crisps can be made with almost any fruit that is good baked. Pear crisp, peach crisp, and blueberry crisp are some good options.

The butterscotch flavor in this apple crisp comes from two kinds of brown sugar used in two different ways. A dark brown sugar sauce bakes with the apples, and a light brown sugar crumbly topping adds flavor and crunch.

This dessert is wonderful served warm from the oven with softly whipped cream. *Yield: Serves 8*

Ingredients

5 Granny Smith apples, peeled and sliced

1 tablespoon lemon juice

1/2 cup packed dark brown sugar

3 tablespoons butter

1/4 cup heavy whipping cream

1/4 teaspoon salt

2 teaspoons vanilla

3/4 cup packed light brown sugar

3/4 cup flour

1 cup quick-cooking oatmeal

1/2 cup butter, melted

Butterscotch Apple Crisp

- Preheat oven to 350°F. Grease 9-inch-square pan. Toss apples with lemon juice in pan.

- In saucepan, combine dark brown sugar and butter; cook until smooth.

- Add cream and salt; cook until sauce blends. Remove from heat and add vanilla. Pour over apples.

- Combine light brown sugar, flour, and oatmeal; stir in 1/2 cup melted butter until crumbly. Sprinkle over apples. Bake 40 to 50 minutes, until apples are tender and top is golden brown. Serve warm.

Blueberry Crisp: Make recipe as directed, except use 5 cups fresh or frozen blueberries in place of apples. If using frozen blueberries, do not thaw before using. Omit dark brown sugar, butter, and cream; mix berries with ½ cup granulated sugar. Top with oatmeal mixture and bake as directed, until blueberries are bubbling and topping is crisp and golden brown.

Peach Crisp: Make recipe as directed, except substitute 6 peaches, peeled and sliced, for apples. Omit dark brown sugar, butter, and whipping cream mixture. Toss peaches with ¼ cup packed brown sugar and ½ cup granulated sugar. Add 12 cups chopped walnuts to oatmeal streusel mixture. Bake crisp as directed until golden brown.

Pour Sauce over Apples

Mix Topping

- Dark brown sugar has more molasses than light brown sugar and therefore has a stronger flavor.

- Cook the brown sugar mixture until the sauce blends. This will take a few minutes on the heat.

- Drizzle the sauce evenly over the apples. The sauce will not completely coat the apples.

- You can use light brown sugar instead of dark brown for a lighter taste. But don't substitute margarine for the butter or light cream for the heavy cream.

- Combine the flour, sugar, and oatmeal before adding the butter to make sure it's evenly mixed.

- The butter should be completely melted before adding to the oatmeal mixture.

- Stir the mixture with a spoon until the butter coats the dry ingredients and the ingredients begin to stick together.

- Crumble the topping evenly over the apples. Don't press down. Bake until the topping is golden and crunchy.

COBBLERS & CRISPS

103

CHERRY CLAFOUTI
Tart cherries are enveloped in a custardy cake

Clafouti is a French dessert that is usually made with cherries baked in a sweetened and spiced cake batter. The batter is poured over the cherries and the whole thing is baked until the cake has a nice golden crust and the cherries are softened and sweet.

The cherries you buy for this dessert should be large, plump, and firm. Remove the stems, and take out the pits using a cherry pitter so the cherries stay whole.

You can use sweet or sour cherries in this simple dessert. Some purists insist that the pits should stay in the cherries while baking to add a slight almond flavor, but that makes the dessert difficult to eat. *Yield: Serves 6–8*

Ingredients

3 cups pitted bing cherries

2 tablespoons orange juice

1 teaspoon grated orange zest

³/₄ cup flour

²/₃ cup granulated sugar

¹/₈ teaspoon salt

¹/₂ teaspoon cinnamon

3 eggs

1 egg yolk

³/₄ cup light cream

2 teaspoons vanilla

¹/₄ cup sliced almonds

2 tablespoons powdered sugar

Cherry Clafouti

- Preheat oven to 350°F. Grease 9-inch baking pan; add cherries, orange juice, and zest.

- In medium bowl, combine flour, sugar, salt, and cinnamon; mix. In small bowl, combine eggs, egg yolk, cream, and vanilla; mix.

- Add egg mixture to flour mixture and whisk until smooth. Pour over cherries; sprinkle with almonds.

- Bake 40 to 50 minutes, until crust is golden brown and toothpick inserted in center comes out clean. Sprinkle with powdered sugar and serve warm.

Pitting cherries is serious business. You must make sure that every cherry has every pit removed, or someone could break a tooth eating your carefully prepared dessert. Cherry pitters work well, but you can also push a drinking straw through the cherry to remove the pit. Make sure that you hear or see the pit come out of each cherry.

• • • • RECIPE VARIATION • • • •

Plum Clafouti: Make recipe as directed, except substitute 14 to 16 ripe purple or red plums for cherries. Slice plums in half and remove pits. Place plums, cut-side down, in prepared baking dish and sprinkle with orange juice, orange zest, and 2 tablespoons packed brown sugar. Prepare batter as directed and pour over fruit. Bake 45 to 55 minutes, until plums are tender.

Prepare Cherries

Add Batter and Bake

- Work over the sink or a large bowl as you pit the cherries so you can hear each one leave the cherry and plop into the hard container.

- Do not pit the cherries ahead of time or they will turn brown, just as peaches and apples do.

- For a different flavor, you can use lemon juice and lemon zest in place of the orange juice and zest.

- If you are using sour cherries, add 2 to 3 tablespoons sugar along with the orange juice.

- This cake batter is a variety of a genoise, a basic French butter cake.

- The traditional genoise cake does not contain any cream, but is made in the same way.

- The batter will not completely cover the cherries. Some will poke through, which gives the dessert a pretty finish.

- This dessert is best served warm, topped with softly whipped cream or slightly softened vanilla ice cream.

COBBLERS & CRISPS

BERRY CRISP
Sweet and juicy berries are topped with a rich and crunchy streusel

Sweet berries release their juices when baked with a crisp granola-and-nut topping in this delicious recipe. And this dessert is relatively healthy. Berries are high in vitamins A and C, and the streusel is a good source of fiber.

When baking with berries, use fresh berries or frozen. The frozen berries should not be thawed before being added to the recipe. The heat of the oven will thaw them, and then they will bake with the rest of the ingredients. Frozen, thawed berries will be too mushy.

Use your favorite granola cereal in this easy recipe. Make sure that it doesn't contain dried fruits that will clash with the flavor of the berries. *Yield: Serves 6–8*

Ingredients

2 cups chopped strawberries

1 cup blueberries

2 cups frozen raspberries, unthawed

$1/2$ cup granulated sugar

2 tablespoons flour

1 tablespoon cornstarch

$2/3$ cup flour

1 cup packed brown sugar

$2/3$ cup quick-cooking oats

$1/2$ cup granola cereal

$1/2$ cup chopped pecans

$1/2$ teaspoon cinnamon

$1/8$ teaspoon cardamom

Pinch salt

$1/2$ cup butter, melted

Berry Crisp

- Preheat oven to 375°F. In 9-inch-square pan, toss berries with granulated sugar, 2 tablespoons flour, and cornstarch.

- In medium bowl, combine $2/3$ cup flour and brown sugar; mix well. Add oats, granola, pecans, cinnamon, cardamom, and salt. Stir in butter until mixture is combined and sprinkle over the berry mixture.

- Bake 30 to 40 minutes, until berries are bubbly and topping is browned. Serve warm with ice cream or Creamy Lemon Sauce (see variation).

Raspberry Crisp: Make recipe as directed, except substitute 4 cups frozen raspberries for strawberries and blueberries. Keep frozen berries frozen if that is what you are using. Omit cardamom; add ⅛ teaspoon grated or ground nutmeg. Substitute walnuts for pecans. Bake as directed; serve warm with Creamy Lemon Sauce.

Creamy Lemon Sauce: In saucepan, combine 2 tablespoons cornstarch with ½ cup granulated sugar and pinch salt. Add 1 tablespoon honey, ⅓ cup lemon juice, 2 tablespoons heavy cream, and ⅔ cup water. Cook, stirring constantly with wire whisk, over medium heat until mixture boils and thickens. Remove from heat and let cool. Store in refrigerator.

Toss Berry Mixture

Mix Topping

- Never wash fresh berries before you are ready to use them, because they can get moldy very quickly.

- Just rinse the berries to wash them. Cut the stems and part of the top from the strawberries and slice lengthwise.

- Rinse blueberries and raspberries and sort over them to remove any that are too soft or soggy.

- Don't try to make the berry filling ahead of time, because the sugar will start leaching liquid from the berries.

- When making a streusel topping, always mix the dry ingredients together first.

- This will let the butter combine evenly with the dry ingredients and form small clusters of streusel.

- These clusters will bake and become crunchy in the heat of the oven as the fruit bubbles.

- Serve this dessert warm from the oven with a creamy dessert sauce, softly whipped cream, or vanilla or fruit-flavored ice cream.

COBBLERS & CRISPS

SUMMER FRUIT SALAD
A lemon-mint syrup adds flavor to this easy salad

Good, perfectly ripe fresh fruit can be a dessert in itself. Sometimes there's no better way to end a meal than to offer a ripe, juicy pear with some sharp Cheddar or Parmesan cheese.

But what if you want to serve something just a bit more special, that takes a little more effort? This recipe, which pairs fresh fruit with a simple and flavorful sauce, is the answer.

You can choose your favorite fruits for this salad, or use whatever looks good in the market or at the farm stand. The recipe can be transformed into a winter fruit salad by using winter fruits like pears, apples, and grapes.

A plain sugar cookie or wafer is a good accompaniment to this healthy dessert. *Yield: Serves 8*

Ingredients

¹/₄ cup sugar

¹/₄ cup honey

3 tablespoons lemon juice

2 tablespoons chopped fresh mint

¹/₄ cup pineapple juice

1 cantaloupe, made into balls

2 peaches, peeled and sliced

2 nectarines, sliced

1¹/₂ cups red grapes

2 cups sliced strawberries

1 cup raspberries

6 mint sprigs

Summer Fruit Salad

- In small saucepan, combine sugar, honey, lemon juice, chopped mint, and pineapple juice; bring to simmer.

- Cook until syrup is clear and has reduced to ⅓ cup, about 10 minutes. Cool 20 minutes, then strain.

- Place cantaloupe, peaches, nectarines, and grapes in serving bowl. Pour syrup over; stir gently. Chill 2 to 3 hours.

- When ready to serve, add strawberries and raspberries. Top with mint and serve immediately.

Simmer Syrup

Drizzle Syrup over Fruit

- This syrup is a variation on Simple Syrup, which is used to sweeten beverages like iced tea and lemonade.

- Simmer the syrup until the sugar and honey dissolve completely.

- The syrup is strained after cooking because the mint will darken when exposed to heat. Use a fine mesh strainer and press on the mint to extract the most flavor.

- You can add more chopped fresh mint to the syrup after it has cooled for even more flavor.

- The syrup is chilled with some of the fruits so they can absorb its flavor.

- The peaches and nectarines will turn brown when sliced or chopped unless they are treated with an acidic ingredient, like the syrup.

- You can use more or less syrup, according to your own taste. Offer more syrup on the side for guests who like a sweeter dessert.

- A dollop of sweetened whipped cream or a spoonful of ice cream will dress up this dessert.

FRUIT DESSERTS ·

POACHED PEARS

Simple poached fruit is flavored with vanilla and garnished with chocolate

Poaching is a cooking technique that cooks food in liquid kept just below the simmering point. The liquid "smiles," according to the French.

It's important that the liquid not come even to a simmer, let alone a boil, when poaching fruits. The fruit will overcook and begin to fall apart if the poaching liquid gets too hot.

You can poach other fruit too. Peaches and apples are commonly poached. The fruit becomes tender and sweeter and will cut perfectly with a dessert spoon.

You can serve poached fruits with just about any sauce, ice cream, or topping. Drizzling pears with chocolate is perfect. *Yield: Serves 4–6*

Ingredients

4 large pears, peeled

1 cup pear nectar

¹/₂ cup dry white wine

¹/₂ vanilla bean

¹/₃ cup sugar

Pinch salt

4 ounces semisweet chocolate, chopped

¹/₄ cup heavy cream

Poached Pears

- Cut a small slice off bottom of pears so they will stand upright.

- In large saucepan, combine nectar, wine, vanilla bean, sugar, and salt; bring to simmer.

- Carefully add pears. Poach 10 minutes, then turn pears and poach 7 to 9 minutes longer, until tender. Spoon liquid over pears as they cook.

- Remove pears and let cool. Remove vanilla bean and boil sauce until reduced by half. Pour over pears. Melt chocolate and cream together; drizzle over pears.

Poached Peaches: Make recipe as directed, except substitute 4 large ripe peaches for pears. Use 1 cup water in place of pear nectar. Peel peaches, cut in half, and remove pit. Poach peaches 5 to 6 minutes, until tender, spooning poaching liquid atop as peaches cook. Cool in syrup, then chill. Serve with Berry Sauce or Creamy Lemon Sauce.

Berry Sauce: In medium saucepan, combine 1 cup raspberries and 1 cup blueberries. In small bowl, combine ⅓ cup granulated sugar, 1 tablespoon cornstarch, and ¼ cup pear nectar; blend well. Add to berry mixture in saucepan. Cook over medium heat, stirring constantly, until boiling. Simmer 2 to 4 minutes, until thickened. Remove from heat and add 1 teaspoon vanilla. Cool.

Peel Pears

Poach Pears

- To peel pears, use a swivel-bladed vegetable peeler. Hold the pear in your non-dominant hand.

- Hold the peeler in your dominant hand. Gently peel the skin from the pear, being careful not to bruise the fruit.

- You can remove the core and seeds from the pear if you'd like. Remove from the bottom so the stem remains intact.

- You can also cut the pears in half and remove the core. Cut the poaching time in half.

- Make sure that the sugar is completely dissolved before you add the pears to the poaching liquid.

- You can simmer the liquid before adding the pears, but don't simmer after the pears are on the heat.

- Watch the mixture carefully as it cooks. If bubbles start to break on the surface, turn the heat down.

- If you like, you can cool the pears in the poaching liquid. This keeps them moist and adds even more flavor.

FRUIT DESSERTS

SUMMER PUDDING

This updated English dessert pairs pound cake with berries

Even though the generic English word for "dessert" is *pudding*, this recipe is a special case. It's not a pudding in the American sense of the word. Cake is layered in a pan, then soaked with fresh fruit and fruit juices.

The whole thing is pressed down and chilled, then unmolded. It holds together because the fruit and cake meld into a sweet and tart dessert with a texture somewhat like, well, pudding.

You can use almost any fruit to make summer pudding, but traditionally soft fruits like berries are used. They have the most juice and blend well with the cake or bread.

Serve this pudding with sweetened whipped cream on a hot summer night, after a meal of cold salads and crusty bread. *Yield: Serves 8*

Ingredients

2 cups cherries, pitted and sliced

1/3 cup cherry juice

3 cups strawberries, sliced

1/2 cup sugar

2 tablespoons lemon juice

2 cups raspberries

1 (16-ounce) package frozen pound cake, thawed

Sweetened whipped cream (see variation)

Summer Pudding

- Line 9x5-inch loaf pan with plastic wrap. In pan, simmer cherries, juice, strawberries, sugar, and lemon juice 8 minutes.

- Add raspberries; cook 6 minutes; cool. Spread 1/3 cup sauce in pan. Cut pound cake into 1/3-inch slices.

- Dip cake slices in berry mixture; line pan with cake. Spread 1/2 cup berry sauce on top; repeat layers until pan is full.

- Cover with plastic wrap, top with smaller pan, and weight down with a can. Chill 6 hours. Unmold; serve with whipped cream.

Classic Summer Pudding: Make recipe as directed, except use 1-pound loaf firm white bread in place of pound cake. Cut off crusts and cut bread into ½-inch slices. Line bowl with bread, fill with fruit mixture, and top with bread. Weight down and chill. When ready to serve, unmold pudding and serve with sweetened whipped cream or Hard Sauce (see page 183).

Sweetened Whipped Cream: In chilled bowl, with chilled beaters, beat 1 cup heavy whipping cream with 1 teaspoon vanilla and ¼ cup powdered sugar until stiff peaks form. Refrigerate up to 1 hour, or make just before serving. To hold for a longer period of time, place dollops on waxed paper; freeze until solid. Thaw in refrigerator 2 hours before serving.

Simmer Berries

- The berry mixture is simmered so the fruits start to break down. They will release more juices when cooked.

- The berries will naturally start to release juice when combined with sugar.

- You can make the berry mixture ahead of time, then keep it in the refrigerator.

- Bring the mixture to room temperature before layering with the pound cake.

Layer Cake with Berry Mixture

- Pound cake is a cake with dense texture. That's why it's important to dip the cake in the liquid before layering.

- The fruit juices have to soak all the way through the cake for the dessert to be successful.

- You can let this dessert stand, well covered, in the refrigerator 2 to 3 days.

- Garnish the dessert with mint sprigs, or sprinkle with toasted slices almonds for a bit of crunch.

FRUIT DESSERTS

STRAWBERRY RASPBERRY FOOL
Fresh fruit is folded into sweetened sour cream in this easy dessert

Fool is an old-fashioned word for an old-fashioned dessert. Traditionally, fools were English. They first appeared in the 1500s, made with pureed fruit folded into whipped cream. They can be made with any fruit, but gooseberries were originally used. The word may have been derived from the French word *fouler,* which means "to crush."

This fool recipe enhances the whipped cream by adding sour cream. This helps cut the sweetness of the dessert and adds more depth of flavor.

One of the nicest things about this type of dessert is that you can make it ahead of time. Then, when it's time to serve, just pull the servings out of the fridge, garnish with fruit or mint, and eat. *Yield: Serves 6*

Ingredients

2 cups sliced strawberries

3 tablespoons sugar

1 tablespoon lemon juice

1 cup raspberries

³/₄ cup sour cream

2 tablespoons packed brown sugar

1 cup heavy whipping cream

3 tablespoons powdered sugar

1¹/₂ teaspoons vanilla

Strawberry Raspberry Fool

- In medium bowl, combine strawberries with sugar; partially mash berries, leaving some whole. Let stand 10 minutes.

- Stir in lemon juice and raspberries; set aside.

- In another bowl, place sour cream and brown sugar; mix well. Beat cream with powdered sugar and vanilla until stiff.

- Fold whipped cream into sour cream; gently fold in berry mixture. Place in stemmed goblets; cover and refrigerate up to 3 hours.

114

Mixed Berry Fool: Make recipe as directed, except substitute 1 cup blackberries and 1 cup blueberries for strawberries. Sprinkle berries with sugar and lemon juice and toss gently. Prepare whipped cream and sour cream mixtures as described. Fold all together, leaving some streaks of whipped cream visible in finished dessert. Chill.

Simple Fruit Fool: Use 3 cups of one type of fruit, either strawberries, raspberries, blackberries, or blueberries. Toss with sugar and lemon juice. Omit sour cream. Increase whipped cream to 1½ cups, and increase powdered sugar to ⅓ cup. Beat cream mixture until stiff. Crush half of berries and fold into cream until blended, then fold in remaining whole fruits. Spoon into goblets and chill.

Prepare Berry Mixture

- Rinse the berries under cool running water only when you're ready to use them. Cut off the tops.

- Slice the berries and sprinkle with the sugar. During the standing time, the berries will release some of their juice.

- The lemon juice accentuates the tart flavor of the berries, and the acid helps make the berries softer.

- You can use frozen berries in a pinch. Thaw them and use about half the juices in this recipe.

Fold Mixtures Together

- The brown sugar adds a floral note to the cream mixture. The sugar will dissolve while the fools chill.

- You can use low-fat or nonfat sour cream in place of full-fat if you'd like.

- The fat in the whipped cream will make the mixture creamy despite using these other products.

- You can fold the mixture together completely, or let some of the berries and cream show separately by simply marbling them.

FRUIT DESSERTS

PEACH PAVLOVA
A Pavlova is crunchy and creamy at the same time

Pavlova is another English dessert, but this one has its roots in Russia and Australia. The dessert is named after Anna Pavlova, a Russian prima ballerina.

Legend has it that the dessert was created in her honor when she toured Australia or New Zealand in the early twentieth century.

This dessert is beautiful, with a fluffy, marshmallow-like meringue topped with whipped cream and crowned with fresh fruit. You can use any single fruit or any combination that you'd like.

It's important to make this dessert ahead of time, so the whipped cream mixture can help soften the meringue a bit and the fruit mixture can flavor the cream.

Drizzle the Pavlova with caramel syrup or chocolate sauce before serving. *Yield: Serves 8*

Ingredients

7 egg whites

1/8 teaspoon cream of tartar

1 cup granulated sugar

1/4 cup packed brown sugar

2 teaspoons cornstarch

2 teaspoons apple cider vinegar

1 cup heavy whipping cream

2 tablespoons powdered sugar

2 teaspoons vanilla

5 peaches, peeled and sliced

Caramel Sauce (see page 125)

Peach Pavlova

- Preheat oven to 350°F. Place parchment paper on cookie sheet.

- Beat egg whites with cream of tartar until soft peaks form. Beat in granulated sugar until stiff, then brown sugar until very stiff.

- Fold in cornstarch and vinegar. Spoon onto paper in 8-inch circle. Place in oven; turn down to 300°F. Bake 1¼ hours.

- Turn off heat; open door; cool completely. Beat cream, powdered sugar, and vanilla. Top Pavlova with cream, add peaches, and drizzle with sauce.

Chocolate Pavlova: Make recipe as directed, adding ⅓ cup cocoa powder to egg whites along with granulated sugar. Beat until stiff peaks form, then fold in cornstarch and vinegar. Bake Pavlova as directed, except bake 1 hour after temperature is reduced to 300°F. Add 2 tablespoons cocoa powder to whipped cream mixture. Drizzle with chocolate sauce.

Egg whites are easy to beat into fluffy mounds as long as you follow rules. Egg whites separate easily when the eggs are cold, and beat to a higher volume when warm. So separate the eggs right from the fridge, then let them stand 1 hour to warm. Separate each egg over a small bowl, and then transfer the white to a large bowl with the rest of the egg whites.

Beat Egg Whites

- To separate eggs, break an egg into your cupped hand. Let the whites slip through your fingers into the bowl; put the yolk in another bowl.

- Or break the egg, then rock the yolk back and forth between the two halves,

letting the white fall into a bowl.

- Don't let any yolk into the egg whites or they won't beat to stiff peaks.

- If a bit of yolk does get into the white, remove it with a piece of eggshell.

Assemble Dessert

- The egg white mixture has to be beaten to stiff peaks. This means that when you lift the beater, the mixture stands up in points.

- The vinegar and cornstarch change the pH of the mixture so the inside of the meringue stays soft.

- You can make the dessert ahead of time and store it in the refrigerator, or serve it as soon as it is assembled.

- Other fruits that are good in this recipe include pomegranate seeds, raspberries, and strawberries.

FRUIT DESSERTS

STRAWBERRY SHORTCAKE

This classic American dessert is also beautiful

Strawberry shortcake is a wonderful dessert for using the best berries of summer. Flaky shortbread is split and layered with whipped cream and slightly sweetened sliced strawberries.

Shortcake is called *short* because the pastry is high in fat. This proportion is called short. It makes the pastry flaky and crumbly. On a side note, this is why hydrogenated fats are called shortening.

You can make Strawberry Shortcake with everything from pound cake to leftover biscuits from breakfast, but this version is classic.

The shortcake can be made ahead of time. Store it well covered at room temperature. Or you can bake the shortcakes, cool for 20 to 30 minutes, then split and fill with cream while still warm. *Yield: Serves 6–8*

Ingredients

- 2¹/₂ cups flour
- ¹/₂ cup packed brown sugar
- 2 teaspoons baking powder
- ¹/₂ teaspoon baking soda
- ¹/₄ teaspoon salt
- ³/₄ cup butter
- ¹/₂ cup light cream
- 1 egg
- 2 teaspoons vanilla
- 4 cups sliced strawberries
- ¹/₄ cup granulated sugar
- 1 cup heavy whipping cream
- ¹/₄ cup powdered sugar
- ¹/₂ teaspoon vanilla

Strawberry Shortcake

- Preheat oven to 375°F. In bowl, combine flour, brown sugar, baking powder, soda, and salt.

- Cut in butter until particles are fine. In bowl, mix cream, egg, and vanilla. Stir into flour mixture.

- Turn out onto floured surface; knead ten times. Divide into six rounds.

- Bake 15 to 20 minutes, until golden; cool. Combine strawberries with granulated sugar. Beat heavy cream with powdered sugar and vanilla. Split shortcakes; fill and top with strawberries and whipped cream.

Chocolate Strawberry Shortcake: Make recipe as directed, except add ⅓ cup cocoa powder to flour mixture. Add 2 tablespoons cocoa powder to heavy cream mixture when beating with powdered sugar. Assemble dessert as described. Melt 3 ounces semisweet chocolate and drizzle over shortcakes just before you serve them.

Peach and Berry Shortcake: Make recipe as directed, except add ¼ cup granulated sugar to flour mixture. Form and bake shortcakes as directed. When ready to serve, peel and slice 4 peaches. Place in bowl; top with 1 tablespoon lemon juice and 2 tablespoons sugar. Let stand 10 minutes, then add 1 cup raspberries. Whip cream, assemble dessert, and serve.

Cut Butter into Flour

Assemble Shortcakes

- When making shortcakes or other short pastry, it's important that the butter or other fat is cold.

- The butter will be cut into small pieces that are surrounded with the protein and starch from the flour.

- When the pastry bakes, the butter melts and creates a flaky, tender texture in the finished product.

- Cut in the butter using a pastry blender or two knives, cutting across the bowl in many directions. You can also use a food processor.

- The shortcakes should naturally split in the middle. Use a fork to split them, or cut with a sharp knife.

- Let the strawberries stand for a few minutes while you whip the cream so the juices start to flow.

- Make sure that the cream, beaters, and bowl are all very cold so the cream will whip quickly.

- Garnish the dessert with strawberry fans, made by cutting a whole berry into thin slices, leaving them attached at the stem.

FRUIT DESSERTS

119

BAKED VANILLA CUSTARD
Three kinds of vanilla flavor this delicious custard

Custard is the original comfort food. A simple combination of sugar, eggs, milk, and vanilla is mixed and baked until silky smooth and set.

Baked custards are thicker and slightly denser than custards and puddings cooked on the stovetop or in the microwave oven.

Most custards are baked in a water bath. The water helps shield the custard from the heat of the oven, and helps moderate the temperature so the outside edges don't overcook before the center is set.

A vanilla bean, vanilla extract, and vanilla sugar all add lots of flavor to this simple recipe. All of the ingredients have to be of top quality because the dessert is so plain and simple. *Yield: Serves 6*

Ingredients

¹/₂ vanilla bean

1 cup whole milk

1¹/₂ cups heavy cream

¹/₂ cup Vanilla Sugar (see variation)

Pinch salt

4 eggs

3 egg yolks

1 teaspoon vanilla

Baked Vanilla Custard

- Preheat oven to 350°F. Grease six 6-ounce custard cups with unsalted butter.

- Split vanilla bean; scrape out seeds. Mix bean and seeds with milk, cream, Vanilla Sugar, and salt in saucepan. Heat until steam rises.

- In large bowl, combine eggs and egg yolks; beat well. Gradually stir in hot milk mixture. Add vanilla. Strain into prepared cups.

- Place in pan in oven. Pour boiling water around cups. Bake 30 to 40 minutes, until centers jiggle slightly. Cool; chill.

• • • • RECIPE VARIATIONS • • • •

Vanilla Sugar: Place 5 cups sugar in large sealed container. Place one vanilla bean in sugar. Cut another vanilla bean in half lengthwise and scrape out seeds. Add seeds and empty pod to sugar as well. Stir well. Cover and let stand for 1 to 2 weeks before using in recipes. You can use this in any recipe calling for granulated sugar where you want a strong vanilla presence.

Caramel Custard: Make recipe as directed, except use ½ cup packed brown sugar in place of Vanilla Sugar. Cook, strain, and bake custards as directed. Remove from oven, cool 30 minutes, then chill 3 to 4 hours, until very cold. When ready to serve, sprinkle each custard with 1 to 2 tablespoons brown sugar. Broil custards 6 inches from heat until sugar melts and forms a crust.

Make Custard

- The vanilla seeds provide lots of intense vanilla flavor. When heated with the milk mixture, essential oils are released. Heat milk until steaming.

- The hot milk mixture will slightly cook some of the egg proteins when stirred together.

- That is why the mixture is strained before baking. Use a very fine-mesh strainer.

- The vanilla seeds will probably be removed when the custard is strained. That's okay, since their flavor has been infused into the custard.

Strain Mixture into Cups

- The mixture is strained after mixing to remove small bits of egg and so the custard is perfectly smooth.

- For safety's sake, place the cups in a large pan, then place the pan in the oven.

- Pour the boiling water around the cups while it's on the oven rack so you don't have to lift a heavy pan full of water.

- Remove the custard cups from the water bath with tongs, then remove the pan from the oven.

121

CHOCOLATE PUDDING
Easy and rich chocolate pudding is cooked on the stovetop

Chocolate pudding is a classic children's favorite. Most people have only had chocolate pudding made from a mix, whether instant or cooked. This recipe is truly decadent, with a rich chocolate flavor and super-creamy texture.

Two kinds of chocolate add to the flavor of this easy pudding. Cocoa makes the pudding silky, and semisweet chocolate chips add creaminess and intense flavor.

This pudding can be used in many ways. It makes an excellent ice cream when frozen in an ice cream maker. It's good as a filling for tartlet shells, and can be used to fill cream puffs or napoleons.

But it's best just given to children with a small spoon, to let them create their own memories of the perfect childhood.
Yield: Serves 6–8

Ingredients

1/2 cup cocoa powder

1/4 cup cornstarch

2 tablespoons flour

3/4 cup granulated sugar

1/2 cup packed brown sugar

1/8 teaspoon salt

1 1/2 cups light cream

3 cups whole milk

1/2 cup semisweet chocolate chips

1 tablespoon butter

2 teaspoons vanilla

Chocolate Pudding

- Sift cocoa powder, cornstarch, and flour together twice. Place in heavy saucepan.

- Add sugars and salt and mix with wire whisk. Gradually stir in light cream until smooth. Whisk in milk and place over medium heat.

- Cook, stirring frequently, until mixture thickens and comes to boil. Boil 1 minute, stirring constantly.

- Remove from heat; stir in chocolate chips, butter, and vanilla until smooth. Pour into six 6-ounce dessert dishes and chill 4 to 5 hours, until set.

• • • • RECIPE VARIATIONS • • • •

Fudgesicles: Make pudding mixture as directed. Cool, then chill until thickened. Use small paper cups to form fudgesicles, along with wooden sticks. Fill each mold or cup almost to top with cold pudding mixture. Freeze for 1 hour, then insert sticks; freeze until firm. To unmold, rinse molds in warm water for a few seconds, or peel paper off fudgesicles.

Vanilla Pudding: Make recipe as directed, except omit cocoa powder and semisweet chocolate chips. Slit a vanilla bean and scrape out seeds; add to flour mixture. Add cream and milk and beat; stir in vanilla pod. Cook pudding as directed, then remove pod when thickened. Increase butter to 2 tablespoons. Pour pudding into glasses, cover with plastic wrap, and chill until cold.

Stir in Cream

- Light cream has about 20 percent butterfat, while whole milk is 3 percent and heavy whipping cream can have up to 38 percent fat.

- The combination of light cream and whole milk makes the perfect fat concentration for this pudding.

- Cornstarch and flour are used to thicken the pudding with starch and protein.

- This helps prevent separation and weeping of the pudding as it is stored in the refrigerator.

Cook Pudding

- Stir the pudding mixture constantly while it comes to a boil and during the boiling period. A wire whisk is the best tool for the smoothest pudding.

- The pudding may form a skin, or harder layer on its surface, while cooling.

- To prevent this, press plastic wrap directly onto the surface of the pudding when it's poured into the dessert dishes.

- To serve, just pull off the plastic wrap. The pudding will be creamy and smooth.

RICE PUDDING
Medium-grain rice is the key to the creamiest pudding

Rice pudding is another classic comfort food. It should be creamy and thick, with very tender rice.

To create the most tender rice, it is cooked twice. First the rice is cooked in water to rehydrate it until it is tender, then it is cooked with cream, sugar, egg, and flavorings. This double cooking process extracts more starch from the rice, making the pudding creamy and thick.

Rice comes in different lengths, with different types of starch. Long-grain rice has the straightest starch, so it stays separate and fluffy, while short-grain rice has branched starch. Medium-grain rice is a good compromise. The rice grains will be separate, but the pudding itself will be thick and creamy. *Yield: Serves 6–8*

Ingredients

- 1 cup medium-grain white rice
- 2 cups water
- 2 cups whole milk
- 1 cup light cream
- 1/2 cup granulated sugar
- 1/4 teaspoon salt
- 1 egg
- 1 egg yolk
- 1/2 cup heavy cream
- 2 tablespoons powdered sugar
- 1 teaspoon vanilla
- 1/4 teaspoon cinnamon

Rice Pudding

- Combine rice and water in large saucepan; bring to boil. Reduce heat, cover, and simmer 20 to 24 minutes, until rice is tender.

- In another large saucepan, combine milk, cream, sugar, and salt. Heat until sugar dissolves. Add rice.

- Cook over medium heat until thick and creamy, stirring frequently. Add egg and yolk; cook 3 minutes.

- Remove from heat; pour into bowl and chill. Beat cream, powdered sugar, vanilla, and cinnamon in medium bowl. Fold into pudding; chill 2 hours.

• • • • RECIPE VARIATIONS • • • •

Baked Rice Pudding: Cook rice as directed in 2 cups of water until tender. Preheat oven to 325°F and grease 2½ quart baking dish. Add milk, cream, sugar, salt, egg, egg yolk, vanilla, and cinnamon to saucepan with cooked rice. Bring just to boil. Pour into baking dish. Bake 55 to 65 minutes, stirring twice during baking time, until thick. Omit heavy cream and powdered sugar.

Caramel Sauce: In small heavy saucepan, place ⅔ cup granulated sugar. Cook over low heat, stirring until sugar starts to melt. Swirl pan occasionally until sugar is completely melted and brown. Carefully add ½ cup peach nectar, ¼ cup water, and 3 tablespoons heavy cream; boil, stirring, until smooth. Stir in 1 teaspoon vanilla.

Cook Pudding

- If you can't find medium-grain rice, long-grain rice will work just as well; the pudding will be a little less creamy.

- If there is any water left unabsorbed by the rice, drain it off before adding the rice to the remaining ingredients.

- The pudding should be stirred frequently. Scrape the bottom as you stir so it doesn't burn.

- Cook the pudding for at least 3 minutes after the egg is added for food safety reasons.

Fold Cream into Pudding

- The pudding will become thicker when it is chilled. The starch released from the rice will set, trapping liquid.

- The whipped cream folded into the rice pudding adds richness, flavor, and even more creamy texture.

- You can omit the whipped cream if you'd like, or serve it on top of the chilled pudding.

- The pudding can also be served warm. Let stand 15 to 20 minutes, stir again, then serve, perhaps with some Caramel Sauce.

CRÈME BRÛLÉE
Silky custard is topped with a melted sugar crust

Crème brûlée is a grown-up pudding, flavored with vanilla bean and topped with a crisp, glassy crust of burnt sugar.

The best crème brûlée is silky smooth, with a deep and rich vanilla flavor. The dessert is heavy with cream and egg yolks, yet it should melt on your tongue. The crisp and brittle sugar coating is made by melting brown or granulated sugar with a small propane torch, or by placing the chilled custard under the broiler.

This dessert isn't difficult to make, but you must follow the steps precisely. The cooked custard must be strained using a very fine-mesh strainer before it is baked. And a water bath during baking is also essential. *Yield: Serves 6*

Ingredients

1 vanilla bean

3 cups heavy cream

7 egg yolks

½ cup granulated sugar

⅛ teaspoon salt

2 tablespoons packed brown sugar

Crème Brûlée

- Preheat oven to 325°F. Grease six 6-ounce custard cups with unsalted butter.

- Split bean; remove seeds. Combine bean, seeds, and cream in heavy saucepan over low heat.

- Beat egg yolks, granulated sugar, and salt. Add ½ cup hot cream to egg yolks. Return to pan; stir 1 minute. Strain into custard cups.

- Bake in water bath 35 to 40 minutes, until set. Let cool 15 minutes; remove from water bath and chill. Top with brown sugar; caramelize with propane torch. Serve.

• • • • RECIPE VARIATION • • • •

Chocolate Crème Brûlée: Make recipe as directed, but add 1 cup semisweet and ½ cup milk chocolate chips to custard mixture after egg yolks have been added. Stir over low heat until chocolate is melted and smooth. Pour into custard cups and bake as directed in water bath. Chill, then top with granulated sugar and caramelize with a torch, or under broiler.

YELLOW LIGHT

No matter how hard or consistently you stir this custard as it cooks, there will still be small bits of cooked egg in the mixture. Also, the chalazae—the bit of protein in the egg that helps keep the yolk anchored to the white—may not blend into the mixture as it cooks. Use the finest-mesh strainer you can find to strain this custard so the finished product is as smooth as possible.

Strain Mixture into Cups

- When you add some of the heated cream to the egg yolk mixture, you are tempering the eggs.

- This just means you are bringing the temperature of the eggs closer to the temperature of the hot cream.

- This step is necessary to minimize the tendency of the eggs to scramble when added to the hot cream.

- Straining the custard before baking removes any undissolved sugar, bits of egg, and larger vanilla seeds.

Melt Sugar Crust

- You can use brown or granulated sugar to form the crust on the crème brûlée.

- Make sure that the crème brûlée is very well chilled before attempting to make the sugar crust.

- If the custard isn't very cold, it will melt and start to liquefy when the sugar is heated.

- Make the sugar crust just before serving the crème brûlée. It can't be made ahead of time, because the crust will soften.

127

PUMPKIN CINNAMON FLAN
Pumpkin adds flavor and color to a silky caramel flan

Flan is a custard dessert that is baked on top of melted sugar. The melted sugar, which creates a hard shell on the baking dish, softens as the custard bakes and creates a caramel sauce. This sauce then spills down over the flan when it is unmolded.

This alchemy happens because the liquid from the custard reacts with the melted sugar in the heat of the oven, gradually softening it. This sauce also makes it easier to unmold the flan after baking.

The combination of caramel, with its complex flavors, and the silky custard is really spectacular. If you have a flair for the dramatic, unmold the flan in front of your guests! *Yield: Serves 6*

Ingredients

- ³/₄ cup granulated sugar
- 1 cup solid-pack canned pumpkin
- 3 eggs
- 5 egg yolks
- 1 (14-ounce) can sweetened condensed milk
- ¹/₃ cup packed brown sugar
- 1 cup heavy cream
- 2 tablespoons orange juice
- 2 teaspoons vanilla
- 1 teaspoon cinnamon
- ¹/₈ teaspoon cardamom

Pumpkin Cinnamon Flan

- Preheat oven to 350°F. Place 9-inch glass dish in larger dish; add hot water to larger dish.

- Melt granulated sugar until brown, swirling pan occasionally. Pour into 9-inch dish; tilt to coat bottom. Return to hot water.

- Place pumpkin in blender; add eggs and yolks; blend. Add milk, brown sugar, cream, juice, vanilla, cinnamon, and cardamom.

- Pour into pan over caramel. Bake 40 to 50 minutes, until just set. Cool on rack; chill 4 to 5 hours. Loosen edges and invert onto plate.

• • • • RECIPE VARIATION • • • •

Caramel Flan: Make recipe as directed, except omit pumpkin, cinnamon, and cardamom. Omit brown sugar; use ⅓ cup granulated sugar instead. Make melted sugar as directed. Combine remaining ingredients in blender and blend until smooth, then pour into cups. Bake as directed, in a water bath. Cool, then chill and unmold to serve.

ZOOM

Melting sugar isn't difficult, but it does take some patience and constant surveillance. It will seem at first like the sugar will never melt, but it will start softening around the edges. When this happens, stop stirring and just swirl the pan occasionally. Then the edges liquefy, and the sugar will gradually develop a deep brown color. When it is completely liquid, quickly pour into the custard cups.

Melt Sugar; Add Custard

- Be careful with the melted sugar; it is very hot and can burn in a second.

- The sugar mixture in the pan should be firm when you add the custard. Still, pour slowly and carefully so the sugar isn't disturbed.

- You can make these flans in individual cups, too. Use six heatproof custard cups.

- Divide the melted sugar between the cups. Pour sugar into each one, swirl to coat, then return to the hot water. Repeat.

Run Knife around Flan

- The magic in this dessert is how the hard sugar caramel turns into a silky sauce.

- The flan should unmold from the dish easily. You will still need to run a knife around the flan edges, though.

- This helps introduce air under the flan, which releases the seal of the sauce to the pan.

- Place a serving plate on top of the dish, invert quickly, shake gently, and then remove the dish to reveal the flan.

POTS DE CRÈME
Rich and velvety chocolate pudding is served in tiny pots

Pots de crème—pronounced *po deh kremm*—is an elegant and rich French dessert that is the perfect finish to a fancy meal. It is served in small quantities simply because it is so rich. Serve with small spoons too, for the complete elegant experience.

The name *pots de crème* refers to the rich chocolate custard as well as to the small cups that hold it. Most pots de crème are flavored with vanilla or chocolate.

This custard is thicker and denser than regular baked custards or flans. Don't substitute light cream or artificial products for the heavy cream and egg yolks or the recipe will not work.

Garnish with some sweetened whipped cream and a sugared or candied violet. *Yield: Serves 6*

Ingredients

2 cups heavy whipping cream

$1/2$ cup whole milk

$1/2$ cup packed brown sugar

6 (1-ounce) squares semisweet chocolate, chopped

5 egg yolks

2 teaspoons dark rum, if desired

$1/8$ teaspoon salt

2 teaspoons vanilla

Pots de Crème

- Preheat oven to 325°F. Grease six small custard cups or demitasse cups with unsalted butter.

- Combine cream, milk, and brown sugar in saucepan; cook, stirring, until sugar dissolves. Stir in chocolate until smooth.

- Beat eggs yolks, rum, salt, and vanilla in medium bowl. Whisk in 1 cup of chocolate mixture, then return to pan.

- Strain mixture into prepared cups. Place in water bath; bake 20 to 25 minutes, until set. Cool 30 minutes, chill 4 hours.

• • • • RECIPE VARIATIONS • • • •

Blender Pots de Crème: Combine cream, milk, and brown sugar in saucepan and cook until sugar dissolves and mixture comes almost to simmer. Meanwhile, place 2 cups semisweet chocolate chips in blender or food processor. Add hot cream mixture with rum, salt, and vanilla. Blend until smooth, then pour into prepared cups. Chill until set.

Vanilla Pots de Crème: Make recipe as directed, except substitute granulated sugar for brown sugar. Omit chocolate. Slit 1 vanilla bean and remove seeds. Add seeds to cream, milk, and sugar mixture along with pod; heat as directed. Continue with recipe. Strain into demitasse cups and bake in water bath as directed, then chill. Garnish with shaved dark chocolate.

Add Chocolate to Cream Mixture

Strain Custard into Cups

- To chop chocolate, place it on a cutting board. Take a chef's knife and cut the chocolate into small pieces.

- Hold the knife with your dominant hand, and press down on the top of the blade with your other hand.

- Stir the cream mixture con- stantly when the chocolate is added, until it is melted and the mixture is smooth.

- Be sure to scrape the bottom of the pan so the chocolate doesn't burn.

- You can substitute 1 cup of chocolate chips in place of the chopped chocolate.

- When you mix some of the hot chocolate mixture into the egg yolks, you are tempering the yolks.

- This brings the two mix- tures closer together in temperature, so the eggs blend with the cream mixture.

- You can strain the mixture into a bowl or a large heat- proof pitcher, then pour into the cups.

- Pots de crème are served cold, but let them stand at room temperature 10 minutes before serving.

ENGLISH TRIFLE
Cake and fruit are layered with pudding in this delicious dessert

Trifle is a classic English dessert that consists of cake, jam, fruits, and pudding layered in a large glass bowl. This beautiful dessert can be made with many different flavors and types of fruit and pudding. A soft sponge cake is the traditional base for this recipe.

This dessert was invented to use up leftover cake and has been found in English cookbooks more than 300 years old. The recipe traditionally uses liqueur, but you can omit that if children are eating the dessert. Substitute orange juice for Grand Marnier, or raspberry juice for framboise.

Make sure that you display the trifle in its bowl before serving so your guests can admire its artistry before digging in. *Yield: Serves 8–10*

Ingredients

Lemon Butter Cake (see page 46)

$2/3$ cup strawberry jam

3 cups strawberries, sliced

2 cups blueberries

2 peaches, peeled and chopped

$1/3$ cup sugar

2 tablespoons orange juice

1 cup heavy whipping cream

3 tablespoons powdered sugar

1 teaspoon vanilla

$1/4$ cup Grand Marnier liqueur

Vanilla Pudding (see page 123)

$1/2$ cup sliced almonds, toasted

$1/4$ cup toffee bits

English Trifle

- Cut cake into three layers. Spread each layer with jam. Cut cake into 2-inch cubes.

- In large bowl, combine strawberries, blueberries, peaches, sugar, and orange juice; let stand 10 minutes. Beat cream with powdered sugar and vanilla.

- Place one-third of cake in large glass bowl; drizzle with half of liqueur. Add one-third of fruit and pudding and repeat layers.

- Top with whipped cream; sprinkle with almonds and toffee bits. Cover and chill 4 to 6 hours before serving.

Easy English Trifle: Make recipe as directed, except use a 1-pound frozen pound cake, thawed, in place of Lemon Butter Cake. Cut pound cake into 1-inch pieces and layer with ingredients as directed. Substitute two 4-serving-size packages vanilla pudding, prepared, for homemade pudding. Layer all ingredients as directed, then chill until serving time.

Individual English Trifles: Make the recipe as directed, except layer the ingredients in eight to ten glass bowls. The amount of food in each bowl depends on the size of the bowls and how large you want the dessert to be. They can be as small as custard cups or as large as dessert bowls. In most individual bowls you'll only be able to fit two layers of all of the ingredients.

Prepare Cake and Ingredients

- To easily cut the cake, use a serrated knife and cut gently. The serrated edge is a good choice for airy sponge cake.

- Spread the jam evenly over the cake, then cut into cubes. Don't perform this step ahead of time.

- You can use other fruits that look good in the market. Raspberries, blackberries, and cherries are delicious.

- Choose the jam you used based on the fruits highlighted in this dessert.

Layer Ingredients

- The cake cubes can be arranged jam-side up, or tumbled in any manner.

- Then spoon on the fruit and its juices that have accumulated in the bowl. If you're not using liqueur, add orange or lemon juice.

- Add the pudding, spreading it into an even layer. Try to keep the layers separate so they are visible.

- The cream is the final layer in the trifle. You can flavor it with liqueurs or other extracts if you'd like.

CLASSIC TIRAMISU

Ladyfingers, mascarpone cheese, and cream combine for a wonderful dessert

Tiramisu is the Italian version of English trifle. The ingredients are a bit different, but the end result is similar. The Italian version uses ladyfingers, a soft cake-like cookie, along with mascarpone cheese and espresso.

You can use coffee liqueur, also known as Kahlúa, in this dessert to add a sophisticated edge. But if you're serving this dessert to children or nondrinkers, just increase the espresso by a few tablespoons and omit the liqueur.

One of the nicest things about trifles and tiramisu is that they must be made ahead of time. This is a great boon when entertaining. All you have to do is take your gorgeous dessert out of the fridge and serve it. *Yield: Serves 8–10*

Ingredients

- 1 egg
- 5 egg yolks
- 2/3 cup granulated sugar
- 1/2 cup whole milk
- 1 (16-ounce) package mascarpone cheese
- 1 1/3 cups heavy whipping cream
- 1/4 cup powdered sugar
- 2 teaspoons vanilla
- 2/3 cup strong espresso, cooled
- 3 tablespoons coffee liqueur
- 2 (7-ounce) packages ladyfingers
- 5 chocolate espresso beans, chopped

Classic Tiramisu

- In large saucepan, combine egg, egg yolks, sugar, and milk. Using electric mixer, beat over medium heat until simmering.

- Simmer and beat 2 minutes. Let cool 20 minutes, then chill 2 hours. Beat in mascarpone. Beat cream with powdered sugar and vanilla until stiff; fold into egg mixture.

- Combine espresso and liqueur. Quickly dip ladyfingers into espresso; place half in 13x9-inch pan.

- Layer half of egg mixture over ladyfingers; repeat layers; sprinkle with beans.

• • • • RECIPE VARIATION • • • •

Easy Tiramisu: Make recipe as directed, except in place of egg yolk mixture, beat a 16-ounce container of mascarpone cheese with ½ cup sugar, 2 tablespoons light cream, and 2 tablespoons amaretto until smooth. Beat 1 cup heavy whipping cream with 2 tablespoons powdered sugar and 1 teaspoon vanilla until soft peaks; fold into mascarpone mixture.

Make Egg Mixture

- Separate the eggs while cold; they are easily to separate at this temperature. Freeze the whites for another use.

- It's important to beat the egg mixture constantly while it's on the stove so it cooks evenly and the eggs don't scramble.

- If you want to be very accurate, the egg mixture should reach 160°F on a food thermometer.

- The egg mixture helps make the tiramisu very rich and creamy.

Layer Ingredients

- You can find ladyfingers in the international foods aisle of the supermarket, or order them online.

- Or make the ladyfingers from scratch for a really authentic, superb dessert.

- The ladyfingers should absorb some of the espresso mixture, but not enough that they start to fall apart.

- Chill this dessert, well covered, for at least 24 hours before serving so the flavors blend and develop.

LEMON TRIFLE PARFAITS

Tangy lemons add a depth of flavor to these individual trifles

Combine trifle ingredients in a parfait style for an easy and delicious dessert that is refreshing on a warm summer evening.

You can transform any large trifle or tiramisu dessert to a parfait simply by layering the ingredients in a goblet or parfait glass. Use pretty wineglasses on a long stem for an elegant look.

Angel food cake is a good choice for this dessert, or you can use the Lemon Butter Cake recipe (see page 46). A white or yellow shortening cake is also a good choice.

Garnish these parfaits with some whipped cream and a sprig of mint or lemon basil for the perfect finishing touch.
Yield: Serves 8–10

Ingredients

- ¹/₂ angel food cake
- ¹/₄ cup frozen lemonade concentrate, thawed
- 1 (8-ounce) package cream cheese, softened
- 1 (14-ounce) can sweetened condensed milk
- ¹/₂ cup fresh lemon juice
- 1¹/₃ cups heavy whipping cream
- ¹/₃ cup powdered sugar
- 1 teaspoon vanilla
- 1 cup hard lemon candies, crushed
- 2 cups fresh raspberries

Lemon Trifle Parfait

- Cut cake into 1-inch cubes and place on baking sheet. Drizzle with thawed concentrate and set aside.

- In large bowl, beat cream cheese until fluffy. Gradually add condensed milk, beating until fluffy. Beat in lemon juice.

- In small bowl, beat cream with sugar and vanilla until stiff peaks form. Fold 1 cup into cream cheese mixture.

- In eight to ten parfait glasses, layer cake, cream cheese mixture, crushed candies, raspberries, and whipped cream. Repeat layers. Chill 4 to 5 hours.

Chocolate Trifle Parfaits: Make recipe as directed, except substitute Chocolate Cake for angel food cake. Omit lemonade concentrate, lemon juice, and lemon candies. Beat cream cheese with 1 cup melted semisweet chocolate chips. Add ¼ cup cocoa powder to whipping cream with powdered sugar. And use chopped dark or semisweet chocolate in place of candies.

Berry Trifle Parfaits: Make recipe as directed, except omit lemon candies. In place of lemonade concentrate, use ¼ cup peach or pear nectar. For fruit, use 1 cup fresh raspberries, 1 cup chopped strawberries, and 1 cup fresh blueberries. Use angel food cake or any white or yellow shortening cake. Garnish with fresh mint sprigs.

Beat Cream Cheese

Layer Ingredients

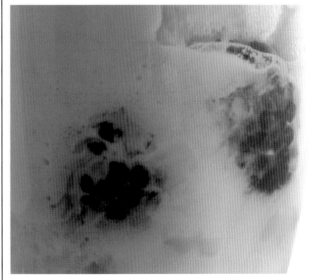

- To soften cream cheese, let it stand at room temperature for 1 hour before using.

- Or you can remove the cream cheese from its wrapping, place on a plate, and microwave at 50 percent power for 50 to 60 seconds.

- The cream cheese has to be beaten before being mixed with other ingredients so it is as smooth as possible.

- The sweetened condensed milk (do not use evaporated milk) adds silkiness and a depth of flavor to the filling.

- For this dessert, the cake is cut into smaller cubes so it will easily fit into the parfait glasses or goblets.

- Layer the ingredients carefully so they are distinct. The glasses have clear sides, so this is important.

- Wipe the rim of the glasses or goblets when you are done, then cover carefully with plastic wrap.

- Serve these parfaits straight from the refrigerator, stopping just to garnish them or arrange on a tray.

STRAWBERRY CHOCOLATE TRIFLE

Fruit and chocolate make a delicious and elegant trifle

Trifles and tiramisus are recipes that can be easily changed with just a few alterations. As long as you keep to the basic proportions of cake, pudding, and liquid flavoring, you can create your own special version of theses desserts.

These types of desserts are the most open to substitutions and interpretation. They are most like cooking, where you are just assembling ingredients that are already prepared. Use a purchased cake or make one from a mix. Prepared pudding can be substituted for pudding made from scratch. And any fresh fruit is delicious in these recipes.

Have fun with creating trifles. And once you do create a masterpiece, be sure to write it down so it isn't lost forever. *Yield: Serves 8–10*

Ingredients

Chocolate Cake (see page 36)

¹/₄ cup chocolate liqueur, if desired

Chocolate Pudding (see page 122)

1¹/₄ cups heavy whipping cream

¹/₄ cup cocoa

¹/₄ cup powdered sugar

1 teaspoon vanilla

1 cup strawberry jam

4 cups sliced strawberries

4 ounces semisweet chocolate, finely chopped

¹/₄ cup toasted sliced almonds

Strawberry Chocolate Trifle

- Cut cake into 1-inch squares and place on baking sheet. Drizzle with chocolate liqueur.

- Prepare Chocolate Pudding and let cool. Beat cream with cocoa, powdered sugar, and vanilla; fold 1 cup cream into pudding mixture.

- In large footed glass bowl, layer cake, jam, pudding mixture, strawberries, cream, and chopped chocolate.

- Continue layering until all ingredients are added. Cover and chill 6 to 8 hours before serving. Top with sliced almonds.

Mixed Fruit Trifle: Make recipe as directed, except use an angel food cake in place of Chocolate Cake. Omit chocolate liqueur. For filling, use Vanilla Pudding (see page 123); omit cocoa. In place of strawberries, use 2 peeled and sliced bananas, 8-ounce can of crushed pineapple (drained), 1 cup raspberries, and 2 peeled and sliced kiwifruit. Garnish with mint.

Apple Cranberry Trifle: Make recipe as directed, except use yellow shortening cake in place of Chocolate Cake. Omit liqueur and chocolate. Use Vanilla Pudding in place of Chocolate Pudding. Omit jam; use butterscotch ice cream topping. Cook 3 chopped apples, 1 cup dried cranberries, ⅓ cup sugar, 2 tablespoons butter; use in place of strawberries.

Prepare Cake and Ingredients

- Any cake, even cupcakes or cake-like cookies, can be used in a trifle. Just make sure that the texture isn't too soft.

- The cake should be moist but shouldn't fall apart when drizzled with the liqueur.

- You can certainly use a chocolate pudding mix in place of homemade pudding. But just once, try it with homemade!

- There are special glass bowls with straight sides made for serving trifle, but any large bowl will do.

Layer Ingredients

- The order in which you layer ingredients isn't critical to the success of the recipe.

- There are only two rules: Cake should be on the bottom, and whipped cream or pudding should be on the top.

- That way the dessert has structure, and it won't dry out while in the refrigerator. Still, cover it tightly so it doesn't absorb other food flavors.

- Other fruits, like peaches or raspberries, would also be delicious in this elegant recipe.

WHITE CHOCOLATE TRIFLE

Raspberries and cake are a beautiful contrast to white chocolate

White chocolate is an indulgent and decadent ingredient transformed into a trifle. Because white chocolate is so sweet, it is best complemented by a tart ingredient like raspberries or peaches. Don't use almond candy coating or confectioner's coating in place of the white chocolate.

Sour cream plays an important part in the pudding mixture. Since the white chocolate is so sweet, another ingredient is needed to temper the sweetness. The sour cream also adds wonderful texture.

You can use low-fat sour cream in place of regular sour cream, but don't substitute a nonfat product. The taste and texture just won't be the same.

Enjoy this elegant dessert after a meal of roast chicken and potatoes. *Yield: Serves 8*

KNACK FABULOUS DESSERTS

Ingredients

1 (11-ounce) package white chocolate chips

2 cups heavy whipping cream

1¹/₂ cups sour cream

2 tablespoons powdered sugar

1 cup frozen raspberries, thawed

1 recipe Yellow Cake (see page 37)

¹/₄ cup raspberry liqueur

3 cups fresh raspberries

2 ounces semisweet chocolate, shaved

White Chocolate Trifle

- In large saucepan, melt chocolate chips in whipping cream. Remove to large bowl; chill 2 to 3 hours, until very cold.

- Combine sour cream, powdered sugar, and frozen raspberries until smooth; set aside.

- Beat white chocolate mixture until fluffy. Cut cake into 2-inch pieces, place on cookie sheet, and sprinkle with liqueur.

- Layer cake, sour cream mixture, white chocolate mixture, and raspberries in large glass bowl. Sprinkle with shaved chocolate; chill.

Melt Chips in Cream

- Place the chips and cream in a heavy-duty saucepan over low heat to melt.

- If you can't watch the mixture constantly, use a double boiler with simmering, not boiling, water in the bottom.

- If the cream mixture gets too hot, the chocolate will seize. That means the mixture will become very thick and grainy.

- You may be able to save it by whisking in a teaspoon of plain vegetable oil, or you may have to start over.

Make Sour Cream Mixture

- Powdered sugar contains some cornstarch, which will help stabilize the sour cream mixture.

- Sift the powdered sugar before using, using a mechanical sifter or a fine-mesh sieve to remove any lumps.

- The raspberries will tint the mixture a beautiful color of pink. You can use pureed thawed frozen strawberries if you'd like.

- Serve this sweet dessert with hot coffee flavored with cream or vanilla sugar, or hot tea flavored with lemon.

CHOCOLATE TIRAMISU CAKE

Chocolate cake, caramel candy bars, and whipped cream create a decadent dessert

Take tiramisu to the next level by creating a cake using its ingredients. This is a special dessert for a birthday or other celebration. The cake stays super-moist because it is drizzled with chocolate liqueur and ice cream sauce. And the layers are smooth and creamy, very decadent.

You can use a scratch or cake mix cake in this recipe. Since you're baking three layers from a two-layer recipe, you'll need to reduce the baking time so the cake isn't too dry. Watch the cake carefully in the oven.

If you're making this dessert for children, omit the chocolate liqueur and substitute 2 tablespoons chocolate milk. *Yield: Serves 8–10*

Ingredients

1 Chocolate Cake (see page 36)

¼ cup chocolate liqueur

2 tablespoons caramel ice cream sauce

1 (8-ounce) package cream cheese, softened

½ cup sour cream

½ cup heavy whipping cream

1 cup semisweet chocolate chips, melted

1 (12-ounce) bag chocolate-covered soft caramels

1 recipe Chocolate Whipped Cream Frosting (see page 207)

Chocolate Tiramisu Cake

- Make cake in three 8-inch layers; bake 17 to 22 minutes; cool. Combine liqueur and sauce in small bowl.

- In large bowl, beat cream cheese until fluffy. Add sour cream and whipping cream, then melted chocolate chips.

- Cut candies in thirds. Place one cake on serving plate; drizzle with one-third of liqueur mixture. Top with half of cream cheese mixture; top with one-third candies.

- Repeat layers. Frost top and sides of cake. Garnish with remaining candies. Chill.

Easy Chocolate Tiramisu Cake: Make recipe as directed, except bake cake in a 13x9-inch pan. Poke holes into cake; drizzle ice cream sauce mixture over all. Top with all of the cream cheese mixture and sprinkle with all of the candies. Chill cake 4 to 6 hours. Omit Chocolate Whipped Cream Frosting, or just top each serving with a dollop of sweetened whipped cream.

Classic Tiramisu Cake: Use Yellow Cake (see page 37) in place of Chocolate Cake; bake in three 8-inch pans. Omit chocolate liqueur; use coffee liqueur. Omit cream cheese; use 1 cup mascarpone cheese. Omit melted chocolate chips. Add ⅓ cup granulated sugar to mascarpone mixture. Use chopped chocolate espresso beans in place of candies. Frost with Chocolate Frosting (see page 209).

Beat Cream Cheese Mixture

- It's important that the cream cheese is soft before you start beating.

- If you try to beat cold or stiff cream cheese, small lumps will form that will never be beaten smooth.

- Make sure that the melted chocolate has cooled slightly before adding to the cream cheese mixture.

- You can make this mixture ahead of time. Let it stand at room temperature for 30 to 40 minutes to soften before assembling the dessert.

Assemble Dessert

- Since the cake layers are thinner than normal, they will be quite delicate; handle carefully.

- You may want to use an extra-large spatula to move the cake layers; find in baking supply stores.

- The dessert is very moist. You may want to use cake skewers to hold it together after it's assembled, as in wedding cakes.

- Remove the skewers before serving the dessert. The cake will become firmer when it is chilled.

CHOCOLATE CHOCOLATE COOKIES

There's extra chocolate in these simple and rich little cookies

There's nothing better than chocolate cookies and a glass of milk. It's the classic after-school snack. These little cookies are simple, yet very special.

Because this dough is high in fat, with all the chocolate, butter, and egg yolks, it is very tender and creamy. The cookies are baked at a slightly lower temperature so they will bake through evenly and not burn on the bottom.

With this much chocolate in a cookie, doneness tests become crucial. Make sure your oven is properly calibrated, then bake a test cookie to discover the proper timing for your oven.

And remember, cookies firm up as they cool. The cookies should be soft in the center when removed from the oven. *Yield: 36–40 cookies*

Ingredients

2 (1-ounce) squares unsweetened chocolate, chopped

8 (1-ounce) squares semisweet chocolate, chopped

²/₃ cup white chocolate chips

¹/₄ cup cocoa powder

1 teaspoon instant espresso powder

¹/₂ cup butter, softened

1 cup packed brown sugar

¹/₂ cup granulated sugar

3 eggs

2 egg yolks

2 teaspoons vanilla

1¹/₄ cups flour

1 teaspoon baking powder

¹/₂ teaspoon baking soda

¹/₄ teaspoon salt

1 cup milk chocolate chips

Chocolate Chocolate Cookies

- In microwave, melt unsweetened and semi-sweet chocolate. In food processor, grind white chocolate chips, cocoa, and espresso powder.

- Beat butter with brown and granulated sugars. Beat in eggs and yolks, one at a time; add vanilla.

- Add melted chocolate, then dry ingredients. Fold in white chocolate mixture and milk chocolate chips.

- Cover; chill. Roll into 1-inch balls; place on parchment-paper-lined cookie sheets. Bake at 325°F 9 to 12 minutes. Remove paper to rack; cool.

Triple Chocolate Nut Cookies: Make cookies as directed, except substitute milk chocolate chips for white chips. Grind with cocoa powder and espresso powder as directed. Stir in milk chocolate chips along with 1 cup chopped pecans and walnuts before baking cookies. Bake as directed. Melt ½ cup white chocolate chips with 1 teaspoon vegetable oil; drizzle over cooled cookies.

Double Chocolate Bars: Make recipe as directed, except instead of forming dough into balls, press it into greased 13x9-inch baking pan. Bake 25 to 35 minutes, until bars are just set. Melt 1 cup semisweet chocolate chips with 1 teaspoon oil, and 1 cup white chocolate chips with 1 teaspoon oil; stir until smooth. Drizzle both mixtures over cooled bars. Cut into squares to serve.

CHOCOLATE

Add Chocolate to Batter

- The chocolate is melted in the first step because it needs to cool before being added to the butter mixture.

- If the chocolate is too hot, it will melt the butter. This destroys the structure you build by beating the butter with the sugars.

- The cookies will still be good, but the texture will be denser.

- To soften butter, let it stand at room temperature for 1 hour. Or you can grate it on a regular box grater.

Shape and Bake Cookies

- Because the dough is chilled and high in fat, it shouldn't stick to your fingers when you shape the cookies.

- If it does, rinse your hands with cold water, or dust them with some cocoa powder. Bake the cookies until their edges are set.

- This dough freezes very well. Form the cookies into balls, then freeze until hard.

- Bake the cookies frozen, adding 3 to 5 minutes to the baking time. Because the cookies are so delicate, move the whole piece of parchment paper to the wire rack to cool.

CHOCOLATE FONDUE

Dip everything from fruit to cookies in this intense fondue

Fondue for dessert is a relatively new phenomenon. It started appearing in restaurants and cookbooks in the 1960s. It quickly caught on and is now considered a classic chocolate dessert.

The rich and silky chocolate mixture is easy to make as long as you follow a few rules. Melt the chocolate over low heat, stir constantly while it melts, and do not use Sterno to keep the fondue mixture hot while serving.

Use your imagination and have fun with the dippers in this easy recipe. You can use any cookie, fresh fruit, or cake cut into squares.

For a larger party or a dessert buffet, make several different flavors of fondue and offer lots of dippers. *Yield: Serves 6–8*

Ingredients

1 cup semisweet chocolate chips

1 cup milk chocolate chips

1 (1-ounce) square unsweetened chocolate, chopped

1/4 cup white chocolate chips

3/4 cup light cream

1 teaspoon vanilla

Dippers: strawberries; chocolate cookies; pound cake, cut into fingers; cherries; pear slices

Chocolate Fondue

- In heavy saucepan over very low heat, combine all ingredients except vanilla and dippers.

- Cook and stir until chocolate is melted and mixture is smooth. Remove from heat and stir in vanilla.

- Pour mixture into fondue pot and place on base. Light tea candle and place under fondue pot. Do not use Sterno; it will be too hot.

- Dip strawberries, cookies, cake fingers, cherries, and pears into the chocolate to eat.

Mocha Fondue: Make recipe as directed, except omit white chocolate chips. Add another ¼ cup semisweet chocolate chips; melt with cream. Stir in 1 to 2 teaspoons espresso powder with vanilla until mixture is smooth and glossy. Serve with fresh fruit and pound cake cut into strips.

White Chocolate Fondue: Make recipe as directed, except omit semisweet chocolate chips, milk chocolate chips, and unsweetened chocolate. Use 2 cups white chocolate chips (11.5-ounce package). Add ¼ cup heavy whipping cream and 2 tablespoons butter when melting white chocolate chips. Add 1 to 2 tablespoons amaretto with vanilla if desired.

Melt Chocolate

Serve Dessert

- The various types of chocolate will melt at slightly different temperatures. That means you must watch the mixture carefully.

- Stir frequently until the mixture is very smooth. If you are unsure, use a double boiler.

- Place water in the bottom part of the double boiler, and add chocolate to the top. Bring the water to a simmer, not a boil.

- Do not allow any water into the chocolate mixture or it may seize (get firm and lumpy).

- The chocolate mixture will stay fairly fluid even when it's not placed over a candle or heat source.

- A small Crock-Pot, on the "keep warm" setting, is a great choice for serving, especially at a buffet.

- Offer large toothpicks or fondue forks with the dippers so people don't double-dip.

- You may need to stir the fondue mixture as it is eaten to keep it smooth.

CHOCOLATE CARAMEL TRUFFLES
Homemade caramel is stirred into chocolate to make these fabulous truffles

Just the word *truffle* is decadent. Truffles are expensive candies when purchased, but when you make them yourself they do not cost very much. And they're fun to make and eat.

Truffles are made from ganache—a mixture of chocolate and heavy cream melted together and allowed to harden in the refrigerator.

You can make the truffles directly from this hardened mixture or, for a silky truffle that melts in your mouth, beat the firm chocolate mixture until it becomes very fluffy and light.

These truffles are delicious on a dessert buffet, and they make excellent gifts for Christmas, a birthday, or Valentine's Day. Pack in pretty boxes. *Yield: 36 truffles*

KNACK FABULOUS DESSERTS

Ingredients

¹/₃ cup granulated sugar

2 tablespoons water

3 tablespoons heavy cream

1 pound semisweet chocolate, chopped

¹/₂ pound milk chocolate, chopped

1 cup heavy whipping cream

2 teaspoons vanilla

¹/₄ cup cocoa powder

Chocolate Caramel Truffles

- In small heavy saucepan, combine sugar with water. Bring to boil; cover pan and boil 30 seconds.

- Uncover; boil until mixture turns golden brown. Remove from heat and add 3 tablespoons cream; stir until smooth. Let cool; chill.

- In large bowl, place chocolates. Heat 1 cup cream until boiling; pour into chocolate. Stir until smooth. Add vanilla. Chill until very cold.

- Add caramel to chilled chocolate; beat until fluffy. Form into balls; roll in cocoa powder. Refrigerate.

Milk Chocolate Truffles: Make recipe as directed, except omit sugar-and-water mixture. For chocolate, use 1 pound chopped milk chocolate and ½ pound chopped semisweet chocolate. Melt as directed, then chill until firm. Do not beat mixture; roll truffle mixture into balls. Coat as desired and chill until firm.

Stuffed Truffles: Make recipe as directed. When forming truffles, mold each around a piece of chopped candy; large piece of toasted walnut, pecan, or cashew; or some mini chocolate chips. Or make small Milk Chocolate Truffles and stuff into center of Chocolate Caramel Truffles, or vice versa. Roll these truffles into chopped nuts or dip into melted chocolate; refrigerate until set.

Melt Sugar with Water

- The sugar is melted with the water because that's a little easier than melting straight sugar.

- This mixture is turned into caramel with the addition of heavy cream.

- It will sputter vigorously when the cream is added, and some of the sugar will become hard.

- Just keep stirring over low heat and it will turn into a smooth sauce.

Beat Chilled Mixture

- The mixture has to be very firm before beating. Chill for at least 6 hours. When you press a finger into the mixture, an indentation should remain.

- If the mixture starts to get soft while you form the truffles, return it to the refrigerator.

- You can coat the finished truffles in everything from cocoa powder to chocolate shot, toasted coconut, and chopped nuts.

- Or use melted chocolate: Melt 1 cup chocolate chips. Stir in ¼ cup milk chocolate chips until smooth.

CHOCOLATE

CHOCOLATE WHOOPIE PIES
Soft chocolate cookies are sandwiched together with chocolate crème

Whoopie pies are a soft cake-like cookie sandwiched together with a fluffy whipped filling. This dessert originated in New England. The most common filling for this delicious chocolate treat is Marshmallow Fluff, a gooey and sticky creation that is like softened marshmallows. Any classic recipe uses fluff in the filling.

These large cookies are made soft through the use of butter, milk, and egg yolks. The cookies are traditionally made very large, about the size of an English muffin, but you can make them any size you'd like.

These cookies beg to be served with a tall glass of icy-cold milk for an after-school snack. *Yield: 24 cookies*

Ingredients

- ¹/₂ cup butter, softened
- ³/₄ cup packed brown sugar
- ¹/₄ cup granulated sugar
- 1 egg
- 1 egg yolk
- 1³/₄ cups flour
- ¹/₈ teaspoon salt
- 7 tablespoons cocoa powder
- ¹/₂ teaspoon baking powder
- ¹/₂ teaspoon baking soda
- ³/₄ cup milk
- 2 teaspoons vanilla
- 2 cups powdered sugar
- ¹/₄ cup cocoa powder
- ¹/₂ cup butter, softened
- 1 cup marshmallow crème
- 1 teaspoon vanilla
- 1–2 tablespoons heavy cream

Chocolate Whoopie Pies

- Beat ½ cup butter with brown and granulated sugars. Beat in egg and egg yolk.

- Sift together flour, salt, 7 tablespoons cocoa, baking powder, and soda. Add alternately to batter with milk. Stir in vanilla. Cover; chill 2 to 3 hours.

- Preheat oven to 350°F. Grease baking sheets. Drop batter by tablespoons onto sheets. Bake 11 to 14 minutes.

- Sift powdered sugar with cocoa. Beat ½ cup butter, marshmallow crème, and vanilla; add cocoa mixture and cream. Assemble.

When softening butter, it's tricky to use the microwave oven. The butter can melt unevenly as a result of the hot spots found in every microwave oven. This can change the texture of the finished cookies. In a pinch, you can use the microwave, but watch the butter very carefully. Microwave for 10 seconds at 30 percent power, then let stand 2 minutes; check the butter. Repeat one or two more times until the butter is properly softened.

Classic Whoopie Pies: Make recipe as directed, except drop batter by ¼-cup portions onto greased and floured cookie sheets. Bake 13 to 17 minutes, until cookies are set. Cool 2 minutes on cookie sheets, then remove to wire racks. Make filling as directed, except omit cocoa powder. Sandwich cookies together with filling mixture. Makes 8 to 10 whoopie pies.

CHOCOLATE

Form Cookies

- This cookie batter is made like cake batter. First the butter and sugar are creamed together, then eggs are added.

- Add the dry ingredients alternately to the batter with the milk.

- This means that you completely stir in some of the flour, then completely stir in some of the milk; repeat.

- The cookies will be soft and puffy and rather fragile when warm. Remove from the cookie sheet carefully, after they have cooled for 2 to 3 minutes.

Sandwich Cookies Together

- This frosting is sticky, creamy, and gooey because of the marshmallow crème. Do not try to substitute another ingredient.

- Because the cookies and the frosting are soft, store these cookies in an airtight container.

- To keep them soft, add a fresh apple wedge to the container. This will keep the environment humid.

- These cookies are best eaten within a few days of being made. And they do not freeze well.

GERMAN CHOCOLATE CAKE

Delicate cake is layered with coconut pecan filling and topped with chocolate frosting

This cake is elegant and very beautiful. The classic coconut pecan frosting is layered between the cake layers and on top, while the sides are coated with a chocolate mixture.

German chocolate is not like dark, semisweet, or milk chocolate. It is slightly sweeter than semisweet chocolate, and contains lecithin, a natural ingredient that helps it melt smoothly and combine beautifully with other ingredients.

You can substitute a combination of semisweet and milk chocolate for the German chocolate if you can't find it in the supermarket. Or use 5 ounces semisweet chocolate for the 5 ounces of German chocolate in this recipe and add another 2 tablespoons sugar. *Yield: Serves 8–10*

Ingredients

5 (1-ounce) squares German chocolate

$^1/_3$ cup water

1 cup butter, softened

1 cup packed brown sugar

$^3/_4$ cup granulated sugar

4 eggs

2 teaspoons vanilla

2 cups sifted flour

2 tablespoons cocoa powder

1 teaspoon baking soda

$^1/_4$ teaspoon salt

1 cup buttermilk

Coconut Pecan Filling (see variation)

Creamy Chocolate Frosting (see variation)

German Chocolate Cake

- Preheat oven to 350°F. Coat two 9-inch-round cake pans with nonstick baking spray.

- Melt chocolate with water in saucepan. Beat butter with sugars; add eggs. Add chocolate and vanilla.

- Sift flour with cocoa, soda, and salt. Add alternately to batter with buttermilk.

- Pour into pans; bake 23 to 28 minutes, until done; remove and cool. Place one layer on plate; add half of filling. Add second layer; cover with remaining filling. Frost sides with Creamy Chocolate Frosting.

Creamy Chocolate Frosting: In bowl, beat 1 (3-ounce) package cream cheese, softened, with 3 tablespoons softened butter. Melt 1 cup semisweet chocolate chips; cool. Beat 1½ cups powdered sugar into butter mixture; add chocolate and 1 teaspoon vanilla. Add 2 tablespoons milk and ½ cup powdered sugar; beat until fluffy.

Coconut Pecan Filling: In saucepan, combine 1 cup light cream, ½ cup sugar, ½ cup packed brown sugar, 2 tablespoons cornstarch, 2 egg yolks, and ½ cup butter. Cook on medium heat, stirring until thick. Remove from heat; add 1 teaspoon vanilla, 1 cup chopped toasted pecans, and 1 cup toasted flaked coconut. Let stand 1 hour; beat well until very thick and fill cake.

Make Batter

Fill and Frost Cake

- When melted chocolate is combined with a tiny bit of water, it will seize. When melted with a lot, it becomes very smooth.

- Make sure to beat the mixture well after each addition of egg. Beat until the egg disappears and the batter is fluffy.

- It's important to sift the flour because this is such a delicate cake.

- Measure the flour before you sift it, not after, or there won't be enough structure in the batter.

- This cake is unusual in that the filling and frosting are two different recipes.

- You can leave the sides of the cake unfrosted for a more classic German Chocolate Cake.

- Use this technique on other cakes to get dif-ferent results. Fill a cake with marshmallow crème, and frost with chocolate frosting.

- Place strips of waxed paper under the bottom layer before you start. Frost the cake, then gently pull the strips out for a perfectly clean cake plate.

153

SOUR CREAM CHOCOLATE CAKE

Sour cream adds richness and depth of flavor to this moist cake

Two kinds of chocolate make this cake rich. It's easy to prepare with ingredients you most likely already have on hand in the kitchen.

You can make a sheet cake or a layer cake with this recipe. Or make cupcakes and top with a variety of frostings.

Sour cream helps temper the sweetness of the cake and also makes the crumb tender and silky. You can use low fat sour cream in this recipe, but avoid nonfat products.

Be careful not to overbake this cake. It's done if the top springs back when lightly touched in the center, or if a toothpick inserted in the cake comes out clean. Internal cake temperature should be 200°F. *Yield: Serves 10–12*

Sour Cream Chocolate Cake

Ingredients

2 (1-ounce) squares semisweet chocolate, chopped

$1/4$ cup light cream

$1/2$ cup water

$1/2$ cup cocoa powder

$3/4$ cup butter, softened

1 cup packed brown sugar

$3/4$ cup granulated sugar

3 eggs

2 teaspoons vanilla

2 cups cake flour

1 teaspoon baking soda

$1/2$ teaspoon baking powder

$1/2$ teaspoon salt

$2/3$ cup sour cream

Whipped Cream Frosting (see page 206)

- Preheat oven to 350°F. Coat a 13x9-inch pan or two 9-inch-round pans with nonstick baking spray.

- In saucepan, combine chocolate, cream, and water; bring to simmer. Stir in cocoa.

- In bowl, beat butter with sugars until fluffy. Add eggs and beat well; add vanilla.

- Sift flour, soda, baking powder, and salt; add alternately with sour cream. Stir in chocolate. Pour into pan(s). Bake 13x9 pan 35 to 45 minutes, 9-inch pans 25 to 35 minutes. Cool and frost.

Sour Cream Chocolate Frosting: In large bowl, mix 1 (12-ounce) package semisweet chocolate chips, ½ cup milk chocolate chips, and ½ cup butter. Microwave on 50 percent power, until melted; stir and let stand 5 minutes. Beat in 1 cup powdered sugar, then add 1 teaspoon vanilla. Add 1 cup sour cream alternately with 3 cups powdered sugar; beat until smooth.

Sour Cream Chocolate Cupcakes: Make recipe as directed, except line 24 muffin tins with paper liners. When batter is completed, fill prepared tins three-quarters full. Bake at 350°F 22 to 27 minutes, until cupcake tops spring back when lightly touched with finger. Let cool in pans 5 minutes, then remove and cool completely on wire racks. Frost as desired.

Add Flour and Sour Cream

Remove Cake from Pans

- Brown sugar is a great addition to chocolate cake batter. It adds a bit of moistness and more flavor than granulated sugar.

- Add the eggs, one at a time, beating well after each addition. This adds more air to the batter.

- Cake flour is made from a special strain of wheat that is lower in protein, and therefore gluten, than all-purpose flour.

- You can substitute ¾ cup plus 2 tablespoons all-purpose flour, plus 2 tablespoons cornstarch, for each cup of cake flour.

- Removing cake layers from pans is a delicate job, but it's not difficult.

- Never let the cake stand in a pan longer than 5 to 10 minutes. If the cake sticks, you can hold it over a burner briefly to melt the cooking spray.

- Run a knife around the edge of the pan. Then gently shake the cake back and forth.

- Place a wire rack atop the cake and invert with the pan. Tap the pan bottom; the cake should drop out.

CHOCOLATE

155

CLASSIC CHOCOLATE MOUSSE
Rich and light, this mousse is the perfect finish for a special dinner

Chocolate mousse is a fancy chocolate pudding. The mixture is light and airy because heavy cream—and sometimes meringue—is folded into the creamy chocolate mixture.

This recipe omits eggs for food safety reasons. The heavy cream provides the fat and creamy mouth-feel of the yolks. When whipped, it also imparts the airiness of the beaten whites.

This is plainly an indulgent recipe. Do not substitute low-fat or nonfat products for the heavy cream and real chocolate.

Mousse is great for entertaining because it must be made ahead of time. You can serve it many ways: in pretty goblets, in a large bowl, garnished with whipped cream, chocolate shavings, edible flowers, or candied violets. *Yield: Serves 8–10*

Ingredients

12 ounces semisweet chocolate, chopped

4 ounces milk chocolate, chopped

2¹/₂ cups heavy cream, divided

2 teaspoons vanilla

¹/₈ teaspoon salt

¹/₄ cup powdered sugar

Classic Chocolate Mousse

- In food processor, place chopped chocolates. Bring 1 cup heavy cream just to boil in small saucepan.

- With food processor running, pour hot cream into chocolate. Blend until smooth. Add vanilla and salt; pour into large bowl.

- Cover mixture and chill until very cold, about 3 to 4 hours. When chocolate mixture is chilled, beat 1½ cups cream with powdered sugar until stiff.

- Beat chilled chocolate mixture until fluffy. Fold in whipped cream; spoon into serving bowl(s). Chill.

Chocolate is creamy because it has a low melting point. Untempered chocolate melts at around 90 to 100°F, or near body temperature. That's why it is creamy when you hold it in your mouth. Tempered chocolate, which is used to make candy bars and commercial chocolate, has a slightly higher melting point. White chocolate has the lowest melting point, which is why it's the creamiest of all.

• • • • RECIPE VARIATION • • • •

Chocolate Mousse Pie: Make recipe as directed; chill mousse for 1 hour. During that time, place 28 chocolate sandwich cookies in food processor. Process until fine crumbs form. Place in medium bowl and stir in ⅓ cup melted butter. Press this mixture into bottom and up sides of 10-inch pie pan; spoon in chocolate mousse mixture. Cover and chill 4 to 6 hours.

Blend Chocolate Mixture

Fold Cream into Chocolate

- The mixture of heated heavy cream and melted chocolate is called a ganache.

- This can be used to make truffles or as a filling for chocolate layer cake.

- Be sure to process the mixture until the chocolate is completely melted and the mixture is very smooth.

- Vanilla is added after the chocolate is melted so the volatile oils will not evaporate with the heat.

- Fold mixtures together until neither can be seen.

- As whipped cream is beaten, it thickens because it turns into a foam. Any dairy product will produce foam when beaten, but to form a stable foam the product needs a certain amount of fat.

- The fat and protein gather around the air bubbles produced during beating and trap the air.

- Powdered sugar contains cornstarch, which stabilizes foam. This is why it's used when making whipped cream.

CHOCOLATE SOUFFLÉ
Soufflés are easy if you follow a few rules

Soufflés can strike fear into the hearts of the most accomplished cook or baker. But these ethereal concoctions are fairly foolproof when you understand the science.

Soufflés rise because the air trapped in protein bubbles from beating egg whites expands in the oven heat. For a successful soufflé, you must have a sturdy sauce or base for flavor and structure, and well-whipped and stable meringue to make it rise.

Use a whisk to make sure the sauce is smooth, and cook the flour mixture well for stability. Beat the egg whites with an acid like lemon juice or cream of tartar until stiff, not soft, peaks form. Then bake the souffle until it's puffy and set.

Finally, serve the soufflé immediately from the oven; it won't wait for guests! *Yield: Serves 6–8*

Ingredients

- ¹/₂ cup cocoa powder
- ¹/₂ cup packed brown sugar
- ¹/₃ cup flour
- ¹/₈ teaspoon salt
- 1 cup milk
- ¹/₃ cup light cream
- 4 egg yolks
- ¹/₂ cup semisweet chocolate chips, melted
- 2 teaspoons vanilla
- 6 egg whites
- 1 teaspoon lemon juice
- ¹/₄ cup granulated sugar

Chocolate Soufflé

- Preheat oven to 350°F. Butter bottom of 2-quart soufflé dish with unsalted butter.

- In saucepan, combine cocoa, brown sugar, flour, and salt; gradually add milk and cream. Cook until boiling.

- Remove from heat; add ½ cup to beaten egg yolks; return to pan. Cook 1 minute. Remove from heat; add chips and vanilla.

- Beat egg whites with lemon juice, then add sugar; beat until stiff. Fold into chocolate mixture; pour into pan. Bake 45 to 55 minutes.

Cook Chocolate Base

Fold in Egg Whites

- The base mixture is a quick version of a white sauce: made from fat, flour, and liquid.

- The cream substitutes for the butter in the sauce and makes the finished dish a bit lighter.

- Because chocolate is so dominant in this recipe, it's important to choose a very good brand, like Callebaut or Ghirardelli.

- The sauce is made first so it can cool for a few minutes before you add the beaten egg whites.

- The acid in the lemon juice helps strengthen the protein in the egg whites so the foam is more stable.

- You can use ½ teaspoon cream of tartar in place of the lemon juice to accomplish the same thing.

- Add the sugar gradually, beating until, when you stop the mixer and lift up the beaters, the egg whites stand up in straight peaks.

- Stir a dollop of the egg whites into the chocolate mixture to lighten, then fold in the rest until combined.

MORE CHOCOLATE

159

CHOCOLATE ICEBOX DESSERT
Plain chocolate cookies are surrounded in chocolate cream

This old-fashioned dessert is very easy to make and impressive and elegant to serve. To make it, you need plain, crisp chocolate wafers or cookies. Famous Wafers is one brand. The cookies gradually soften in the whipped cream, absorbing moisture from it, to create a cake-like texture.

When serving this dessert, it's important to cut 1-inch-thick slices on the diagonal. That way the cookies will all be sliced,

and they will create a pattern in the whipped cream mixture reminiscent of a zebra stripe.

This dessert must be made ahead of time so the consistency is correct when served. Garnish with chocolate shavings or some rich Chocolate Sauce (see page 161). *Yield: Serves 8*

Ingredients

- ¹/₂ cup semisweet chocolate chips
- ¹/₂ cup milk chocolate chips
- 2 cups heavy cream, divided
- ¹/₄ cup powdered sugar
- 1¹/₂ teaspoons vanilla
- 1 (9-ounce) box plain chocolate wafer cookies
- 1 (1-ounce) square semisweet chocolate

Chocolate Icebox Dessert

- In saucepan, combine semisweet and milk chocolate chips with 1 cup heavy cream.

- Melt over low heat, stirring frequently, until smooth. Cover and chill 2 to 3 hours.

- Beat remaining 1 cup cream with powdered sugar and vanilla. Beat chocolate mixture until fluffy; fold two mixtures together.

- Spread large spoonful of chocolate cream on cookies; stack them on their sides in long log shape. Frost generously. Shave chocolate on top. Cover; chill 4 to 6 hours.

Individual Chocolate Icebox Desserts: Make recipe as directed, except when assembling dessert, do not stack all cookies in a row. Frost 4 cookies with whipped cream mixture, using about 2 tablespoons cream for each. Stack one atop another, then frost top and sides of little stack. Repeat with remaining cookies and whipped cream. Each stack will serve 1.

Chocolate Sauce: In saucepan, combine 1 (12-ounce) package semisweet chocolate chips, 1⅓ cups light cream, 3 cups powdered sugar, and ½ cup butter. Bring to simmer. Boil mixture 7 to 8 minutes, until thickened, stirring often. Remove from heat and stir in 1 teaspoon vanilla. Cool sauce, stirring frequently. Store, covered, in refrigerator. Heat in microwave or saucepan before use.

Spread Cream on Cookies

- You can flavor the cream mixture any way you'd like. Omit the chocolate or use white chocolate instead.

- Another good variation would be peanut butter. Melt with the cream and the semisweet chocolate.

- Make sure you put enough cream mixture on each cookie; it should be about ¾ inch thick.

- You can start by stacking the cookies on top of one another, but you'll have to lay the whole thing on its side after a while.

Finish Dessert

- Make sure that the cream mixture covers the cookies thickly all the way around.

- The cookies will gradually absorb moisture from the cream mixture and soften as the dessert stands in the refrigerator.

- This will also make the cream a bit stiffer. The dessert will keep its shape when sliced.

- Garnish this dessert by reserving a bit of the whipped cream; pipe along the edges.

MORE CHOCOLATE

MOLTEN CHOCOLATE CAKES

These little cakes have a smooth molten center of pure chocolate

Either a chef in New York or one in France invented the molten chocolate cake in the 1980s. Whoever created this dessert deserves the Nobel Prize. It is very simple, very rich, and the perfect ending to a special meal.

The little cakes have a liquid, or literally molten, chocolate center that oozes out when the cake is cut.

There are several ways to make this cake. In one, a truffle is made and put in the center of a thick cake batter. In another, the cake is simply underbaked slightly so the center is undercooked. The cake does get warm enough to alleviate food safety concerns.

Like a soufflé, this dessert should be served as soon as it is made. *Yield: Serves 6*

Ingredients

2 tablespoons unsalted butter

2 tablespoons cocoa powder

³/₄ cup unsalted butter

4 (1-ounce) squares semisweet chocolate

¹/₃ cup milk chocolate chips

3 eggs

1 egg yolk

5 tablespoons granulated sugar

1¹/₂ teaspoons vanilla

3 tablespoons flour

Molten Chocolate Cakes

- Grease six 6-ounce custard cups with unsalted butter; sprinkle with cocoa powder.

- In saucepan, melt ¾ cup butter with semisweet and milk chocolate until smooth; set aside.

- Beat eggs and yolk with sugar and vanilla until light.

- Beat in melted chocolate mixture and flour.

- Pour into prepared cups; cover and chill 3 to 4 hours. Bake in preheated 425°F oven 12 to 15 minutes, until puffed. Let stand 1 minute; run knife around edges and invert onto plates; serve.

White Chocolate Sauce: Place 1 cup white chocolate chips or 1 cup chopped white chocolate in heatproof bowl. In saucepan, place 1¼ cups heavy whipping cream; bring to simmer. Immediately pour over white chocolate. Whisk until chocolate is melted and mixture is smooth. Stir in ½ teaspoon vanilla. Serve warm or refrigerate until cold; reheat in double boiler before serving.

Molten Chocolate White Lava Cakes: Make recipe as directed except, before you make cakes, make filling. Melt ½ cup white chocolate chips with ½ cup heavy whipping cream; chill until firm. Form into six balls. Fill custard cups with batter; press white chocolate ball into center. Bake as directed. Increase baking time to 14 to 19 minutes.

Prepare Batter

Bake Cakes

- This simple dessert is easy to make, and a good choice for beginning cooks.

- Watch the chocolate mixture carefully as it melts. The two chocolates do have different melting points.

- The chocolate mixture does have to cool before you mix it with the egg-and-sugar mixture.

- Dusting the cups with cocoa is a neat trick for working with any chocolate cake. This prevents sticking but doesn't change the color of the cake.

- The key to success in this dessert is to not overbake the little cakes. Watch them carefully.

- They will still be delicious if overbaked, but the center will not be "molten."

- For a lovely presentation, drizzle several kinds of chocolate sauce on the plates before you add the cakes.

- Or serve the cakes with vanilla or chocolate ice cream for a temperature contrast.

MORE CHOCOLATE

CHOCOLATE MERINGUE TORTE

This luscious torte is perfect for a special occasion

When you want a spectacular dessert for a birthday, large party, or Valentine's Day party, this is it. A delicate cake is layered with luscious and rich chocolate frosting and tender meringue.

While this dessert is impressive, it doesn't have to be difficult to make. Follow directions carefully. Also think about dividing the work over several days. The cake and meringue

will keep well, if thoroughly wrapped, for a day or two. Bake one day, then assemble the dessert the next.

The meringue will absorb some of the moisture from the frosting as it sits, becoming soft and tender like a Pavlova.

Serve this cake on fancy china, accompanied by flavored tea. *Yield: Serves 10–12*

Ingredients

2 egg whites

¹/₈ teaspoon cream of tartar

Pinch salt

¹/₂ cup sugar

2 teaspoons vanilla, divided

1 cup butter, softened

5–6 cups powdered sugar

4–6 tablespoons heavy cream

3 (1-ounce) squares unsweetened chocolate, melted

2 tablespoons cocoa powder

Chocolate Cake (see page 36), baked in 2 9-inch pans

Chocolate Meringue Torte

- Preheat oven to 275°F. Beat egg whites, cream of tartar, and salt until foamy. Beat in sugar and half of the vanilla.

- Shape meringue into 9-inch round on parchment paper. Bake 1 hour. Cool.

- Beat butter, 2 cups powdered sugar, and 1 tablespoon cream. Stir in chocolate and cocoa. Then beat in remaining sugar, cream, and vanilla.

- Place one cake layer on serving plate; frost. Top with meringue; frost. Add final cake layer; frost top and sides. Cover and let stand 6 hours.

Easy Chocolate Cake: Make recipe as directed, except instead of scratch cake, start with 1 (18.25-ounce) box chocolate cake mix. To dry mix, add ½ cup sour cream, 1 cup chocolate milk, ¼ cup vegetable oil, and 4 eggs. Beat until combined, then beat at high speed 2 minutes. Pour into two 9-inch greased cake pans; bake at 350°F 30 minutes.

When making a meringue, it's important that the beaters and bowl be totally free of any fat or grease. And make sure there isn't a trace of yolk in the egg whites. Add the sugar gradually, beating until the meringue is stiff. The points of the meringue should not droop when the beater is lifted, and the sugar should be dissolved. Bake the meringue at a low temperature so it becomes crisp throughout.

Make Meringue

- The meringue is ready for shaping when you rub a bit of it between your fingers and can't feel any sugar crystals.

- To shape the meringue, draw a circle on the parchment paper by outlining a cake pan.

- Make sure that the meringue is even. Use a spatula to smooth the top so there are no peaks or valleys.

- The peaks can burn in the oven. Also make sure the sides are straight.

Assemble Dessert

- Pile the frosting on the meringue layer, both top and bottom.

- You want the meringue to soften so it's easier to cut and eat. This also makes the texture very pleasant.

- The dessert should be refrigerated if the day is very warm. Let it stand at room temperature 30 to 40 minutes before slicing.

- A cake stand with a glass dome is the best utensil for storing and displaying this cake.

FLOURLESS CHOCOLATE CAKE
This rich and dense dessert is a chocoholic's dream

Flourless chocolate cake is exactly what it sounds like. There is no flour in this recipe, which makes it a wonderful dessert for those who cannot eat gluten. Of course, it's a fabulous dessert for anyone who loves chocolate!

The protein in eggs forms the structure of this dessert. When the eggs are beaten with the other ingredients, the proteins unwind and form a web that holds everything else in suspension. The cake is very flat and dense, almost like a truffle.

Because it is so rich, you must serve this dessert in very small pieces. A spoonful or two of Crème Anglaise placed on the plate, with a wedge of this cake nestled on top, is the perfect ending to a special meal. *Yield: Serves 12–16*

Ingredients

¹/₄ cup Grand Marnier liqueur

¹/₃ cup granulated sugar

2 tablespoons packed brown sugar

6 (1-ounce) squares bittersweet chocolate

4 (1-ounce) squares semisweet chocolate

¹/₃ cup milk chocolate chips

³/₄ cup unsalted butter

3 eggs

2 egg whites

Flourless Chocolate Cake

- Grease 9-inch springform pan and wrap in foil; set aside. Preheat oven to 300°F.

- In saucepan, combine liqueur and sugars; heat until sugar dissolves. Chop chocolates and add to mixture; stir until smooth; pour into bowl.

- Cut butter into small pieces and beat into warm chocolate mixture, then add eggs and egg whites.

- Pour into prepared pan; set in hot-water bath. Bake 35 to 40 minutes. Cool 1 hour, then chill overnight. Unmold and serve.

Crème Anglaise: In a small heavy saucepan, place 1 cup cream with seeds and pod from a vanilla bean. Heat over low heat until mixture starts to steam. Meanwhile, beat 4 egg yolks with ½ cup granulated sugar in small bowl. Slowly beat ½ cup of hot cream mixture into eggs. Remove vanilla pod, then beat egg mixture into cream. Cook over low heat, whisking constantly, until thickened.

Flourless Chocolate Cupcakes: Make recipe as directed, except grease six 4-ounce custard cups with unsalted butter and dust with cocoa powder. Divide batter among cups. Bake in water bath for 15 to 20 minutes or until cakes are just set. You can unmold these, or serve them in the custard cups, drizzled with some Crème Anglaise.

Add Butter to Chocolate

- It's important for this recipe that the butter is unsalted. It may not seem like it would make much of a difference, but it does.

- Unsalted butter is used in rich sauces and in recipes like this. It makes the finished product much creamier.

- Because the chocolate is so important in this recipe, use the best quality you can find and afford.

- The butter will just barely melt as it is beaten into the warm chocolate mixture.

Place Cake in Water Bath

- Make sure there are no holes or small tears in the foil you use to wrap the springform pan.

- You might want to wrap the pan in two layers of foil. The water must not touch the chocolate mixture.

- Set the large pan in the oven, then use a pitcher to pour in the hot water. Finally, place the pan in the water for safety reasons.

- To unmold, run a knife around the edge, then remove the sides of the pan. Serve right from the pan bottom.

LEMON SHERBET
Cool and tangy sherbet is the perfect summer dessert

Sherbet is a simple low-fat frozen dessert that, unlike sorbet, contains eggs, milk, or other dairy products. The terms are often used interchangeably; even though they are not technically the same thing, it doesn't matter that much.

Sherbet is served as a light dessert, or can be used as a palate cleanser between courses in a formal dinner. The light, clean taste of this food helps prepare the palate for courses to come.

This recipe can be flavored with any citrus juices. Use lime juice and zest along with lime liqueur, or orange juice and zest with Grand Marnier. Or omit the liqueur if you are serving this refreshing recipe to children. *Yield: Serves 8*

Ingredients

1 cup lemon juice

2 tablespoons limoncello liqueur, if desired

2 teaspoons finely grated lemon zest

1¹/₂ cups sugar

2 cups whole milk

1 cup heavy cream

2 cups buttermilk

Pinch salt

Lemon Sherbet

- Combine juice, liqueur (if using), and zest in large bowl. In large saucepan, combine sugar with milk. Heat, stirring, until sugar dissolves.

- Beat sugar mixture into juice mixture along with cream, buttermilk, and salt; beat well until smooth.

- Freeze in ice cream maker according to manufacturer's directions, or pour into 13x9-inch pan.

- Freeze until firm, stirring every hour, about 4 to 5 hours. Pack into freezer containers and freeze 2 to 3 hours before serving.

When you're peeling lemons and using the peel (also called zest) in recipes, make sure you only use the colored part. The white part between the colored skin and flesh is called the pith; this is very bitter. Using a microplane grater to zest lemons and oranges is the best way to avoid the pith. Move the fruit on the grater frequently for best results.

• • • • RECIPE VARIATION • • • •

Lemon Sorbet: Make recipe as directed, except omit milk, cream, and buttermilk. Increase lemon juice to 1½ cups and add 1 cup water. Heat these ingredients together until sugar dissolves completely, then cool and chill until cold. Freeze in ice cream maker, or as directed in recipe, using 9-inch-square or -round cake pan.

Beat Mixture

Pour Sherbet into Pan

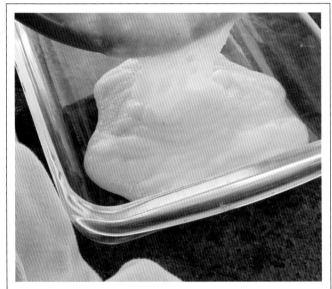

- The sugar is heated with the milk so it dissolves completely before being mixed with the other ingredients.

- It's important to beat the mixture together well, but don't beat too long. You don't want to add much air to the mixture.

- The best-quality ice cream and sherbet has less air added. In technical terms, the percentage of added air is called overrun.

- Stir well with a wire whisk until the mixture is smooth. Don't use a stand or hand electric mixer.

- An ice cream maker works by introducing air into the mixture as it freezes.

- This keeps the ice crystals that form small, making the ice cream or sherbet creamier.

- Without an ice cream maker, the mixture must be disturbed occasionally. That's why you stir it during the freezing period.

- The sherbet is "ripened" for a few hours after freezing so the flavors have a chance to bloom and develop.

HONEY ICE CREAM
Honey adds a rich floral note to this ice cream

Ice cream, real homemade ice cream, is a wonderful summertime treat. It's not difficult to make, but it does take some time.

You do need an ice cream maker for this type of dessert. The mixture has to be agitated or stirred constantly while it freezes for the best, creamiest texture.

There are several different types of ice cream makers. The old-fashioned kind needs rock salt and ice. This mixture melts, lowering the temperature of the ice cream well below the freezing point of 32°F. The brine should be around 10°F.

Automatic ice cream makers are much easier to use: You just freeze the insert, add the ice cream, and turn it on. *Yield: Serves 8*

Ingredients

- 2 cups milk
- 1 cup heavy whipping cream
- 2/3 cup honey
- 1/4 cup packed brown sugar
- 4 egg yolks
- 1 teaspoon vanilla
- 1/8 teaspoon salt

Honey Ice Cream

- In large saucepan, combine milk, cream, honey, and brown sugar. Cook and stir over low heat until honey and sugar dissolve.

- Beat egg yolks in small bowl until fluffy. Add ½ cup hot milk mixture and beat; stir into remaining milk mixture.

- Cook over low heat, stirring constantly, until mixture thickens enough to coat back of spoon. Remove from heat; add vanilla and salt.

- Cool completely; chill. Freeze in ice cream maker according to manufacturer's directions.

170

Chocolate Ice Cream: Make recipe as directed, except omit honey. Add ½ cup granulated sugar and ½ cup cocoa powder to milk-and-cream mixture. Cook as directed, then chill thoroughly. Freeze in ice cream maker according to manufacturer's directions, adding ½ cup ground milk chocolate chips or white chocolate chips when ice cream is almost frozen.

Vanilla Ice Cream: Make recipe as directed, except omit honey and brown sugar. Add ⅔ cup granulated sugar to milk-and-cream mixture, along with seeds from a vanilla bean pod. Add pod to cream mixture too, and heat until sugar dissolves. Remove pod, add egg yolks, and continue with recipe.

Cook Custard

- Stir the mixture constantly while the sugar and honey are dissolving.

- Add the hot milk mixture slowly to the egg yolks. This tempers the yolks so they won't scramble or cook when added to the custard.

- Make sure that you beat the egg yolks constantly while adding the hot milk mixture so they don't curdle.

- Like all custards, this mixture is done when it becomes thick enough to coat a spoon; your finger will leave a trail through it.

Freeze Ice Cream

- Be sure that the freezable insert for the ice cream maker is very well frozen. This usually takes at least 4 hours.

- Add the chilled custard and attach the dasher, then fasten the top onto the machine.

- Turn it on and let it run according to the manufacturer's directions. When the ice cream is done, pack into another container.

- This last step, called ripening, lets the ice cream become firm enough so it's easy to scoop and serve.

ICE CREAM

VANILLA GELATO

Gelato is a rich Italian ice cream with a very smooth and creamy texture

Gelato, a dessert from Italy, is richer than ice cream because it contains less air. The gelato is churned at a slower pace in special machines. So you can't make authentic gelato in American ice cream machines! A home gelato maker is expected to be available in this country soon.

Technically, gelato has less fat than American ice cream.

This puzzles people, since it tastes creamier and has more intense flavors. Less air is the answer. Also, the lower amount of fat means the gelato doesn't coat your taste buds, so the flavor can reach them more easily.

To mimic gelato's texture, sweetened condensed milk and mascarpone cheese are used in this recipe. *Yield: Serves 8*

Ingredients

1 vanilla bean

2 cups light cream

1 (14-ounce) can sweetened condensed milk

2 egg yolks

1/2 cup mascarpone cheese

1 teaspoon vanilla

Pinch salt

Vanilla Gelato

- Split vanilla bean and scrape out seeds. Combine light cream, sweetened condensed milk, and egg yolks in saucepan.

- Beat in vanilla seeds, then add split bean. Cook over low heat, stirring constantly, until mixture is thick enough to coat spoon.

- Remove from heat and remove the vanilla bean from the custard. Whisk in cheese, vanilla, and salt. Cool 30 minutes, then chill until very cold.

- Freeze in ice cream maker according to manufacturer's directions.

Chocolate Gelato: Make recipe as directed, except omit mascarpone cheese. Add 4 ounces chopped bittersweet chocolate to cream mixture. Cook and stir until chocolate is melted, then cook and stir until thickened. Add ⅓ cup unsweetened cocoa powder with vanilla and salt. Chill mixture and freeze as recipe directs.

Pistachio Gelato: Make recipe as directed, except omit mascarpone cheese. Grind 1 cup shelled unsalted pistachio nuts (the green ones, not the dyed red ones) with 2 tablespoons sugar until very fine. Combine with cream and other ingredients in saucepan; cook as directed. Add 2 or 3 drops green food coloring to mixture, if desired. Chill and freeze as directed.

Cook Custard

- Sweetened condensed milk is used instead of granulated sugar in this recipe to make the gelato creamier.

- Do not substitute evaporated milk for the sweetened condensed milk or the recipe will not be sweet.

- Do not cook the cheese with the cream mixture or it may separate or curdle. Add it after the custard is cooked.

- Chill the mixture, tightly covered, in the refrigerator until it is very cold, at least 4 to 6 hours.

Freeze Gelato

- If you use an old-fashioned ice cream maker instead of an automated one, you can more closely approximate the true texture of gelato.

- The old-fashioned ice cream maker is stirred by hand with a crank.

- Stir it slowly, much more slowly than you would normally, to add less air to the gelato.

- When packing the gelato into a container to ripen, pack down firmly to remove some air.

ICE CREAM

MINT CHOCOLATE CHIP ICE CREAM

Refreshing mint ice cream is speckled with chocolate

Flavored ice creams can be made of almost any sweet or savory ingredient. Mint is a popular flavor because it is so simple and refreshing.

There are several ways to create a mint-flavored dessert. Fresh mint leaves are potent. If soaked in liquid—also known as an infusion—the flavor is pure and clean. Mint and peppermint extracts are another way to create the flavor, and flavored liqueurs like crème de menthe are delicious too.

The quality of the chocolate is very important in this recipe. Melted chocolate is stirred into very cold ice cream, creating flakes of chocolate. Buy a good-quality, flavorful chocolate for this delicious ice cream. *Yield: Serves 6*

Ingredients

1 1/2 cups fresh mint leaves

1 cup heavy whipping cream

1 cup light cream

1 cup whole milk

10 tablespoons granulated sugar

5 egg yolks

2 tablespoons crème de menthe

5 (1-ounce) squares semisweet chocolate, chopped

Mint Chocolate Chip Ice Cream

- Combine mint leaves, heavy cream, light cream, and milk in large saucepan. Heat until steaming.

- Remove from heat, cover, and let stand 40 minutes. Strain into another saucepan. Whisk in sugar and egg yolks.

- Cook, stirring constantly, until simmering; simmer 5 minutes, until thick; add crème de menthe.

- Chill until cold; freeze in ice cream maker. When almost done, melt chocolate. Turn off machine; add melted chocolate. Turn machine on; let mix 1 minute. Freeze.

Peppermint Bonbon Ice Cream: Make recipe as directed, except omit crème de menthe. Add ½ teaspoon peppermint extract and 5 to 6 drops green food coloring to mixture. Chill as directed, freeze in ice cream maker, and add chocolate as directed, substituting melted milk chocolate for semisweet.

Cookies and Cream Ice Cream: Make recipe as directed, except omit mint leaves and crème de menthe. Make ice cream and chill. Freeze as directed in ice cream maker. When ice cream starts to freeze, chop 20 chocolate sandwich cookies and add to ice cream maker. Process for another few minutes, then add melted chocolate and process until flakes form.

Steep Mint Leaves

- Mint comes in several varieties, including spearmint, peppermint, pineapple mint, orange mint, and chocolate mint.

- Rinse off the leaves and shake off excess water. Bruise the leaves slightly by pressing down on them with the back of a spoon.

- Then combine with the creams and milk in a saucepan and heat gently.

- The volatile oils in the mint leaves will transfer to the cream while the mixture heats and is standing.

Add Melted Chocolate

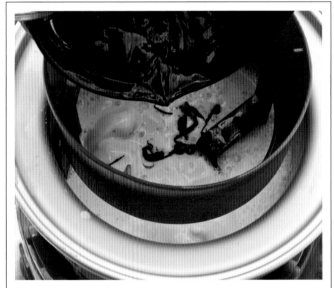

- Adding melted chocolate to ice cream is a neat way to make a chocolate chip dessert.

- The chocolate will solidify in small flakes, blending in better with the ice cream than would chocolate chips or chopped chocolate.

- Pour the chocolate in a thin steam over the frozen ice cream.

- If you want larger pieces of chocolate, add the chocolate quickly to the cold mixture. Or just fold in chopped chocolate or chocolate chips.

ICE CREAM

175

CHOCOLATE SEMIFREDDO

Meaning "half cold" in Italian, this luscious dessert is soft and sweet

Semifreddo sounds like an exotic dessert, but it is very simple and easy to make. This is a very rich dessert, made with an egg custard combined with meringue and whipped cream. You don't need an ice cream maker for this dessert. The fat content keeps the mixture soft and creamy even when frozen in an ordinary freezer.

The meringue and whipped cream also add air into the mixture, replicating the action of an ice cream maker.

For another version of semifreddo, layer the custard mixture with a sponge cake to create a frozen type of tiramisu.

Serve this elegant dessert with Chocolate Sauce (see page 161) and shaved chocolate on fancy dessert plates with silver spoons. *Yield: Serves 8*

Ingredients

4 eggs, separated

¹/₂ cup sugar

1 cup semisweet chocolate chips

2 teaspoons vanilla

2 tablespoons chocolate liqueur

2 tablespoons powdered sugar

1 cup heavy whipping cream

¹/₂ cup hazelnut chocolate spread

1 cup shortbread cookie crumbs

¹/₂ cup chopped hazelnuts

Chocolate Semifreddo

- In saucepan, combine egg yolks with ½ cup sugar. Whisk constantly over low heat until mixture is light yellow. Stir in chips, vanilla, and liqueur; set aside.

- In bowl, beat egg whites with powdered sugar until stiff; set aside. Using same beaters, beat cream with spread until stiff.

- Fold mixtures together. Pour into 9x5-inch loaf pan lined with plastic wrap.

- Sprinkle with cookie crumbs and hazelnuts. Cover; freeze 4 to 6 hours. Unmold; lift off plastic wrap, and slice.

Add Chocolate Chips to Custard

- The egg-yolk-and-sugar mixture is quite fragile. Be careful to constantly whisk it, not stir it, when it's on the heat.

- The chocolate chips will melt when added to the egg yolk mixture. Stir until the chips are melted and the mixture is smooth.

- The custard will cool in the time it takes you to beat the egg whites and whipped cream.

- Be sure that you beat the egg whites first, then the whipping cream, in that order.

Place Mixture in Prepared Pan

- Semifreddo can be shaped into almost any form. Choose decorative molds, tart pans, small loaf pans, or cake pans.

- The crumb mixture can go on the bottom of the pan or on the top, to form a crust when the mixture is unmolded.

- Or you can fold the crumb mixture into the custard to create a different dessert.

- You can use cake cubes instead of the cookie crumbs for a softer texture. Layer them with the ice cream.

ICE CREAM

177

ICE CREAM CAKE

Make a cake just like specialty ice cream shops

Ice cream cakes became popular in the 1980s as a variety of birthday cakes, even though bombes, or fancy ice cream desserts, have been around since the nineteenth century. Chain stores offer the cakes, decorated to your specifications, but it's easy and much less expensive to make your own. Plus, it's fun!

All you need are cookie crumbs, ice cream sauce, ice cream, and candies. Whipped cream or frosting and a piping bag are

optional for decorating your creation.

Get the kids involved in this type of recipe. Since you don't need the oven, a mixer, or knives to make this dessert, it's ideal for beginning cooks.

Use your imagination when decorating these fun cakes, and have fun serving and eating them! *Yield: Serves 8*

Ingredients

12 Chocolate Chip Cookies (see page 48)

¹/₃ cup butter, melted

1 cup Hot Fudge Sauce (see variation), divided

¹/₂ quart vanilla ice cream

¹/₂ quart chocolate chip ice cream

1 (2-ounce) milk chocolate bar

Ice Cream Cake

- In food processor, place cookies. Process until crumbly. Add melted butter; process until mixed. Press into bottom of 9-inch springform pan.

- Spread ½ cup sauce over crust; freeze 30 minutes. Top with vanilla ice cream; freeze 30 minutes.

- Spread with ½ cup Sauce; freeze 30 minutes. Then top with chocolate chip ice cream; freeze 4 to 6 hours, until firm.

- Remove sides of pan and place on serving plate. Grate chocolate over top of cake; cut into slices to serve.

Hot Fudge Sauce: In heavy saucepan, combine 1 cup light cream, 1 cup semisweet chocolate chips, ¼ cup milk chocolate chips, 1½ cups powdered sugar, and ¼ cup butter; cook over medium heat, stirring frequently, until boiling. Boil 7 to 9 minutes, until thick. Remove from heat; add 1 teaspoon vanilla. Cool, stirring occasionally, to room temperature. Store covered in refrigerator.

Brownie Ice Cream Cake: Make recipe as directed, except use 9-inch pan of brownies as base. Or you can chop pan of brownies into 1-inch pieces and fold them into ice cream to use as cake. Top with Mint Chocolate Chip Ice Cream and Hot Fudge Sauce. Whip 1 cup heavy cream with ¼ cup powdered sugar and 1 teaspoon corn syrup. Use this to frost cake and pipe decorations.

Press Crumbs into Pan

- Any cookie can be used as crumbs for this type of recipe. Use homemade or purchase mass-produced cookies.

- Or you can fold the cookies into some of the ice cream. There are many different ways to assemble this dessert.

- Press the crumbs into the bottom of the pan using the back of a spoon or a measuring cup.

- Or you can press the crumbs down using a smaller pan that just fits inside the springform pan.

Layer Ice Cream and Sauce

- You can build up as many layers of ice cream and sauce as you want.

- Fill the pan or even go over the pan edge. To make the pan deeper, fold a long strip of foil several times, then place around the pan.

- Hold the foil in place with kitchen string or a paper clip. Add ice cream and toppings to the pan.

- Freeze the cake until firm, then unmold and decorate as desired before serving.

ICE CREAM

179

BANANAS FOSTER

This classic dessert is easy and last minute

Bananas Foster first appeared in Brennan's Restaurant in New Orleans in the 1950s. Bananas were imported into the United States through the port of New Orleans, and the restaurant wanted to feature them in a new dessert.

This simple, yet elegant, dish is simply made of sliced bananas sautéed in a butter-and-sugar mixture, flavored with spices and sometimes flamed before being spooned over ice cream.

Use bananas that are ripe but still firm for this recipe. The peel should be bright yellow with some dark spots. Don't peel the bananas until you're ready to make the sauce and serve dessert.

If you have a chafing dish, you can make the recipe in that; flame it at the table! Just use care and enjoy this spectacular dish. *Yield: Serves 6*

Bananas Foster

Ingredients

4 bananas, peeled

1 tablespoon lemon juice

1/3 cup butter

3/4 cup packed dark brown sugar

3 tablespoons rum or lime juice

2 teaspoons vanilla

1/2 teaspoon cinnamon

1/8 teaspoon cardamom

6 cups Honey Ice Cream (see page 170)

1/2 cup crushed toffee bits

- Cut bananas lengthwise in half, then cut each half into three pieces; sprinkle with lemon juice.

- In large skillet, combine butter and brown sugar; heat until butter melts. Cook 1 to 2 minutes, stirring frequently, until mixture combines.

- Stir in rum, vanilla, cinnamon, and cardamom, then add bananas. Cook 1 to 2 minutes, until bananas are hot. Spoon into six serving dishes.

- Top with ice cream and sprinkle with toffee bits; serve immediately.

GREEN ●LIGHT

To flame Bananas Foster, you need either a gas cooktop or a long match and liqueur in the recipe. Rum is the traditional ingredient used; it's added when the bananas are done. Cook the mixture for a minute until it is hot, then tip the pan so the fumes ignite on the gas burner. Or light with a long-handled match. The flames will burn out in a minute or two; serve the dessert.

•••• RECIPE VARIATION ••••

Bananas Foster Crepes: Make recipe as directed. Have Crepes Helene (see page 192) on hand. Let ice cream stand at room temperature 20 minutes to soften. Fill each crepe with ⅓ to ½ cup of ice cream; place in freezer. Prepare banana mixture, then pour over filled crepes. Top with Hot Fudge Sauce (see page 179) and serve immediately.

Cook Butter Mixture

- Measure out all of the ingredients before you start the recipe; it goes together as quickly as a stir-fry.

- The butter mixture will look separated at first, but keep stirring. As the mixture heats up it will blend.

- When you add the rum and the spices, the mixture will bubble up. Be careful, since the rum could ignite at this stage.

- Stand back from the pan and make sure your clothes or hair aren't hanging over the pan or the heat.

Add Bananas; Serve

- Add the bananas carefully to the hot sauce mixture so it doesn't splatter.

- You might want to put them on a spatula and slide carefully into the sauce.

- This recipe has to be served as soon as the bananas are heated through and

softened. It can't be made ahead of time and reheated.

- Think about using other fruits in this recipe: sliced pears or apples, cooked for a few minutes longer in the sauce, would be delicious.

BREAD PUDDING
Warm and comforting bread pudding is an easy dessert

Bread pudding is the ultimate in comfort food. It was originally developed as a way to use up leftover bread in more frugal times. But it has been upgraded to an elegant dessert with the addition of ingredients like chocolate, dried fruits, and sauces.

You can use any type of bread in this recipe, except for the very soft, fluffy processed bread so beloved by children. The bread should have some type of character and texture so it stands up to the creamy custard.

You can serve this comforting pudding with Hard Sauce (see variation), with a warm caramel sauce (see page 125), or chocolate sauce (see page 161). *Yield: Serves 8–10*

(see page 125), chocolate sauce (see page 161).

Ingredients

1 loaf sliced raisin bread

1 cup cinnamon chips

$^1/_2$ cup butter

1 cup packed brown sugar

$^1/_3$ cup granulated sugar

2 cups heavy whipping cream

2 cups whole milk

2 eggs

2 egg yolks

2 teaspoons vanilla

2 teaspoons cinnamon

$^1/_2$ teaspoon nutmeg

$^1/_8$ teaspoon cardamom

KNACK FABULOUS DESSERTS

Bread Pudding

- Bake bread slices on cookie sheet at 250°F 10 to 15 minutes. Cool and cube.

- Place bread and chips in buttered 13x9-inch pan. Melt butter with sugars in saucepan; cook and stir until combined.

- In large bowl, combine cream, milk, eggs, egg yolks, vanilla, cinnamon, nutmeg, and cardamom; beat well. Beat in sugar mixture.

- Pour over bread mixture in pan. Let stand 20 minutes. Bake at 350°F 60 to 70 minutes, until set. Serve warm with sauce.

• • • • RECIPE VARIATIONS • • • •

Hard Sauce: In small bowl, beat 10 tablespoons softened butter until light. Add ½ cup powdered sugar and ¼ cup packed brown sugar; beat until sugar dissolves. Add 2 tablespoons heavy cream, 1 teaspoon vanilla, and ⅛ teaspoon cinnamon. Beat until light and fluffy. You can add 1 to 2 tablespoons of dark rum to this recipe if you'd like. Chill until ready to serve.

Chocolate Bread Pudding: Make recipe as directed, except substitute semisweet chocolate chips for cinnamon chips. Use chocolate-filled croissants, cubed, or cubed French bread in place of raisin bread. Add ½ cup cocoa powder to cream-and-milk mixture. Omit nutmeg and cardamom. Serve finished bread pudding with Caramel Sauce (see page 125) or Chocolate Sauce (see page 161).

Beat Sugar Mixture

- Sugars are melted with butter to form a caramel sauce. This makes the recipe richer and adds a depth of flavor to the custard.

- This step also helps the sugar melt so the finished bread pudding is smooth and velvety.

- Let the sugar mixture stand and cool slightly while you combine the eggs with the cream and spices.

- Beat well using a wire whisk, not a spoon, so the custard is smooth and evenly blended.

Pour over Bread Mixture

- The bread slices are baked so they are dry enough to absorb some of the moisture from the custard.

- Pour the custard slowly over the bread so it can absorb some of it.

- Using a spoon, push the bread down into the custard mixture as it stands. Some may bob up above the custard.

- The top should be crusty and nicely browned when the pudding is done for a wonderful texture contrast.

PEANUT BRITTLE

Homemade peanut brittle is a wonderful holiday gift

Peanut brittle is a wonderful candy for the holidays. It makes a delicious gift, especially when packed into a keepsake tin, box, or cookie jar.

This recipe is special because real peanut butter is stirred into the brittle mixture after it is cooked. This makes the brittle slightly less hard, with a creamier texture. It also ramps up the candy's flavor.

You can make this recipe with any type of nut. Try using hazelnuts, and stirring in chocolate hazelnut spread in place of the peanut butter. Or use pistachios and add pistachio butter.

Be careful when making this recipe. The sugar syrup is very hot and can burn in a second. Use hot pads and pay attention in the kitchen! *Yield: 1½ pounds candy*

Ingredients

- 1 cup granulated sugar
- ¹/₂ cup packed brown sugar
- ¹/₂ cup water
- 1¹/₂ cups shelled peanuts
- ³/₄ cup light corn syrup
- 3 tablespoons butter
- ¹/₃ cup peanut butter
- ¹/₂ teaspoon salt
- ¹/₂ teaspoon baking soda

Peanut Brittle

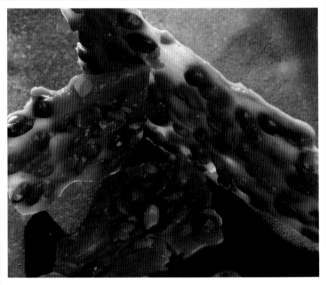

- Have all ingredients ready before you start. Grease large cookie sheet with unsalted butter.

- In heavy saucepan, combine sugars with water; bring to simmer. Stir in peanuts and corn syrup; bring to simmer again.

- Add candy thermometer and cook to 295°F. Remove from heat; add butter, peanut butter, and salt. Mix well.

- Add baking soda; mixture will foam. Beat well and immediately pour onto sheet. Spread with two forks; let cool, then break.

····RECIPE VARIATIONS····

Creamy Old-Fashioned Fudge: In saucepan, combine 3 cups sugar, 3 tablespoons cocoa, 1 cup milk, 1 table-spoon heavy cream, and 1 teaspoon corn syrup. Bring to boil, then add 2 (1-ounce) squares unsweetened choco-late. Wipe down pan with wet brush. Boil to 233°F. Add 3 tablespoons butter and 1 teaspoon vanilla; let stand until 110°F. Beat until thickened; pour into greased 8-inch pan.

Caramels: In saucepan, combine 1 cup packed brown sugar, 1 cup granulated sugar, 2 cups light cream, 1½ cups corn syrup, and a pinch of salt. Cook until mixture starts boiling; cover pan to wash down sides. Cook to 243°F. Add ½ cup butter and 1 tablespoon vanilla. Pour into buttered 9-inch pan. Let stand, then cut into squares. Wrap each square in waxed paper.

Candy Thermometer

- Any candy is made by con-centrating sugar syrup so it will form a certain structure.

- Soft-ball stage (234°F) makes a creamy candy; hard-ball stage (255°F), a firm consistency.

- Light or soft crack (280°F) and hard crack (300°F) are used for taffy, toffee, and brittles.

- The candy thermometer must be properly placed so it is not touching the bot-tom or sides of the pan.

Finish Cooking and Cool

- It's important that the sugar crystals be removed from the interior sides of the pan.

- After the mixture comes to a boil, wash down the sides above the boiling liquid with a wet brush.

- Or cover the pan so steam washes off the crystals. One sugar crystal can crystallize a whole pan, ruining it.

- Pour the mixture quickly into the prepared pan and spread to your desired thickness. Then let the brittle cool and break it into pieces.

BOSTON CREAM PIE
Soft yellow sponge cake is layered with rich custard and topped with chocolate glaze

Boston Cream Pie is a misnomer. This recipe isn't a true pie; it's a layered cake. It got its name because New England bakers were in the habit of making cakes in pie tins. This dessert was originally made in the 1800s at the Parker House Hotel, which is also the source of Parker House Rolls. It is the official Massachusetts State Dessert.

When properly made, this cake is an elegant and delicious dessert. Tender vanilla sponge cake is layered with a rich vanilla-scented cream, and a satiny chocolate glaze finishes the top.

This cake is sliced into wedges like a pie, and served like a pie, not turned onto its side like a cake. *Yield: Serves 8*

Ingredients

1¹/₂ cups flour

2 tablespoons cornstarch

1¹/₂ teaspoons baking powder

¹/₄ teaspoon salt

¹/₄ cup butter, softened

³/₄ cup sugar

2 eggs, separated

1¹/₂ teaspoons vanilla

¹/₃ cup milk

¹/₂ Creamy Vanilla Custard (see variation)

2 ounces semisweet chocolate, chopped

¹/₃ cup milk chocolate chips

¹/₂ cup heavy cream

Boston Cream Pie

- Preheat oven to 350°F. Spray 9-inch cake pan. Sift together flour, cornstarch, baking powder, and salt.

- Beat butter and sugar until light. Add egg yolks and vanilla. Alternately add flour mixture and milk. Beat in unbeaten egg whites. Pour into pan.

- Bake 25 to 30 minutes, until done; cool completely. Slice in half horizontally and fill with custard.

- Melt chocolate with cream until smooth; cool 5 minutes. Pour over cake. Let stand 1 hour; serve. Store leftovers in refrigerator.

···· RECIPE VARIATION ····

Creamy Vanilla Custard: Combine ⅓ cup sugar, 1 egg
yolk, 2 tablespoons flour, 1 tablespoon cornstarch, ½
cup light cream, and ½ cup milk in saucepan. Beat.
Cook over low heat, stirring constantly, until thick.
Remove from heat and beat in 1 tablespoon butter,
1 teaspoon vanilla, and 3 ounces cream cheese. Cool.
Whip ¼ cup heavy cream and fold into mousse; chill.

Assemble Cake

- To slice the cake, place toothpicks around the center.

- Use a long-handled ser-rated knife to cut through the cake, keeping the blade on top of the toothpicks. You can also use unflavored dental floss to cut through the cake.

- Then gently lift off the top part, using a large round spatula; set it aside.

- Place the bottom part of the cake on the serving plate and top with the custard.

Add the Glaze

- Don't make the glaze until the cake has been assem-bled with the custard filling.

- Chop the semisweet choco-late using a large knife, then combine with the chips in a saucepan.

- Add the cream and heat, watching the mixture care-fully. Stir frequently so it doesn't burn.

- Pour the glaze over the cake and, using a spatula or spoon, smooth it evenly on top. Let some of the glaze drip down the sides of the cake.

POUND CAKE

A velvety and dense pound cake is a classic dessert

Pound cake was named because the original recipes used a pound each of butter, sugar, eggs, and flour. These proportions make a dense and creamy cake with a small crumb.

This is a very old cake, probably first made in England in the 18th century. It appeared in the first American cookbook in 1796, called *American Cookery*.

Modern pound cakes are not as dense as the original recipe. Other ingredients, like cream cheese and heavy cream are used to lighten the crumb and produce a silky texture.

Use pound cake to make a rich variation on Strawberry Shortcake (see page 118), use it as an ingredient in Tiramisu (see page 134), or serve it plain with flavored tea as the perfect morning treat. *Yield: Serves 12–14*

Ingredients

- ⅓ cup coconut oil
- 2½ cups granulated sugar, divided
- 1 cup butter, softened
- 1 (8-ounce) package cream cheese, softened
- ¼ teaspoon salt
- 2 teaspoons vanilla
- 7 eggs, room temperature
- 3⅓ cups cake flour
- ½ cup heavy cream

Pound Cake

- Preheat oven to 325°F. Grease two 9x5-inch loaf pans with unsalted butter.

- In large bowl, beat coconut oil with ½ cup sugar until fluffy. Add butter and beat well. Add cream cheese and beat well.

- Add remaining sugar, salt, and vanilla; beat 5 minutes at high speed. Beat in eggs, one at a time. Beat in flour, then cream.

- Pour into pans. Rap pans on counter. Bake 40 to 45 minutes, until done. Cool 15 minutes; cool completely on wire rack.

• • • • RECIPE VARIATION • • • •

Chocolate Pound Cake: Omit cream cheese and add ⅓ cup butter in its place. Sift ½ cup cocoa powder with cake flour. When all ingredients are combined, add 3 (1-ounce) squares semisweet chocolate, chopped and melted with 1 teaspoon espresso powder. Bake cakes as directed. Melt ½ cup semisweet chocolate chips with 2 tablespoons cream; glaze cooled cakes.

• • • • GREEN ● LIGHT • • • •

If you don't have cake flour on hand, or can't find it in your market, it's easy to make a substitute: Use ¾ cup plus 2 tablespoons flour and add 2 tablespoons cornstarch. Then sift the flour and cornstarch mixture together twice before adding to the remaining ingredients. This will blend the two dry ingredients so the flour protein is interspersed with starch from the cornstarch.

Add Sugar to Butter Mixture

- It's very important that the butter, cream cheese, eggs, and cream are all at room temperature before you start making this cake.

- The ingredients must combine well or the texture of the cake will not be smooth and dense.

- Coconut oil is hard at room temperature, so it is beaten separately with sugar until fluffy.

- Make sure that the mixture of oil, butter, and cream cheese is thoroughly combined before continuing with the recipe.

Beat in Eggs

- To bring eggs to room temperature, let them stand out of the refrigerator for 1 hour.

- Or you can put the eggs in a bowl filled with warm water for 5 to 10 minutes.

- The eggs won't want to combine with the butter mixture easily; keep beating until the mixture is smooth.

- The pans are rapped on the counter before baking to remove any large air bubbles and create a dense crumb texture.

OATMEAL CAKE

A hearty oatmeal cake is a good choice for lunchboxes or even breakfast on the run

Oatmeal is a whole-grain product that adds flavor, nutrition, and texture to a simple shortening cake. The type of oatmeal you use does matter. There are four basic types of oatmeal: instant, quick-cooking, rolled oats, and steel-cut oats, proceeding in order from most to least processed.

Quick-cooking and rolled oats are the ones to use in baking.

Quick oats will make a milder product with a softer texture, while rolled oats have a stronger flavor and more chewy texture. Use the product you want for the result you want.

This easy and classic cake can be frosted with a broiled frosting, any buttercream or cream cheese frosting, or just dusted with powdered sugar before serving. *Yield: Serves 16*

Ingredients

1¼ cups quick-cooking oatmeal

½ cup butter

1 cup water

½ cup milk

1 cup packed brown sugar

½ cup sugar

2 eggs

1¾ cups flour

½ teaspoon baking soda

½ teaspoon baking powder

1 teaspoon ground cinnamon

¼ teaspoon ground cardamom

¼ teaspoon salt

Broiled Frosting (see page 210)

Oatmeal Cake

- Preheat oven to 350°F. Coat 13x9-inch baking pan with nonstick baking spray containing flour.

- In large bowl, place oatmeal and butter. In small saucepan, combine water and milk; bring just to boil. Pour over oatmeal mixture.

- Let cool 10 minutes, then stir in sugars and eggs until smooth. Add flour, soda, baking powder, spices, and salt.

- Pour into prepared pan. Bake 30 to 40 minutes, until set. Frost with Broiled Frosting.

190

•••• RECIPE VARIATIONS ••••

Upside-Down Cake: Cut all cake ingredients in half. Peel two small pears and slice. Toss with 1 tablespoon lemon juice. Melt 2 tablespoons butter in 9-inch round cake pan. Sprinkle with ⅓ cup brown sugar and 2 tablespoons chopped pecans. Arrange pears on top. Pour cake batter over. Bake 350°F 30 to 35 minutes, until done. Cool 5 minutes, then invert onto serving plate.

Oatmeal Cupcakes: Make recipe as directed, except line 24 muffin tins with paper liners. Stir 2 cups raisins or 2 cups semisweet chocolate chips into batter. Divide batter among prepared cups, filling each three-quarters full. Bake cupcakes at 350°F 20 to 25 minutes, until tops spring back when lightly touched. Cool completely, then frost as desired.

Pour Water over Oatmeal

- The oatmeal is soaked in hot liquid so it will blend well with the remaining cake ingredients.

- This softens the oatmeal . The grain will absorb water, making the cake more tender.

- This step also helps dissolve the sugar when it's added with the eggs so the cake is creamy and not gritty.

- The butter will melt when the hot liquid is added. The oatmeal, eggs, and flour create the texture in this easy cake.

Add Flour and Bake

- Stir in the flour and spices until combined, then beat the batter 30 to 40 seconds.

- This helps develop the gluten in the flour's protein, which creates the cake's structure.

- To test for doneness, lightly touch it with a fingertip; the cake should spring back.

- This cake keeps well because it is so moist. It will last, well covered, for 3 to 4 days—if it isn't eaten first.

CREPES HELENE

Dessert crepes are so versatile and can be filled many ways

With crepes in the freezer, you can whip up a dessert in seconds with ingredients you have on hand. Learn to make them and use them in this delicious recipe that combines tender pears with a brown sugar sauce and Hot Fudge.

Crepes are simply very thin pancakes. They have a higher liquid-to-flour proportion than typical breakfast pancakes, so the batter spreads out more in the pan.

The trick to crepes is getting the batter to evenly coat the pan as soon as it's added. The batter should be the consistency of heavy cream. Add to the pan and immediately swirl and twist the pan to coat.

Fill these easy crepes with everything from cooked fruit to ice cream. *Yield: Serves 8*

Ingredients

3 eggs

1 egg white

1 cup milk

¹/₃ cup light cream

1 cup flour

3 tablespoons sugar

1 tablespoon cornstarch

Pinch salt

1 teaspoon vanilla

6 tablespoons butter, divided

¹/₃ cup packed brown sugar

3 pears, peeled and sliced

1 cup Hot Fudge Sauce (see page 179)

2 tablespoons powdered sugar

Crepes Helene

- Beat eggs, egg white, milk, and cream until smooth. Add flour, sugar, cornstarch, salt, vanilla, and 2 tablespoons melted butter.

- Let batter stand 30 minutes. Heat 7-inch nonstick skillet over medium heat. Add 1 tablespoon melted butter. Using ¼-cup measure, add 3 tablespoons batter; swirl. Cook 1 to 2 minutes per side. Repeat.

- Melt 3 tablespoons butter and brown sugar in pan; add pears; cook until simmering. Spread Hot Fudge Sauce on crepes; add pear mixture. Roll up. Sprinkle with powdered sugar.

192

Crepes Suzette: Make crepes as directed and cool. Fold each crepe in half, then in half again to form triangle. Melt ½ cup butter in large saucepan. Add 3 tablespoons sugar and cook until melted. Remove pan from heat and add ¼ cup Grand Marnier; flame. Add crepes to pan with tongs, turning to coat with sauce. Heat through. Serve crepes with Honey Ice Cream (see page 170) and sauce.

Lemon Cream: In medium bowl, beat 1 cup heavy cream until soft peaks form. Add 1 cup mascarpone cheese, 3 tablespoons powdered sugar, ¼ cup lemon juice, and ½ teaspoon vanilla. Beat until smooth and thick. Use as a filling for crepes, or thin with some more heavy cream and use as a dessert sauce. Vary this recipe by using orange juice and adding some Grand Marnier.

Swirl Batter in Pan

- Make a test crepe at first to make sure the batter is the correct consistency. If the batter doesn't spread easily, add more milk.

- The pan should be heated for no more than 30 seconds. Use your wrist to turn the pan so the batter spreads out.

- This just takes practice. You may need to discard the first crepe or two. That's okay.

- Do not stack the crepes to cool; let them stand on a kitchen towel in a single layer.

Finish Crepes

- Pears cooked in brown sugar are a nice filling for crepes, but you can use other fruits.

- The crepes can be rolled up or folded as in Crepes Suzette.

- You can freeze these crepes for later use. Stack them, with waxed paper in between, then wrap in heavy duty foil.

- Mark the package and freeze up to 3 months. To thaw, let stand at room temperature, then use in any recipe or fill with ice cream, whipped cream, or fresh fruit.

ALMOND BISCOTTI

Make your own biscotti to dunk into your morning coffee

If you've become addicted to expensive biscotti from your favorite coffee shop, make your own! They're much less expensive, fun to make, and so much better.

Even though biscotti are a fairly new addition to the coffee-house scene, they have been around for thousands of years. They were first made for Roman travelers because they kept well on long journeys.

The word *biscotti* is derived from the Latin for "twice cooked." The cookies are literally baked two times to create the crunchy and dry texture characteristic of the product.

Enjoy making biscotti and have fun creating new flavors. Use dried fruits, nuts, citrus peel, and chocolate to make the recipe your own. *Yield: 48 biscotti cookies*

Ingredients

- ¼ cup light olive oil
- ½ cup butter, softened
- 1 cup packed brown sugar
- ½ cup granulated sugar
- 3 eggs
- 1 teaspoon vanilla
- 1 teaspoon almond extract
- 3 cups flour
- ½ teaspoon salt
- 1 teaspoon cinnamon
- ½ cup ground almonds

Biscotti

- Preheat oven to 350°F. Line cookie sheet with parchment paper.

- Beat olive oil, butter, and sugars until smooth. Add eggs, vanilla, and almond extract.

- Beat in flour, salt, cinnamon, and almonds. Form into three 2x12-inch strips crosswise on cookie sheet. Bake 30 to 35 minutes, until firm.

- Spray with 1 tablespoon water and cover with foil. Let cool. Cut into ¾-inch slices; place on sides on cookie sheet. Bake 10 minutes, turn, bake 10 minutes, until crisp; cool.

Chocolate Glaze: Combine 1 cup semisweet or milk chocolate chips in heavy small saucepan with 2 table-spoons heavy cream and 1 teaspoon butter. Melt over low heat, stirring frequently, until chocolate melts and mixture is smooth. Add ¼ teaspoon vanilla. Dip cooled biscotti into this mixture to coat half of each cookie. Let cool on waxed paper until set.

Chocolate Biscotti: Make recipe as directed, except omit almond extract, cinnamon, and ground almonds. Reduce flour to 2⅔ cups. Add ½ cup cocoa powder to batter with flour. When dough is mixed, stir in 1 cup dark chocolate chips and ½ cup chopped pecans. Bake, then slice and bake cookies as directed. Drizzle with Chocolate Glaze when they have cooled.

Arrange Dough on Cookie Sheet

Slice Cookies

- The olive oil adds a mild fruity flavor to the cookies. It's traditional in many Italian biscotti recipes.

- Handle the dough as little as possible so the gluten in the flour doesn't develop.

- Round off the sides and make sure that the dough strips are even and about the same size.

- This simple dough doesn't rise much in the oven. The first baking is to set the dough so it can be sliced.

- Use a serrated knife to cut the baked dough into individual cookies. Use a gentle sawing motion to cut through the dough.

- The dough will be firm but not crisp. The cookies become crisp during the second baking.

- You can cut the dough logs straight across, or cut on a diagonal to make longer biscotti.

- Leave the cookies plain or dip them in Chocolate Glaze for the perfect finishing touch. Store the biscotti in airtight containers.

CHURROS

Cream puff batter is deep fried until crisp and served with a spicy chocolate sauce

This fun and delicious dessert comes from Spain and Latin America, where street vendors sell them for midmorning or afternoon snacks.

You need a pastry bag to make this recipe. A cream puff dough, made in a saucepan, is spooned into the bag, then forced into hot oil through a star tip. The tip creates ridges in

the churros that add to the crunchy texture.

The dough is made by boiling water and butter together, then adding flour and cooking the dough. Eggs are beaten in to act as the leavening agent that makes the dough puff in the heat. Serve these churros warm for a snack. *Yield: Serves 8–10*

Ingredients

1 cup water

1 cup whole milk

3 tablespoons packed brown sugar

1/2 teaspoon salt

3 tablespoons butter

2 cups flour

1/2 teaspoon cinnamon

2 eggs

1/2 cup granulated sugar

1 1/2 teaspoons cinnamon

4 cups vegetable oil

Churros

- In saucepan, bring water, milk, sugar, and salt to a boil. Add butter, flour, and ½ teaspoon cinnamon; stir until a ball forms.

- Beat in eggs, one at a time; let cool 30 minutes. Mix granulated sugar and 1½ teaspoons cinnamon on plate.

- Heat oil to 375°F in large pan. Place dough in pastry bag. Pipe dough in 5-inch rods into oil; fry 3 to 6 minutes, until brown.

- Drain on paper towels; roll in cinnamon sugar and serve warm with dipping sauce.

Cream Puffs: Make recipe as directed, except increase eggs to 4 and increase butter to ½ cup. Omit milk, and reduce flour to 1¼ cups. Boil water with sugar, salt, and butter; add flour and cook. Add eggs and beat well. Drop mixture by ¼-cup measure onto greased cookie sheets. Bake at 400°F 25 to 35 minutes, until puffed and golden brown. Fill with pudding or ice cream when cool.

Spicy Fudge Dipping Sauce: In saucepan, combine 1 cup Hot Fudge Sauce (see page 179), ¼ cup light cream, and ½ to 1 teaspoon cinnamon, along with pinch cayenne pepper. Heat, stirring frequently, until sauce is combined and smooth. Pour into serving bowl and let stand while preparing churros. Drizzle or serve in cups for dipping. Increase cayenne pepper according to taste.

ETHNIC DESSERTS

Cook Churro Dough

- Make sure that the water mixture comes to a full rolling boil before you add the butter-and-flour mixture.

- Cook until the mixture comes together and cleans the sides of the pan.

- Add the eggs and beat well. You can use a hand mixer for this step because it's difficult to incorporate the eggs into the stiff dough.

- Spoon the dough into the pastry bag and attach the star tip.

Pipe Dough into Oil

- A thermometer is also necessary for this recipe to make sure the oil is at the correct temperature.

- Don't crowd the pan with too many churros at once: add only 4 or 5 at a time. Any more will cool the oil.

- If the oil isn't hot enough, the dough will absorb the oil and become greasy.

- Turn the churros in the oil with a slotted spoon as they cook, then remove to paper towels to drain, then roll in sugar.

BAKLAVA

Paper-thin phyllo dough is layered with sweet nuts and spicy sugar syrup

This classic and ancient dessert is a real showstopper, but it's easy to make once you know how to work with phyllo dough.

Baklava probably began in Assyria, and was incorporated into cuisines of Greece and Turkey by merchants traveling to Mesopotamia.

Phyllo is paper-thin dough that is almost always purchased in the store. You can find it in the frozen foods aisle of the supermarket. It is layered with butter, sugar, and nuts in a pan. The mixture is baked until crisp, then a sweet syrup is poured over all. *Yield: Serves 12–14*

Baklava

Ingredients

1 cup butter, melted

³/₄ cup water

¹/₂ cup apple juice

³/₄ cup granulated sugar

¹/₂ cup packed brown sugar

²/₃ cup honey

2 tablespoons lemon juice

2 teaspoons vanilla

2 cups finely chopped walnuts

2 cups finely chopped pistachios

3 tablespoons sugar

2 teaspoons cinnamon

1 (16-ounce) package frozen phyllo dough, thawed

- Preheat oven to 350°F. Coat 13x9-inch pan with butter. Combine first seven ingredients in saucepan; simmer 30 minutes; cool.

- Mix nuts, 3 tablespoons sugar, and cinnamon. Place one sheet phyllo in pan. Brush with butter. Repeat with five sheets; sprinkle with ¼ cup nuts.

- Add two buttered sheets and ¼ cup nuts. Continue, with six more sheets.

- Cut into diamond shapes almost through to bottom of pan. Bake 45 to 50 minutes, until crisp. Pour syrup over baklava.

• • • • RECIPE VARIATION • • • •

Baklava Rolls: Make recipe as directed, except make equal stacks of phyllo dough, layered with sugar-and-nut mixture, eight sheets high. Roll up each sheet, starting with short side. Brush with melted butter and cut each roll into 2-inch slices. Place slices, cut-side up, in greased 13x9-inch pan. Bake at 350°F 35 to 45 minutes. Cool, then pour syrup over all.

Layer Phyllo-and-Nut Mixture

- The nuts should be finely chopped so they will layer evenly with the phyllo dough.

- Chop them in a food processor or a nut grinder, or use a chef's knife. You can use any combination of nuts you'd like in this recipe.

- Sprinkle the nut mixture very evenly over the entire phyllo surface.

- The butter helps create the flaky texture of the finished dish and adds wonderful flavor. Do not substitute margarine in this recipe.

Pour Syrup over Baklava

- It's important to cut all the way through the phyllo layers before baking.

- When this is done, the syrup can penetrate to the bottom of the pan and the baklava will be evenly flavored.

- The basic rule of baklava is to pour hot syrup over cooked phyllo dough, or cold syrup over hot phyllo dough.

- The crisp pastry absorbs the syrup, creating a sticky, crisp, and crunchy dessert.

MACAROONS

Chewy and rich coconut cookies are easy to make

Macaroons are simple cookies made of egg whites, sugar, and either coconut or ground almonds. These cookies are quite sweet with a chewy and moist texture. Macaroons can also be light and crisp like a meringue.

The first macaroons were made in Italy in the eighteenth century, and were adopted by the Jewish community in Eastern Europe. The cookies are a great choice for Passover since they do not contain any leavening.

Coconut macaroons are the most common. They are made from sweetened egg whites and flaked or shredded coconut. Almond macaroons are usually made with almond paste. They are slightly less sweet and chewier.

Serve macaroons with tea or coffee or a big glass of milk for any holiday or snack time. *Yield: 36 cookies*

Ingredients

1/2 cup sweetened condensed milk

1/2 cup cream of coconut

1 tablespoon honey

2 teaspoons vanilla

2 1/2 cups flaked coconut

2 1/2 cups shredded coconut

3 egg whites

1/2 teaspoon salt

2 tablespoons sugar

Macaroons

- In large bowl, combine condensed milk, cream of coconut, honey, and vanilla; whisk until blended. Add both types of coconut.

- In medium bowl, beat egg whites with salt until foamy; gradually add sugar and beat until stiff. Fold into coconut mixture.

- Cover and refrigerate 1 to 2 hours. Preheat oven to 350°F.

- Drop batter onto cookie sheets lined with parchment paper. Bake 15 to 19 minutes, until lightly browned. Place parchment on damp towels for 10 minutes; remove cookies.

Almond Macaroons: Place 1 (8-ounce) can almond paste in food processor. Add 2 egg whites, ½ cup packed brown sugar, and ¾ cup granulated sugar; process. Add 1 cup chopped slivered almonds and mix. Drop by teaspoons onto parchment-paper-lined cookie sheets. Bake at 325°F 18 to 22 minutes. Cool on paper, then peel off paper; store in airtight container.

Chocolate Macaroons: Omit cream of coconut. Omit 1 cup flaked coconut; add 1 cup chopped almonds. Add 1 cup melted semisweet chocolate chips to condensed milk mixture. Fold in egg whites, then drop by teaspoons onto parchment-paper-lined cookie sheets. Bake at 350°F 13 to 18 minutes, until set. Cool on paper, then peel off paper. Store in airtight container.

Add Coconut

- The sweetened condensed milk and coconut milk add a creamy taste and rich texture to these cookies.

- Don't substitute coconut milk for the cream of coconut or the recipe won't work properly. You can use all cream of coconut.

- Cream of coconut is thick and sweet. It's usually used in mixed drinks.

- The two types of coconut have different textures. Using them both adds interest to the cookies, but you can use all of one or the other.

Fold in Egg Whites

- The egg white mixture helps leaven the cookies and lightens the texture.

- The egg whites will deflate quite a bit when they are folded into the coconut mixture; that's okay.

- Drop the mixture by teaspoons onto parchment-paper-lined sheets, or use Silpat sheets. Nothing will stick to those silicone liners!

- Make these cookies fancier by drizzling them with a bit of melted chocolate after they have been baked and cooled.

RAISIN KUGEL

Matzos, applesauce, and cinnamon sugar make this Jewish recipe delicious

This traditional Jewish dessert takes many forms, using as its basic ingredients matzo, farfel, and noodles. It can be made as a savory side dish, but it is most commonly known as a sweet dessert.

The word *kugel* means "ball" or "cannonball." This was probably a reference to the original recipe, made from bread and flour. Jews in Germany began to make the dessert using eggs, matzos, and noodles.

You can flavor your kugel with everything from raisins and applesauce to chocolate. The basic ingredients used depend on the holiday and the cook's preference. For Passover, matzos (unleavened crackers) are used. *Yield: Serves 8–10*

Ingredients

1 cup apple juice

1 cup water

2 cups crushed matzo crumbs

¹/₃ cup packed brown sugar

¹/₂ cup granulated sugar, divided

¹/₃ cup applesauce

1 egg yolk

1 teaspoon vanilla

1 cup raisins

1 teaspoon cinnamon, divided

¹/₂ teaspoon ground nutmeg

3 egg whites

Raisin Kugel

- Preheat oven to 375°F. Coat 13x9-inch pan with cooking spray.

- In saucepan, combine juice and water; heat until steaming. Remove from heat; add crumbs. Cool 15 minutes.

- Add brown sugar, ¼ cup granulated sugar, and applesauce. Beat in egg yolk, vanilla, raisins, ½ teaspoon cinnamon, and nutmeg.

- Beat egg whites until stiff; fold into batter. Pour into pan. Combine remaining sugar and cinnamon; sprinkle on top. Bake 50 to 60 minutes, until brown.

Farfel Kugel: Make recipe as directed, except omit juice, water, matzo crumbs, egg yolk, and egg whites. Place 2 cups farfel in large bowl and add 3 cups cold water. Soak for 10 minutes, then drain well. Return to bowl. Add both kinds of sugar, applesauce, 4 eggs, and vanilla; beat well. Add raisins. Pour into greased 9-inch pan; sprinkle with cinnamon sugar. Bake 350°F 45 to 55 minutes, until set.

Apricot Noodle Kugel: Cook 8 ounces medium egg noodles until tender; drain and add 3 tablespoons butter. Combine 1 cup cottage cheese, 3 eggs, and ½ cup packed brown sugar. Stir in 1½ cups apricot nectar, ½ cup pineapple juice, and 1 cup chopped dried apricots. Add noodles. Place in 9-inch greased pan; sprinkle with cinnamon sugar. Bake at 350°F 40 to 50 minute.

Mix Ingredients

- You can crush the matzo fine, or leave some larger pieces for more texture in the kugel.

- Don't let the matzo stand in the hot juice mixture longer than 15 minutes, and don't make this part of the recipe ahead of time.

- You can substitute golden raisins, dried currants, or sweetened dried cranberries for the plain raisins.

- Increase the spices for a more flavorful dish, or use exotic spices like cardamom.

Fold in Egg Whites; Bake

- The egg whites will deflate rather quickly when folded into the matzo batter.

- They do provide some lightness to the dish, and add protein to the structure.

- First stir a dollop of the egg whites into the batter, then fold in the remaining egg whites.

- Serve the kugel warm, cut into squares. You can top with a dusting of powdered sugar for more sweetness.

CREAM CHEESE FROSTING
Cream cheese helps temper the sweetness of frosting

Cream cheese, that ubiquitous dairy product, turns ordinary frosting into something special. The slightly tangy taste of the cream cheese modulates the sweet frosting, adding a depth of flavor and extra-creamy texture.

This frosting is really best on cupcakes or a sheet cake. It does remain fairly soft and isn't quite strong enough to support a layer cake unless the cake is refrigerated.

Vary this frosting by adding coconut or chopped nuts, especially if you're using it on a carrot or apple cake. Try it on simple chocolate cookies, chocolate cupcakes, or Red Velvet Cupcakes for a nice change of pace. Or sandwich the frosting between two graham crackers for a quick snack. *Yield: 2½ cups*

Ingredients

3¹/₂ cups powdered sugar

1 (8-ounce) package cream cheese, softened

1 (3-ounce) package cream cheese, softened

¹/₃ cup unsalted butter, softened

¹/₂ teaspoon salt

2 teaspoons vanilla

1–2 tablespoons heavy cream

Cream Cheese Frosting

- Sift powdered sugar before measuring it, then place in medium bowl.

- In large bowl, beat together cream cheese with butter until very light, about 4 to 5 minutes.

- Gradually add half powdered sugar, beating constantly. Stir in salt and vanilla and beat well.

- Add remaining powdered sugar and beat well. Add heavy cream if needed for desired spreading consistency.

• • • • • RECIPE VARIATION • • • •

Fluffy Cream Cheese Frosting: Make recipe as directed, except omit butter and powdered sugar. Use ¾ cup granulated sugar instead; beat with cream cheese for 3 minutes. Add salt and vanilla, then gradually pour in 1½ cups heavy cream and whip until peaks form. You may need to refrigerate this frosting for 1 to 2 hours before using so it stiffens slightly.

Beat Cream Cheese

Add Sugar and Beat

- The cream cheese must be well softened before it is combined with the butter and remaining ingredients.

- Beat the cream cheese well until it is smooth and fluffy. Do not skip this step or scrimp on the time beating.

- If you add the sugar before this point, lumps will develop that cannot be beaten out no matter how long you work.

- An electric hand or stand mixer works best for making this frosting. A whisk won't stand up to the mixture.

- Powdered sugar is very finely ground so it will dissolve easily into the cream cheese and butter used in this recipe.

- Powdered sugar contains cornstarch, which helps stabilize the frosting. Do not substitute granulated sugar, and don't make your own powdered sugar in a blender.

- Instead of vanilla, try adding 3 tablespoons of lemon juice for a tangy flavor.

- Or add ½ cup cocoa powder, sifted with the powdered sugar, for a Chocolate Cream Cheese Frosting.

WHIPPED CREAM FROSTING

The easiest frosting of all requires little more than chilled cream and a beater

Whipped cream is the simplest frosting, but you must still follow a few rules for the fluffiest result. This frosting is excellent on chocolate cake or as a topping for almost any dessert. It is also perfect for filling a cake. Use another frosting for the top and sides of the cake for more interest.

Make sure that you purchase heavy whipping cream for this

frosting. The cream must have a butterfat content of around 40 percent. If the fat content is less, the cream will simply not whip into peaks, or hold peaks.

If you can, avoid ultra-pasteurized heavy cream. It takes longer to whip and sometimes will not whip to the proper consistency. *Yield: 4 cups*

Ingredients

2 cups chilled heavy whipping cream

¾ cup sifted powdered sugar

Pinch salt

1½ teaspoons vanilla

Whipped Cream Frosting

- Make sure cream is very well chilled. Chill large bowl and beaters to your mixer.

- Pour cream into chilled bowl and start beating at low speed.

- Gradually add powdered sugar, beating until stiff peaks form. Beat in salt and vanilla.

- For more stabilization, dissolve 1 teaspoon unflavored gelatin in 1 tablespoon water and add to cream with sugar.

Chocolate Whipped Cream Frosting: Make recipe as directed, except sift ⅓ cup cocoa powder with half of the powdered sugar. Add it to heavy cream and mix well. Cover and chill for 1 to 2 hours before you start beating. Then add remaining sugar, salt, and vanilla to finish frosting, beating until stiff peaks form.

Caramel Whipped Cream Frosting: Combine heavy cream, 2 tablespoons packed brown sugar, and 1 tablespoon caramel ice cream topping in heavy bowl; whisk until combined. Cover and chill 1 to 2 hours. Beat until soft peaks form; add ⅓ cup powdered sugar, pinch salt, and 1 teaspoon vanilla. Beat until stiff.

Chill Ingredients

Beat to Stiff Peaks

- At a minimum, the cream must be very well chilled. Store it in the coolest part of your refrigerator.

- Chilling the bowls and beaters will help speed things up considerably, but this step isn't strictly necessary.

- Chill all of the equipment for at least 1 hour so it is very cold. Or you can put it in the freezer for 15 to 20 minutes.

- When you take the cream and equipment out of the refrigerator, start making the frosting immediately.

- Start beating at low speed to begin developing the air bubbles and the fat-and-protein web.

- Add the powdered sugar gradually, beating constantly. Stop occasionally to scrape down the sides of the bowl.

- If you are making this recipe for a topping, decrease the sugar to ½ cup.

- You can freeze the whipped cream in small portions. Pipe or dollop some onto waxed paper, then freeze until firm. Let thaw in the fridge before topping desserts.

FROSTINGS

OLD-FASHIONED FROSTING

A flour paste is added to frosting for a super-creamy and fluffy texture

This frosting is very creamy and velvety, with a rich and smooth texture only achieved through a flour paste. This may sound strange, but the flour stabilizes the frosting and contributes a creamy mouth-feel.

For this recipe to work properly, the flour must be well cooked in the milk. If it isn't cooked enough, the frosting will have a raw grain taste. Cooking the flour will swell its starch granules. These granules absorb the liquid in the milk, making a thick paste.

This paste creates the creamy texture of the frosting. It looks like whipped cream and is an excellent frosting to be used on any cake. This recipe is also less sweet. *Yield: 2 cups*

Ingredients

5 tablespoons flour

1/4 teaspoon cornstarch

1/8 teaspoon salt

2/3 cup milk

2/3 cup butter, softened

4 cups sifted powdered sugar

2 teaspoons vanilla

Old-Fashioned Frosting

- In small saucepan, combine flour, cornstarch, and salt; gradually stir in milk with wire whisk.

- Cook over low heat until mixture thickens and just starts to boil, stirring constantly. Remove from heat; let stand until lukewarm.

- In large bowl, beat butter with powdered sugar until very fluffy, about 4 minutes. Gradually add flour mixture and beat until fluffy, another 4 to 5 minutes. Add vanilla.

- Use to frost 13x9-inch pan or one 8- or 9-inch layer cake. Or frost 48 cookies.

Chocolate Frosting: Make recipe as directed, except add 3 tablespoons cocoa powder to flour-and-milk mixture; cook as directed and let cool, stirring occasionally. Meanwhile, melt 2 (1-ounce) squares semisweet chocolate and cool. Beat butter and powdered sugar, then add flour mixture. Beat in vanilla and melted chocolate mixture until smooth.

Granulated Sugar Frosting: Make recipe as directed, except omit powdered sugar. Add ¼ cup solid shortening to butter; beat until smooth. Then add 1 cup granulated sugar and beat until very light and fluffy. Add cooled flour mixture gradually and beat until fluffy. Add vanilla and salt. Cover frosting and refrigerate for 1 day so sugar dissolves, then use frosting on cakes or cookies.

Cook Flour Paste

Beat Frosting

FROSTINGS

- Make sure to measure the flour by spooning it into the measuring spoon and leveling off the top.

- Too much flour will make the frosting thick and gummy. Whisk the flour before adding the milk.

- Stir the flour and milk mixture constantly while it's on the heat, using a wire whisk.

- Make sure that the mixture just comes to a boil, with bubbles rising to the surface. Stir the mixture occasionally while it cools.

- Beat the butter with the powdered sugar until the mixture is pale yellow and very light.

- Add the flour paste in small amounts, about a spoonful at a time, beating constantly.

- This is a good frosting for use in decorating cakes, especially with a pastry bag and piping tips.

- The frosting will not harden completely, but will stay fairly soft. Be sure to use it only on completely cooled cakes, bars, and cookies.

BROILED FROSTING
Sometimes called Lazy Daisy, this frosting is super-easy and quick

Aside from topping a cake with sifted powdered sugar or serving it plain, broiled frosting is the easiest finish. A mixture of butter, sugar, cream, and nuts or coconut is spread onto a baked cake, then broiled until the mixture bubbles. This cooks the mixture and melts the sugar, making a moist, creamy, and flavorful topping.

This frosting was developed in the 1950s when cooking and baking were changing dramatically. Cake mixes were introduced to homemakers, and everyone was looking for shortcuts.

The only trick to broiled frosting is to watch it carefully when it's under the broiler. The frosting can go from perfectly cooked to burned in seconds. *Yield: Frosts 13x9-inch cake*

Ingredients

- ¹/₃ cup butter
- ¹/₂ cup packed brown sugar
- ¹/₂ cup granulated sugar
- ¹/₈ teaspoon salt
- ¹/₃ cup heavy cream
- 1 cup chopped pecans
- 1¹/₄ cups flaked coconut
- 1¹/₂ teaspoons vanilla

Broiled Frosting

- While cake is in oven, melt butter in medium saucepan. Add sugars and salt; remove from heat.

- Add cream and mix well until mixture combines. Stir in pecans, coconut, and vanilla.

- When cake is done, remove from oven and place oven rack 6 inches from heating coils.

- Gently spoon and spread frosting mixture over cake surface. Place under broiler and broil, watching very carefully, 3 to 5 minutes, until frosting bubbles all over surface. Cool.

Chocolate Broiled Frosting: Make recipe as directed, except add ¼ cup cocoa powder to butter with brown and granulated sugars. Add remaining ingredients. Spread frosting on cake and broil as directed. Remove cake from oven and immediately sprinkle with 1 to 2 cups semisweet or milk chocolate chips. Let stand 5 minutes, then gently swirl chips into frosting to marble.

Self-Frosted Cake: Any cake can be finished with this method. When cake batter is divided into pans, mix ¼ cup packed brown sugar with 1 cup semisweet chocolate chips for 8- or 9-inch cake, or ½ cup packed brown sugar with 2 cups chocolate chips for 13x9-inch cake. Sprinkle over batter and bake as directed. You can also add chopped nuts to chocolate chip mixture.

Spread Frosting on Cake

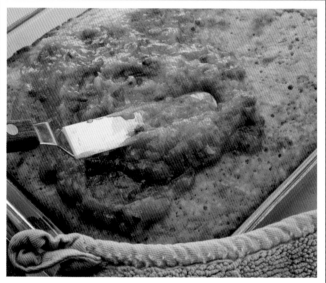

- The frosting has to be spread on the delicate cake with care.

- Use a small spoon to place small dollops of the frosting mixture evenly on the cake.

- Then use an offset spatula to very gently coax the frosting to cover the cake's surface.

- You can take your time with this process, because there's no rush. The frosting won't harden until it is cooked under the broiler.

Broil Frosting

- First arrange the rack in the oven so it is 6 inches away from the heating coils.

- Then preheat the broiler for 5 to 10 minutes to make sure it's at the correct temperature.

- Place the cake in the oven and leave the door ajar. Watch the cake carefully as the frosting cooks.

- You will need to turn the cake around and perhaps move it back and forth under the broiler so it cooks evenly.

EASY BUTTERCREAM FROSTING
This simple one-bowl frosting can be varied many ways

Buttercream frosting is the classic frosting recipe everyone is familiar with. It's just a mixture of butter, sugar, and cream, flavored with a bit of salt and vanilla.

The key to making the best buttercream is to beat it long enough. Even powdered sugar, as fine and powdery as it is, needs to dissolve in the frosting for it to be fluffy and creamy. This takes time and effort.

The butter must be thoroughly softened, but not melted, for best results in this recipe. Let it stand at room temperature for 2 to 3 hours before starting the frosting.

You can use milk or light cream in place of the heavy cream in this creamy frosting. *Yield: 2½ cups*

Ingredients

1 cup butter, softened

¹/₈ teaspoon salt

2 teaspoons vanilla

5–6 cups sifted powdered sugar

6 tablespoons heavy cream, divided

Easy Buttercream Frosting

- Soften butter by letting it stand at room temperature for 2 to 3 hours. In large bowl, beat butter 5 minutes.

- Add salt, vanilla, and 1 cup sugar; beat 2 minutes. Alternately add remaining sugar and 3 tablespoons cream, beating well.

- When desired consistency is reached, beat frosting for 5 minutes longer, until very fluffy.

- Add 2 to 3 squares melted semisweet chocolate or ½ cup cocoa powder for chocolate frosting.

Silky Chocolate Frosting: Make recipe as directed, but add 3 tablespoons cocoa powder to powdered sugar and sift together to blend. Melt 3 (1-ounce) squares semisweet chocolate in microwave or heavy saucepan; cool 20 minutes. Add melted chocolate along with heavy cream. Beat frosting until fluffy. Use to fill and frost cake layers or frost cupcakes.

Coconut Frosting: Make recipe as directed, but use coconut cream instead of light cream as liquid. Substitute ½ teaspoon coconut extract in place of 1 teaspoon of the vanilla. Stir in ½ cup flaked sweetened coconut before using frosting. Top cake, cupcakes, or cookies with more coconut after frosting. You can toast coconut before adding to frosting for more intense flavor.

FROSTINGS

Beat Butter

- Beating the butter before adding any other ingredients adds air into the frosting, making it light and fluffy.

- Don't skip this step, as air is an important ingredient in the best frosting.

- You can use an electric hand mixer or a stand mixer. A spoon can be used, but that takes a lot of strength.

- Stop the mixer and scrape the sides and bottom of the bowl fairly often as you work; scrape the beaters too.

Add Sugar and Cream

- Sift the sugar before you measure it. Be sure to remove any lumps of sugar or anything not fine enough to go through the sifter.

- Add some of the sugar, then beat until it is completely combined with the butter.

- Then add some of the liquid and beat until that is completely combined.

- Continue until the frosting is desired consistency. As you use the frosting you may need to add more liquid to keep the consistency smooth.

SEVEN MINUTE FROSTING

It takes longer than seven minutes to make this frosting, but it's so good

Seven Minute Frosting is an old-fashioned recipe that is basically a cooked meringue. It has a consistency similar to marshmallow crème, but much fluffier and less sticky.

This frosting does tend to "climb" the beaters as it is being made. You may want to cut a piece of waxed paper and place over the mixer beater holes. Stick the beaters through the paper to keep the frosting out of the mixer itself.

Don't let the water in the double boiler bottom touch the bottom of the double boiler top or the egg mixture will cook too quickly.

Enjoy this fluffy frosting on any of your cakes or cookies. It's also good spread on graham crackers. *Yield: 2½ cups*

Ingredients

3 egg whites

1³/₄ cups sugar

¹/₄ cup cold water

2 tablespoons light corn syrup

¹/₈ teaspoon salt

¹/₄ teaspoon cream of tartar

1¹/₂ teaspoons vanilla

Seven Minute Frosting

- This frosting must be made with an electric mixer. In top of double boiler, combine all ingredients except vanilla; beat 1 minute.

- Bring water to boiling in bottom of double boiler. Add top of double boiler and start beating.

- Beat constantly for 8 to 12 minutes, until the frosting stands in stiff peaks.

- Remove from heat and beat in vanilla. Beat until thick and spreadable. Frost cakes, cookies, or cupcakes immediately.

Marshmallow Seven Minute Frosting: Make recipe as directed, except when frosting is thick, at end of cooking and beating time, add ½ cup miniature marshmallows. Beat until marshmallows melt and frosting is thick and fluffy. This is a good frosting for chocolate cake or chocolate cupcakes.

Lemon Seven Minute Frosting: Make recipe as directed, except add 2 tablespoons lemon juice in place of half of the water. Cook frosting over boiling water, beating constantly with electric mixer, until it is thick, smooth, and fluffy. You can tint this recipe with a drop or two of yellow food coloring after it's done.

Beat Frosting

Add Vanilla

FROSTINGS

- Make sure that the double boiler and beaters are free from any fat or grease.

- If you'd like a chocolate Seven Minute Frosting, add ¼ cup sifted cocoa powder with the egg whites.

- Start a timer when the mixture is placed on the double boiler. You still need to determine doneness by the consistency of the frosting.

- A hand mixer is the ideal tool for making this frosting, because it's portable and strong.

- The corn syrup and cream of tartar help prevent sugar crystals from forming, so the frosting stays creamy.

- You may need to beat the frosting for several more minutes after removing the pan from the heat.

- Spread the frosting on the cake as soon as it is stiff and fluffy. It does harden quickly.

- This frosting will be more difficult to make on a rainy or humid day, unless your home is air-conditioned.

ANGEL FOOD CAKE

Like its name, this cake is fluffy and light

Airy, sweet, and fluffy angel food cake is a classic low-fat dessert. It is so popular that many people don't recognize it as low fat!

This light and airy cake may have made its first appearance in the southern United States, baked by slaves, although it was very popular among the Pennsylvania Dutch. Before mixers, making this cake required a lot of strength.

Always use a serrated knife or a cake fork to cut angel food cake, and use a sawing motion. Don't press down on the cake to cut or you will squish it.

All of the tools for making this cake must be free of any trace of grease or fat. *Yield: 1 10-inch tube cake*

Ingredients

10–12 egg whites

1 teaspoon cream of tartar

¹/₄ teaspoon salt

1 cup granulated sugar

2 teaspoons vanilla

³/₄ cup sifted flour

2 tablespoons cornstarch

¹/₃ cup powdered sugar

Angel Food Cake

- Preheat oven to 350°F. Separate eggs while cold; measure out 1⅓ cups egg whites.

- Place egg whites in large bowl; let stand at room temperature 25 minutes. Add cream of tartar and salt; start beating.

- Gradually add granulated sugar, beating until stiff peaks form. Beat in vanilla.

- Sift flour, cornstarch, and powdered sugar; fold into egg whites, ⅓ cup at a time. Spoon into 10-inch tube pan. Bake 45 to 50 minutes, until golden brown. Invert pan; cool completely.

Chocolate Angel Food Cake: *Make cake as directed, except add 6 tablespoons sifted cocoa powder to granulated sugar and beat into egg whites. Bake cake at 325°F for 55 to 65 minutes, until it springs back when lightly touched. Invert cake to cool. Frost with Seven Minute Frosting (see page 214) or glaze with 1 cup semisweet chocolate chips melted with 2 tablespoons heavy cream.*

Lemon Angel Food Cake: *Make recipe as directed, except beat in 2 tablespoons lemon juice and 2 teaspoons very finely grated lemon zest just before you fold flour into mixture. Bake as directed, and invert to cool. Glaze cake with mixture of 1½ cups powdered sugar, 1 tablespoon melted butter, 2 tablespoons lemon juice, and ½ teaspoon grated lemon zest.*

Beat Eggs; Fold in Flour

- Cream of tartar is an acidic ingredient. It helps strengthen the protein bonds in the egg whites, making the foam stronger.

- Salt also helps keep the foam strong. Never add salt until you're ready to beat the egg whites or it will make them runny.

- You know the sugar is dissolved when you rub a bit between your fingers and can no longer feel any grains.

- Fold in the flour carefully, cutting through the batter, down to the bottom, then over the top.

Invert Cake to Cool

- Because the structure of this cake is so delicate, the pan should never be greased. The batter has to cling to the sides as it rises.

- And the cake has to be inverted while it cools. This stretches the foam so it keeps its shape as it cools.

- To remove the cake from the pan, use a sharp knife and cut around the sides.

- Remove the sides, then cut around the center hole and bottom and remove those.

LOW-FAT & LOW-CAL

LIGHT BROWN SUGAR CHEESECAKE

Brown sugar adds moistness and flavor to a low-fat cheesecake

Cheesecake doesn't immediately spring to mind when you think of low-fat and low-calorie desserts. But by the judicious use of light and nonfat products, you can make a cheesecake with wonderful taste and texture.

The key is to combine low-fat and nonfat products along with a tiny amount of full-fat ingredients. Lots of flavor also helps make this dessert exceptional.

You can top this cheesecake with fruit for more flavor, color, and interest. Sauté some apples in apple juice with a bit of lemon juice and sugar and pour over the cheesecake. Or make a praline topping, or use low-fat frozen whipped topping. Caramel sauce would be another wonderful garnish. *Yield: Serves 10*

Ingredients

¹/₂ cup graham cracker crumbs

³/₄ cup chocolate wafer cookie crumbs

3 tablespoons butter, melted

1 tablespoon corn syrup

2 (8-ounce) packages light cream cheese, softened

1 (8-ounce) package fat-free cream cheese, softened

¹/₂ cup fat-free sour cream

2 teaspoons vanilla

1 cup packed brown sugar

2 eggs

3 egg whites

Light Brown Sugar Cheesecake

- Preheat oven to 325°F. Coat 9-inch springform pan with baking spray. Wrap pan in foil.

- In bowl, combine crumbs, melted butter, and corn syrup. Press into bottom of pan; bake 10 minutes; cool.

- Beat cream cheese, sour cream, and vanilla until combined. Add sugar, then eggs and egg whites.

- Pour over cooled crust. Place in large pan; add 1 inch hot water. Bake 55 to 65 minutes, until set. Run knife between cheesecake and pan sides. Cool 1 hour; chill 4 to 6 hours.

Praline Topping: While cheesecake is in oven for last 10 minutes, combine ½ cup packed brown sugar, 2 tablespoons granulated sugar, 1 tablespoon corn syrup, ¼ cup butter, and 2 tablespoons heavy cream in saucepan. Bring mixture to simmer. Cook, stirring frequently, until mixture blends together. When cheesecake comes out of oven, pour mixture over top and spread to coat.

Low Fat Chocolate Cheesecake: Substitute ½ cup chocolate wafer crumbs for graham cracker crumbs. Add 6 tablespoons cocoa powder to cream cheese along with brown sugar. Pour cheesecake filling into crust. Combine ½ cup chocolate wafer crumbs, ¼ cup chopped walnuts, and ½ cup mini semisweet chocolate chips; sprinkle over cheesecake. Bake as directed.

Beat in Sugar

Loosen Cheesecake from Pan

- The corn syrup in the crust adds moisture without adding any fat. You could use honey instead.

- Make sure the crust is completely cool before you add the cheesecake filling.

- Don't beat the cheesecake mixture too much—you don't want to add much air. Beat until the ingredients are combined and smooth.

- Too much air in the cheesecake filling will make the filling rise in the oven, and then settle. This creates cracks.

- The water bath is necessary to add moisture to a low-fat cheesecake while it bakes in the dry oven heat.

- This will also prevent cracks from developing. Cracking cheesecake is a common problem when low-fat products are used.

- Run the knife around the cheesecake when it comes out of the oven; this reduces stress on the filling.

- This step also helps reduce the likelihood of cracking. Chill the cheesecake thoroughly before serving.

TOFFEE MERINGUE COOKIES

Brown sugar and toffee candies add great flavor to crisp meringue cookies

These little cookies are fat-free and delicious. And they are easy to make as long as you follow the directions carefully. Don't make meringues on a humid day unless you have an air-conditioned kitchen, or the egg whites just won't stiffen.

Meringues in themselves are not very flavorful, although they are sweet. So add flavor by folding in different ingredients after the foam has been created.

Crushed hard candies are a wonderful, low-fat way to add flavor to these cookies—or really, any dessert. Extracts, such as almond or peppermint, are another good way to make low-fat desserts more flavorful. *Yield: 36 cookies*

Ingredients

- **3 egg whites**
- **¹/₂ teaspoon cream of tartar**
- **¹/₈ teaspoon salt**
- **2 tablespoons granulated sugar**
- **³/₄ cup packed brown sugar**
- **1 teaspoon vanilla**
- **¹/₂ cup finely crushed toffee bits**

Toffee Meringue Cookies

- Preheat oven to 250°F. Line two cookie sheets with parchment paper and set aside.

- Beat egg whites with cream of tartar, salt, and granulated sugar until stiff. Gradually add brown sugar, beating until stiff again. Stir in vanilla and toffee bits.

- Drop mixture by heaping teaspoons onto cookie sheets, about 1½ inches apart. Bake 1 hour, then turn off heat and let cookies stand in oven 30 minutes.

- Peel cookies gently off parchment paper and store in airtight container.

Meringue Sandwich Cookies: Make cookies as directed; bake and cool. Melt 1 cup semisweet chocolate chips in microwave. Remove from heat and stir in ¼ cup milk chocolate chips. Stir until chips are melted and mixture is smooth. Spread this mixture on flat side of one cookie and top with another. Hold together briefly so they stay together. Let stand until firm.

Lemon Meringue Cookies: Make recipe as directed, except omit brown sugar and 2 tablespoons granulated sugar. Use 1 cup granulated sugar instead. Omit cream of tartar; beat egg whites with 1 tablespoon lemon juice and the salt. Omit vanilla; add ½ teaspoon lemon extract. Fold in ½ cup finely crushed hard lemon candy in place of toffee bits. Form and bake cookies as directed.

Add Brown Sugar

- Brown sugar contains more moisture than granulated sugar, which hinders the formation of the foam.

- To overcome this, beat the egg whites with the cream of tartar, salt, and granulated sugar until stiff peaks form.

- Then slowly beat in the brown sugar. Beating to stiff peaks may take a few minutes; don't give up!

- The sugar should be dissolved when the meringue is completed. Rub a bit between your fingers; you shouldn't feel any grains.

Drop Batter onto Sheets

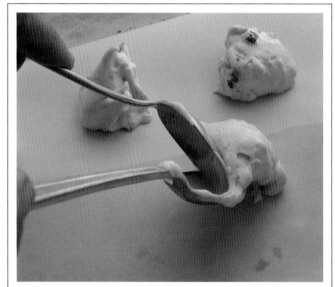

- You must use parchment paper or Silpat (silicone) liners when baking these cookies. They'll stick to even a greased cookie sheet.

- You can spoon the meringue onto the paper, or use a piping bag to make fancier cookies.

- A star tip is always nice. You can make other shapes too, such as logs or small circles for Christmas.

- To make the meringues easier to remove, place the paper on a damp kitchen towel to let the cookies cool.

LOW-FAT & LOW-CAL

BANANA-CHERRY TURNOVERS
Phyllo dough is layered with baking spray, then filled with a sweet fruit mixture

Turnovers are usually made with puff pastry, which is very high in fat, or with phyllo dough layered with a lot of melted butter. Even with lots of fruit, that makes turnovers a high-fat, high-calorie dessert.

But here's a trick to transform this recipe. You can alternate butter and nonstick cooking spray while layering the phyllo

dough. This reduces the fat content while preserving the butter flavor and flaky crunchiness of the pastry.

You can fill these turnovers with just about any fruit mixture, as long as you keep the proportions the same. Canned pie filling is a good substitute too. *Yield: 12 turnovers*

KNACK FABULOUS DESSERTS

Ingredients

2 large bananas, peeled and chopped

1 tablespoon lemon juice

$1/2$ cup cherry preserves

$1/2$ cup dried cherries

2 tablespoons packed brown sugar

3 tablespoons granulated sugar

1 teaspoon cinnamon

$1/4$ cup graham cracker crumbs

12 (14x9-inch) sheets frozen phyllo dough, thawed

2 tablespoons butter, melted

Nonstick cooking spray

Banana-Cherry Turnovers

- Preheat oven to 350°F. Mix bananas with lemon juice, preserves, cherries, and brown sugar.

- Mix granulated sugar, cinnamon, and graham cracker crumbs. Lay one sheet phyllo dough on counter.

- Brush lightly with butter;

sprinkle with 1 tablespoon crumb mixture. Repeat, using spray instead of butter, then top with third sheet. Cut into three 14-inch strips.

- Place scant 2 tablespoons filling on short edge. Fold into triangles; spray. Bake 18 to 23 minutes.

Apple Cranberry Turnovers: Make recipe as directed, except for filling, omit bananas, lemon juice, preserves, cherries, and brown sugar. Instead, peel and cube 2 Granny Smith apples. Cook with 2 tablespoons sugar and 1 tablespoon lemon juice in small saucepan until tender. Add ½ teaspoon cinnamon and ½ cup dried cranberries. Fill and form pastries as directed, then bake.

Pear Chocolate Turnovers: Make recipe as directed, except omit bananas, lemon juice, preserves, dried cherries, and brown sugar. Peel and cube 2 pears. Place in pan with 2 tablespoons brown sugar and 1 tablespoon lemon juice. Cook and stir until tender. Add ¼ teaspoon nutmeg. Cool; add ½ cup miniature semisweet chocolate chips. Use this mixture as filling for phyllo. Shape and bake.

Prepare Filling for Pastries

Fold Pastries

- The lemon juice helps keep the bananas from turning dark when they are cut and adds flavor.

- You can substitute another flavor of preserves for the cherry preserves. Apricot or orange would be delicious.

- The graham cracker crumb mixture adds flavor and crunch to the recipe and helps compensate for less fat.

- Make sure that you scatter the crumb mixture evenly and thinly on the phyllo so it's easy to roll up.

- Start at the end of the pastry strip that holds the filling. Fold the bottom at an angle over the filling so it meets the right edge.

- Then fold the triangle that contains the filling straight up onto the phyllo.

- Repeat, folding the phyllo as you would fold a flag, until you reach the end of the strip.

- Spray with cooking spray and press down gently on the edge of the strip so it stays folded.

BAKED STUFFED APPLES
Baked apples, stuffed with dates, are a comforting dessert

Baked apples are easy, aromatic, and a delicious healthy dessert that no one will suspect is low fat.

The apples become tender and sweet when they are baked, and the filling adds wonderful texture, color, and flavor. The secret ingredients in this recipe include cinnamon-flavored baking chips, dates, and rum.

You can omit the rum if you're serving this to children. But it adds wonderful depth of flavor for an adult dessert.

These apples can be stuffed with any combination of fruits and nuts you'd like. Try golden raisins combined with chopped cashews, or dried sweetened cranberries mixed with pecans.

Serve with a scoop of low-fat ice cream for a wonderfully comforting dessert. *Yield: Serves 6*

Ingredients

6 large Granny Smith apples

$^1/_2$ cup finely chopped dates

3 tablespoons chopped walnuts

2 tablespoons packed brown sugar

1 cup cinnamon chips

2 tablespoons butter

1$^1/_4$ cups water

$^1/_4$ cup rum

$^1/_2$ cup granulated sugar

Baked Stuffed Apples

- Preheat oven to 350°F. Peel 1-inch strip from top of apples and remove core, but leave ½ inch at bottom. Prick apple skin with fork.

- In bowl, combine dates, walnuts, brown sugar, and cinnamon chips. Fill apples, mounding filling high.

- Place in baking dish; top each with 1 teaspoon butter. Bring water, rum, and granulated sugar to boil.

- Pour around apples. Bake 40 to 50 minutes, until apples are tender. Serve warm.

Apple Crisp Apples: Cut 3 medium apples in half. Remove cores. Place apples in microwave pie plate, cut-side up, and brush with 1 tablespoon lemon juice. Combine 1 cup granola, ½ teaspoon cinnamon, ¼ cup packed brown sugar, and 2 tablespoons melted butter. Fill cavities of apples. Cover with plastic wrap. Microwave on high 7 to 9 minutes, until apples are tender.

To remove the core of the apples without breaking through the bottom skin, an apple corer is a great help. This tool will neatly remove the core and seeds without damaging the apple. If you don't have one, use a very sharp, small paring knife to cut a hole around the stem. Then use a small spoon to remove the seeds and enlarge the cavity.

Core Apples

- Work slowly and carefully while you are coring the apples. They will crack or break fairly easily.

- Even if this happens, your dessert isn't ruined. Cut the apples in half and remove the core.

- Then place them cut-side up in the pan and fill with the date mixture. These apples should be baked for half the time specified.

- The strip of skin is removed from the top so the apple is less likely to split in the oven's heat.

Fill and Bake Apples

- Fill the apples to overflowing with the date mixture, but do not push the mixture down into the core.

- The filling will shrink somewhat as it bakes, but if it is packed too tightly the apples could split in the oven.

- For a sauce to serve with the apples, pour the juice from the baking dish into a saucepan.

- Add 2 tablespoons cornstarch and bring to a simmer. Simmer until thickened and serve with apples.

LOW-FAT & LOW-CAL

FLOATING ISLAND
Puffs of meringue are poached, then served with a light custard

Floating Island is an elegant dessert, perfect for company, which consists of fluffy meringues poached in water until they set, served in a velvety custard sauce and drizzled with a caramel sauce.

The soft meringues look like islands floating in the custard, hence the name. This dessert originated in France, Poland, or another part of southeastern Europe. Its name in French is *Oeufs à la Neige*.

You can poach the meringues in milk instead of water for a slightly different taste. Discard the milk after the meringues are cooked.

Drizzle the finished dessert with caramel or chocolate sauce, or sprinkle with crushed toffee or toasted chopped nuts or coconut for a nice texture contrast. *Yield: Serves 8*

Ingredients

1 1/2 cups skim milk

2 tablespoons cornstarch

3/4 cup 1 percent milk

1 egg yolk

1/2 cup sugar

Pinch salt

2 teaspoons vanilla

4 egg whites

1/4 teaspoon cream of tartar

1/2 cup sugar

Floating Island

- In saucepan, combine ½ cup skim milk and cornstarch; whisk. Add remaining skim milk.

- Beat in 1% milk, egg yolk, sugar, and salt. Cook over medium heat, whisking constantly, until mixture coats spoon. Stir in vanilla. Cool; chill.

- Beat egg whites with cream of tartar until foamy. Gradually add ½ cup sugar, beating until very stiff.

- Simmer water. Scoop out spoonfuls of meringue onto water; poach 5 minutes, turning once. Pour custard on plates; top with meringues and sauce.

Low-Fat Caramel Sauce: In saucepan, combine 1 cup granulated sugar and ½ cup water. Boil until golden, about 8 minutes. Remove from heat; add ⅔ cup evaporated skim milk (mixture will bubble up furiously). Cook 1 to 2 minutes longer, whisking until sauce is smooth. Add 1 tablespoon butter and 1 teaspoon vanilla. Let cool; store tightly covered in refrigerator.

Baked Floating Island: Make custard sauce as directed; cool and chill. Beat egg whites with cream of tartar and ¾ cup sugar as directed until stiff peaks form. Coat 8x4-inch loaf pan with nonstick baking spray and add meringue; smooth top. Bake at 350°F 20 to 30 minutes, until puffed and set. Remove from pan and cool 30 minutes. Slice and drizzle with Low-Fat Caramel Sauce.

Make Sauce

Poach Meringues

- Whisk the sauce constantly while it is cooking to help prevent lumps.

- When the mixture is done, it will coat the spoon. Blow on the spoon slightly to cool the sauce, then run your finger over it.

- Your finger should leave a distinct trail in the sauce, which means it has been cooked long enough.

- Whisk the sauce occasionally as it cools, to help it cool down evenly and keep it silky smooth.

- To poach the meringues correctly, keep the water at just below a simmer.

- If the water boils, the meringues will become tough. Regulate the heat carefully.

- When you remove the meringues from the water, let the slotted spoon rest briefly on a towel to remove excess moisture. Place the meringues on a buttered plate.

- You can serve the meringues warm, right out of the poaching liquid, or chill them for a few hours before serving.

SUBSTITUTIONS

These are ingredients that can be substituted for one another

Substitutions

1 cup honey = $3/4$ cup sugar + $1/4$ cup water

1 cup cream = $1/3$ cup butter + $3/4$ cup milk

1 cup whole milk = $1/2$ cup evaporated milk + $1/2$ cup water

1 cup cake flour = $3/4$ cup plus 2 tablespoons flour + 2 tablespoons cornstarch, sifted

1 ounce unsweetened chocolate = 3 tablespoons cocoa powder + 1 tablespoon solid shortening

1 ounce semisweet chocolate = 1 ounce unsweetened chocolate + 1 tablespoon sugar

1 ounce milk chocolate = 1 ounce semisweet chocolate + 1 tablespoon sugar

1 teaspoon baking powder = $1/4$ teaspoon baking soda + $1/2$ teaspoon cream of tartar

1 cup packed brown sugar = 1 cup granulated sugar + 2 tablespoons molasses

1 cup buttermilk = 2 tablespoons lemon juice + $3/4$ cup plus 2 tablespoons milk

1 tablespoon cornstarch = 2 tablespoons flour

1 cup chopped nuts = 1 cup rolled oats

$1/2$ teaspoon cream of tartar = $1/2$ teaspoon lemon juice

1 cup sour cream = 1 cup yogurt

1 egg = $1/4$ cup egg substitute

10 large marshmallows = 1 cup miniature marshmallows

1 vanilla bean = 2 teaspoons vanilla extract

1 teaspoon apple pie spice = $1/2$ teaspoon cinnamon + $1/4$ teaspoon nutmeg + $1/8$ teaspoon allspice

$1/4$ cup rum or brandy = 1 teaspoon imitation rum or brandy extract + $1/4$ cup water

1 cup evaporated milk = 1 cup light cream

EQUIVALENTS
These are equivalent measures of common ingredients

Equivalents

1 pound apples = 3 or 4 medium

1 banana = 1 cup sliced = 1/3 cup mashed

1 peach = 1/2 cup slices

1 pint berries = 2 cups

1 stick butter = 4 ounces = 1/2 cup

3 ounces dried cherries = 1/2 cup

30 vanilla wafers = 1 cup crumbs

20 chocolate wafers = 1 cup crumbs

16 gingersnaps = 1 cup crumbs

15 graham crackers = 1 cup crumbs

7 ounces coconut = 2 1/2 cups

3 cups flaked cereal = 1 cup crumbs

1 cup heavy cream = 2 cups whipped cream

1 egg white = 2 tablespoons

1 pound brown sugar = 2 1/4 cups

1 apple = 1 cup sliced

1 lemon = 3 tablespoons juice

1 lemon = 1 teaspoon grated rind

1 orange = 1/2 cup juice

1 orange = 2 teaspoons grated zest

14-ounce can sweetened condensed milk = 1 1/4 cups

1 pound nuts = 4 cups chopped

Measuring Equivalents

1 cup all-purpose flour = 125 grams = 4.5 ounces

1 cup powdered sugar = 125 grams = 4.5 ounces

1 cup oatmeal = 85 grams = 3 ounces

1 cup granulated sugar = 200 grams = 7.1 ounces

1 cup packed brown sugar = 220 grams = 7.7 ounces

1 cup honey = 340 grams = 12 ounces

1 cup milk = 8 ounces

1 cup sour cream = 8.6 ounces

1 cup vegetable oil = 7.7 ounces

1 cup cocoa = 3.3 ounces

METRIC CONVERSION TABLES

Approximate U.S. Metric Equivalents

Liquid Ingredients

U.S. MEASURES	METRIC	U.S. MEASURES	METRIC
¼ TSP.	1.23 ML	2 TBSPS.	29.57 ML
½ TSP.	2.36 ML	3 TBSPS.	44.36 ML
¾ TSP.	3.70 ML	¼ CUP	59.15 ML
1 TSP.	4.93 ML	½ CUP	118.30 ML
1¼ TSPS.	6.16 ML	1 CUP	236.59 ML
1½ TSPS.	7.39 ML	2 CUPS OR 1 PT.	473.18 ML
1¾ TSPS.	8.63 ML	3 CUPS	709.77 ML
2 TSPS.	9.86 ML	4 CUPS OR 1 QT.	946.36 ML
1 TBSP.	14.79 ML	4 QTS. OR 1 GAL.	3.79 L

Dry Ingredients

U.S. MEASURES	METRIC	U.S. MEASURES		METRIC
1/16 OZ.	2 (1.8) G	2⅘ OZ.		80 G
⅛ OZ.	3½ (3.5) G	3 OZ.		85 (84.9) G
¼ OZ.	7 (7.1) G	3½ OZ.		100 G
½ OZ.	15 (14.2) G	4 OZ.		115 (113.2) G
¾ OZ.	21 (21.3) G	4½ OZ.		125 G
⅞ OZ.	25 G	5¼ OZ.		150 G
1 OZ.	30 (28.3) G	8⅞ OZ.		250 G
1¾ OZ.	50 G	16 OZ.	1 LB.	454 G
2 OZ.	60 (56.6) G	17⅗ OZ.	1 LIVRE	500 G

WEB RESOURCES

These Internet resources will help improve your baking skills

Baking and Dessert Web Sites

AllRecipes.com

http://allrecipes.com/Recipes

AllRecipes, which features reader-submitted recipes that are rated by members, is a reliable source of hundreds of dessert recipes.

Baking and Desserts at About.com

http://baking.about.com

This time-tested site is full of information and recipes about everything from the best brownies to cakes, cookies, and bread.

BH&G

www.bhg.com/recipes

Better Homes and Gardens offers hundreds of simple and interesting dessert recipes, all tested in their kitchens.

RESOURCES

Candy at About.com

http://candy.about.com

This wonderful site has inventive candy recipes, lots of hints and tips, and some of the best pictures.

Epicurious Desserts

www.epicurious.com/recipesmenus/desserts

This Web site features many easy and elegant dessert recipes, some with flavor twists.

Joy of Baking

www.joyofbaking.com

This site has wonderful recipes for everything from puddings to cheesecake to cookies. Information about conversions and substitutions.

RecipeZaar

www.recipezaar.com

Thousands of dessert recipes are submitted by readers and rated by viewers.

Dessert Preparation Videos

About.com

http://video.about.com/food.htm

Thousands of videos will teach you how to make gingerbread men, carve a watermelon basket, or bake a pecan pie.

Expert Village

www.expertvillage.com

You'll learn how to make everything from chocolate chip cookies to chocolate layer cake in these videos.

Gourmandia Videos

www.gourmandia.com/video-recipes-cooking-videos/category/36

Gourmandia has a lot of excellent videos showing how to make crème brûlée, apple tart, and other recipes created by chefs.

Kraft Dessert Videos

www.kraftfoods.com/kf/cookingschool/videos/DessertsVideos
.aspx

Lots of great videos on making everything from a sunflower cake to chocolate passion bowl and layered brownies.

Taste of Home

www.tasteofhome.com/Videos/Desserts

Videos detail how to make different desserts, like pastry crust and ice cream.

Dessert TV Cooking Shows

America's Test Kitchen

www.cooks.illustrated.com

Cook's Illustrated is responsible for this show on PBS that teaches you how to cook. Lots of excellent dessert recipes.

Robin Miller on the Food Network

www.foodnetwork.com/quick-fix-meals-with-robin-miller/index
.html

Robin Miller in her show *Quick Fix Meals* makes easy desserts and quick sweet treats.

Semi-Homemade Cooking with Sandra Lee on the Food Network

www.foodnetwork.com/semi-homemade-cooking-with-sandra
-lee/index.html

Sandra Lee developed the concept of "30 percent fresh food, 70 percent prepared food." She makes lots of easy desserts.

Farmer's Markets

Farmer's Markets

www.farmersmarketla.com

Los Angeles Farmer's Market Web site; the original farmer's market.

Farmer's Market Search

http://apps.ams.usda.gov/FarmersMarkets

The USDA site lets you search for farmer's markets by state, city, county, and zip code, as well as methods of payment.

National Directory of Farmer's Markets

http://farmersmarket.com

This site has an index of US farmer's markets listed by state.

COOKBOOKS AND MAGAZINES
These books and magazines focus on fabulous desserts

Dessert Books

Baggett, Nancy. *The All-American Dessert Book*. Houghton Mifflin Harcourt, 2005. An excellent collection of 150 dessert recipes including fruit desserts, candies, and gifts.

Chattman, Lauren. *Dessert Express*. Taunton, 2008. An excellent collection of quick and easy desserts that can be made in 30 minutes or less.

Deen, Paula. *The Lady & Sons Just Desserts*. Simon & Schuster, 2006. A collection of delicious southern dessert recipes like chess pie and butter cake.

Fabricant, Florence. *The New York Times Dessert Cookbook*. St. Martin's Press, 2002. This book offers 400 recipes for all types of desserts, including gratins, tarts, custard, and biscotti.

Ghirardelli Chocolate Company. *The Ghirardelli Chocolate Cookbook*. Ten Speed Press, 2007. Delicious, classic chocolate recipes, including instructions on the best ways to work with chocolate.

Heatter, Maida. *Maida Heatter's Book of Great Chocolate Desserts*. Andrews McMeel Publishing, 2006. The doyenne of desserts, in her newest book, focuses on chocolate.

Kimball, Christopher. *The Dessert Bible*. Little, Brown and Company, 2000. Not only does this book have wonderful recipes, but it also describes the science behind them and excellent techniques.

Wemischner, Robert. *The Dessert Architect*. Delmar Cengage Learning, 2009. An extensive book with many photos and charts, this is a guide to building desserts. Menus and plating techniques included.

Yard, Sherry, and Wolfgang Puck. *Desserts by the Yard.* Houghton Mifflin Harcourt, 2007. Wolfgang Puck's pastry chef offers a good selection of desserts including soufflés, cheesecake, and crumbles.

Dessert Magazines

Better Homes & Gardens
Tons of dessert recipes that follow the seasons.

Bon Appétit
This venerable publication offers high-end dessert recipes, many from famous chefs.

Dessert Professional
This magazine offers lots of dessert recipes and menus, seasonal recipes and tips.

Family Circle
This magazine offers lots of dessert recipes and menus, seasonal recipes and tips.

Gourmet
Excellent dessert recipes span the seasons. Beautiful pictures and commentary.

Taste of Home
This venerable magazine focuses on reader-submitted recipes, tested in their kitchens.

Woman's Day
Many cake, cookie, pie, and tart recipes in each issue, along with cooking lessons and tips.

FIND EQUIPMENT AND INGREDIENTS
Find ingredients and equipment

RESOURCES

Catalogs and Online Resources

Amazon Grocery
www.agrocerydelivery.com
Amazon.com has a grocery delivery service with general foods and hard-to-find items.

The Baker's Catalog
From King Arthur Flour, this catalog offers cooking equipment and baking ingredients, including specialty flours and flavorings.

Peapod
www.peapod.com
This online grocery store serves some areas of the United States.

Safeway.com
A grocery chain offering delivery of food items, as well as recipes and tips for healthy living.

Schwan's
A home delivery service for groceries, serving parts of the United States.

Catalogs for Baking Equipment

Brylane Home
Lots of kitchen equipment, including specialty tools, utensils, and dishware.

King Arthur
This company offers thousands of unusual baking ingredients, such as unusual spices and gourmet chocolates.

Solutions
Lots of new equipment and tools to make baking quick and easy.

Sur la Table
All sorts of kitchen equipment along with dishes, serving utensils, and flatware.

Williams-Sonoma
Top-of-the-line equipment, along with cookbooks and many appliances, tools, and accessories.

Hotlines

Crisco Pie Hotline

(877) 367-7438

The hotline is available during the holidays for troubleshooting dessert recipes.

King Arthur Flour Hotline

(800) 745-4000

Open during the month of December, this hotline answers consumer questions about baking and desserts.

Land O'Lakes Baking Hotline

(800) 782-9606

The hotline is open during the holidays with baking tips and help.

Nestlé Toll House Baking Line

(800) 637-8537

A holiday hotline that helps consumers with questions about chocolate and baking.

USDA Meat and Poultry Hotline

(800) 535-4555

This year-round line offers information about food safety and answers consumer questions about food preparation.

Manufacturers of Equipment

All-Clad

www.all-clad.com

Excellent, professional-grade cookware and bakeware.

Cuisinart

www.cuisinart.com

This company can completely outfit your kitchen, from ranges to stockpots.

GE Appliances

www.geappliances.com

Outfit your entire kitchen with GE appliances. Online service and customer support.

Kitchenaid

www.kitchenaid.com/home.jsp

Lots of high-quality appliances, from refrigerators and stoves to slow cookers.

Rival

www.rivalproducts.com

Manufacturer of the original Crock-Pot, with product information, recipes, and an online store.

Web Sites for Baking Equipment

Chefsresource.com

www.chefsresource.com

Cutlery, flatware, gadgets, tools, knives, and brands like Cuisinart are featured.

Cooking.com

www.cooking.com

Kitchen fixtures, large appliance, cutlery, cookbooks, and tools can be found at this site.

Crockpot.com

www.crock-pot.com

The Web site for Rival slow cookers, this site offers customer service, replacement parts, and recipes.

KitchenManualsonline.com

http://kitchen.manualsonline.com/manuals/device/slow_cooker.html

This Web site offers contact information for many manufacturers of baking equipment.

GLOSSARY
Learn the language of baking

Al Dente: This Italian phrase, meaning "to the tooth," describes doneness of pasta.

Bake: To heat food rapidly, using dry heat, as in an oven.

Baking Powder: A leavening agent used in baked goods, made of baking soda and an acid such as cream of tartar.

Baking Soda: Bicarbonate of soda is a leavening agent used to make baked goods rise.

Beat: Manipulating food with a spoon, mixer, or whisk to combine.

Blind Bake: To bake a piecrust without a filling. The crust is filled with pie weights or dried beans to keep its shape and prevent puffing.

Chill: To refrigerate a product to quickly lower its temperature.

Chop: To cut food into small pieces, using a chef's knife or a food processor.

Cream: This word has two meaning: The first is a dairy product with a significant amount of butterfat. The second is a verb, meaning to manipulate fat with sugar.

Cut In: A process of working fat such as butter or shortening into flour and other dry ingredients to produce a fine mixture.

Dice: To cut food into small, even portions, usually about ¼ inch square.

Dock: To mark a piecrust or pastry with a docking tool or a fork to prevent puffing.

Fold: Combining two soft or liquid mixtures together, using an over-and-under method of mixing.

Ganache: A mixture, used to coat baked goods, of chocolate and cream, melted together over low heat.

Gluten: The main protein in flour, produced in the presence of water. Gluten consists of two protein molecules, glutenin and gliadin.

Grate: A grater or microplane is used to remove small pieces or shreds of skin or food.

Grill: To cook over coals or charcoal, or over high heat.

Melt: To turn a solid into a liquid by the addition of heat.

Mince: To cut a food or herb into very small and even pieces, about ⅛ inch square.

Peel: To remove the skin of a fruit or vegetable. And, as a noun, the skin of a fruit or vegetable.

Poach: To cook at a temperature just below a simmer.

Seize: When chocolate is overheated or when water is accidentally added to melted chocolate, it can seize—that is, become thick and grainy.

Simmer: A state of liquid cooking, where the liquid is just below a boil.

Stir: To use a whisk, spoon, or electric mixer to move ingredients in a bowl.

Temper: Chocolate is tempered by heating and cooling, or by adding chopped chocolate to melted chocolate. The term also refers to heating egg yolks by adding a heated ingredient.

Toss: To combine food using two spoons or a spoon and a fork until mixed.

Whisk: Both a tool, which is made of loops of steel, and a method, which combines food until smooth.

Zest: This word has two meanings. The verb means removing the peel from citrus fruits. As a noun, the word refers to the actual peel.

INDEX